The Laissez-Faire Peasant

The Laissez-Faire Peasant

Post-socialist rural development in Serbia

Jovana Diković

First published in 2025 by
UCL Press
University College London
Gower Street
London WC1E 6BT

Available to download free: www.uclpress.co.uk

Text © Author, 2025
Images © Author and copyright holders named in captions, 2025

The author has asserted her rights under the Copyright, Designs and Patents Act 1988 to be identified as the author of this work.

A CIP catalogue record for this book is available from The British Library.

Any third-party material in this book is not covered by the book's Creative Commons licence. Details of the copyright ownership and permitted use of third-party material is given in the image (or extract) credit lines. If you would like to reuse any third-party material not covered by the book's Creative Commons licence, you will need to obtain permission directly from the copyright owner.

This book is published under a Creative Commons Attribution-NonCommercial 4.0 International licence (CC BY-NC 4.0), https://creativecommons.org/licenses/by-nc/4.0/. This licence allows you to share and adapt the work for non-commercial use providing attribution is made to the author and publisher (but not in any way that suggests that they endorse you or your use of the work) and any changes are indicated. Attribution should include the following information:

Diković, J. 2025. *The Laissez-Faire Peasant: Post-socialist rural development in Serbia.* London: UCL Press. https://doi.org/10.14324/111.9781800087637

Further details about Creative Commons licences are available at https://creativecommons.org/licenses/

ISBN: 978-1-80008-759-0 (Hbk.)
ISBN: 978-1-80008-762-0 (Pbk.)
ISBN: 978-1-80008-763-7 (PDF)
ISBN: 978-1-80008-764-4 (epub)
DOI: https://doi.org/10.14324/111.9781800087637

In loving memory of my father

Contents

List of figures ix
List of tables xi
Glossary xiii
Acknowledgements xvii

1 The laissez-faire mentality: towards an understanding of
   peasant resilience, autonomy and institutional change 1
2 Peasants in theoretical and historical perspective 27
3 Nesting the laissez-faire mentality 53
4 Laissez-faire practices versus rural development policies 93
5 Local politics and rural development 133
6 Whose rural development? 157
7 Roma and rural development 187
8 Conclusion 207

References 217
Index 229

List of figures

1.1	The Catholic church in Gaj.	19
1.2	Peasants at work threshing the wheat with a combine harvester.	20
3.1	The generations work together; a great-grandfather and his great-grandson stand proudly in front of the family's grain trucks, 2013.	55
3.2	*Fijakerijada*, a festival of horse carriage riding that takes place in Gaj.	61
3.3	*Gajački kotlić*, the contest of fish stew-making that takes place in Gaj during the summer months.	62
3.4	A celebratory atmosphere at *Gajački kotlić*.	62
3.5	A view of the backyard of a household in Gaj.	66
3.6	A field of sunflowers in bloom, ready to harvest.	69
3.7	A large field of wheat, ready to harvest.	69
4.1	The informal outdoor Saturday market in Gaj.	105
4.2	The dirt track leading up to the summer ranches.	106
4.3	A summer ranch, set against the hillside.	107
4.4	Cows grazing beneath electricity pylons at the summer ranch pastures.	113
4.5	Milk canister used to collect milk from the shepherd at the summer ranch.	115
4.6	A shepherd tending pigs (shepherds tend not only sheep but also pigs and cattle).	116
4.7	An improvised watering place for cattle at the summer ranch pastures.	116
4.8	A corn cob ripening on the stalk, one of the crops commonly grown.	118
6.1	The street through central Gaj, showing typical houses of the area.	164
6.2	The baker at work.	169
6.3	Heating the wood-fired bread oven in the bakery.	170
6.4	The tailor's work in progress.	172

List of tables

2.1 General overview of agricultural development, 1955–90. 46
4.1 Reported number of slaughtered cattle for 2013, 2014 and 2015 (thousands). 108
6.1 Land utilized by agricultural households in Vojvodina (hectares). 181

Glossary

Ajvar: The most popular traditional canned food originally made of red paprika. See also *zimnica*.

Bačija or supon: Traditional, customary, oral agreement between a livestock breeder and a shepherd. An appointed shepherd gets paid in money and in kind to live in a hut next to the summer ranch and take care of sheep, cattle or other animals during grazing season from early April until late November.

Banaćani: Families of Banat origin living there for many generations and working in agriculture ever since.

Banatski mentalitet: A mentality ascribed to the region of Banat in Vojvodina.

Banjaši: An ethnic group of Orthodox Roma people originally from Romania.

Buša: Busha, an autochthonous breed of short-horned cattle.

Češka beseda: Czech association in Gaj.

Cigani: A common Serbian expression for Roma people (Gypsies).

Cigani čergari: Nomadic Roma people (nomadic Gypsies).

Čova: A field scarecrow, made of wood with a birch broom which personifies guardianship. *Čova* may have different functions and one of them is to prohibit gleaning. See also *pabirčenje*.

Domaći Cigani: A local term meaning 'domesticated' Roma who have settled in the village and have lived and assimilated into the dominant village culture through work, marriage, religion and language over a long period of time.

Domaćin: A vernacular term for a hospitable householder. In villages it is used interchangeably with the term *gazda*. A slight difference between the two is that a *domaćin* can be a person who does not necessarily have land. See also under *gazda*.

Došljaci: Newcomers. See also under *kolonisti*.

Društvena svojina: A form of collective property established in socialist Yugoslavia and dismantled by the Constitution of the Republic of Serbia in 2006.

Dužan kao Grčka ('be up to your neck in debt' in English): A vernacular expression that signifies when someone runs into debt.

Fijakerijada: Festival of horse carriages taking place in Gaj on the second day of *Spasovdan*. See also **Spasovdan**.

Gajački kotlić: The contest of fish stew taking place in Gaj during summer months.

Gazda: In villages, it signifies a landowner and a good householder. The term **gazda** is used interchangeably with the term **domaćin**. A gazda is a person who is not neglectful, who gets jobs done in the household and fields in due time; someone who is a good planner, and whose household is tidy and neat, who is hospitable and generous and who possesses everything one village household needs. One cannot be a **gazda** without land.

Kolonisti: Resettled people, most of whom were settled down in Vojvodina (or some other partes of Yugoslavia) during the implementation of the first (1919–1941) and the second (1945–1953) agrarian reforms.

Kolonizacija: Organized political resettlement of people in First and Second Yugoslavia. See also under **kolonisti**.

Laissez-faire: Entails three meanings. According to the first, economic, view laissez-faire refers to a minimal government which does not have many laws that regulate and control the buying and selling of goods and services. The other meaning refers to individual behaviour or freedom of action, in which individuals usually try not to interfere with or influence the activities of others and to maintain the same boundaries for themselves. The third, common, meaning refers to cooperation and interaction among people that develop in a highly spontaneous environment with self-regulating mechanisms.

Lakše vučem za selo ('getting things more easily for the village' in English): A local expression according to which people with some political function believe they can employ their clientelist networks to easier access financing or approval of projects necessary for the village.

Mentalitet: Mentality.

Mesna zajednica: Local village council authorized and financed by the state.

Moba: Shared voluntary work by villagers (cousins, friends and neighbours), who join hands during hay collection, picking, building and other strenuous work. People who call for *moba* are expected to return the favour when those who helped them need it.

Naći se u neobranom grožđu: A vernacular expression when someone finds himself in a legally or morally impermissible act or situation. Such a connotation may refer to gleaning. See also **pabirčenje**.

Okućnica: A courtyard attached to the household, consisting of the front yard, a back yard for animals, and a garden. The area varies from a couple to 50–60 acres, where everything needed for daily consumption of the household is produced.

Pabirčenje ('gleaning' in English): A customary arrangement in which a landlord allows poor people to gather leftover crops from the fields after the first harvest. In other contexts it may also refer to gathering woods in forests after logging or gathering coal leftovers in mines which digger machines have left behind.

Paor: An archaic term for a peasant predominantly used in Vojvodina.

Polutani: A vernacular expression for people who in socialist Yugoslavia combined work in factories with farming. They were considered neither fully socialist workers nor fully peasants.

Salaš: Summer ranch for livestock breeding placed outside of the village area.

Samodoprinosi: A local tax inaugurated in socialist Yugoslavia in 1946 for covering the maintenance work in villages. In the name of the tax, the local municipality would automatically deduct 3 per cent from salaries of all employed people. After the liberal-democratic shift in 2000, villages in Serbia gradually abolished this tax.

Šapurina: Crowned corn head used as firewood.

Seljački mentalitet: Peasants' mentality.

Seljak: A vernacular term for a peasant.

Seoska zavetina or *village slava*: Is the main religious festival in Serbian villages celebrating the Orthodox saint, patron of the village.

Slava: The most important family religious celebration of the Orthodox saint, patron of the family.

Slepac: A vernacular derogatory term for a person without family, property, employment or any job. An English equivalent would be 'a bum'.

Spasovdan: A religious celebration that falls on the 40th day after Orthodox Easter. Spasovdan is celebrated as *village slava* of Gaj.

Svinjari: A local derogatory expression for people who breed pigs. An English equivalent would be 'piggers'.

Tito: A nickname of Josip Broz, a communist revolutionary and political leader of the second Yugoslavia from 1945 until 1980.

Veresija: A means of delayed payment. An English equivalent would be 'credit to trust', or 'putting something on the slate'. It is a form of economic transaction that is predominantly based on trust.

Zadruga: Extended patriarchal family household consisting of several kinship members and generations living under the same roof. *Zadruga* was a single unit of production and consumption where family members jointly shared and controlled resources. The property of *zadruga* remained in undivided collective ownership until its dissolution. Although similar family households existed in other parts of Europe, this exclusively village phenomenon was a dominant form of family household self-organization and protection in the Balkans in the nineteenth century. *Zadruga* existed in countries liberated from the Ottoman Empire (Serbia, Montenegro, Bulgaria) and in regions under the control of the Austro-Hungarian Empire. *Zadruga* was slowly abandoned after the Second World War.

Zimnica: Traditional Serbian canned food made of paprika, tomato, cauliflower, pickles in form of a thick sauce, stew or sour vegetables. It is prepared in autumn as a food supply for the winter months.

Žitnice: A local term for storehouses usually built within the household for keeping wheat and crops, designed to store larger amounts of grain. In the past, *žitnice* were built as floor storage, or even an attic could serve sometimes for keeping smaller amounts of grain.

Acknowledgements

Every piece of the book keeps reminding me of the inspiration, encouragement and destinations that contributed to its creation. An interest in studying the development of a post-socialist Serbian village brought me to the University of Zurich. There I met Peter Finke, an anthropologist of a rare scholarly orientation, who intrigued my curiosity by introducing me to the theory of neo-institutionalism. Although over time I grew critical of neo-institutionalist explanations of the post-socialist rural change, it, nevertheless, influenced the development of some of my arguments in the book. Before I met Deirdre McCloskey in Belgrade, and later in Zurich and Chicago, I already admired her 'Bourgeois' trilogy and avidly absorbed the art of erudite writing. If I succeeded in advancing theoretical reaffirmation of virtue ethics it is her influence. My understanding of the importance of self-governance was deepened through a formative discussion with Ilia Murtazashvili at the University of Pittsburgh. Jeremie Forney at the University of Neuchatel and Eszter Krasznai Kovács in Budapest shared with me their knowledge about valuable books on agrarian thought and the concept of a good farmer.

The earliest version of my manuscript was presented at the Lecture Series in Social Anthropology at Department of Social Anthropology and Cultural Studies (ISEK) at the University of Zurich, where I was advised on how to weave better descriptions with analyses. Colleagues from ISEK read and discussed pieces of my work at several workshops and retreats. I am grateful for their comments as they unerringly pointed to the flaws that had to be fixed. Emilia Roza Sulek and Lena Kaufmann have been great conversationalists whose work and books on Tibet fungi miners and China migrant farmers provided me with many important parallels and insights. Agnieszka Joniak-Lüthi has encouraged and critically read my work and helped me in manifold ways to finish what I started.

And I started my study in 2013 in the villages of Gaj, Malo Bavanište, and Beli Breg in south-east Banat in Vojvodina Province. Evica Ignja, Jaroslav Frič, Slavica and Jovan Šefer were not only hosts but friends who became integral parts of my family. Biljana Ilić, Vesna Vuković, Tanja Milutinović, Nena Stefanović, Ivica Žurž and the people from my neighbourhood as well as my interlocutors were invaluable companions. In each of our numerous conversations they would reveal pieces of fascinating local history, and of their personal lives. Their views helped me to grasp the multilayeredness of local resilience, love for land and importance of the community.

With my Belgrade friends Andrej and Svetlana Stanimirović, Slobodan Radosavljević, Tanja Mitrić and Srđan Milošević I enjoyed long intellectual conversations which usually took place under one particular vineyard tree. Such an experience enabled me to translate the culture of debating onto paper.

The open-mindedness of Chris Penfold, the *spiritus movens* of the project, made possible my manuscript's progress into being a book. Elliot Beck competently led me through the process of obtaining permissions and copyrights. Organizational effectiveness of the remainder of the UCL Press team, Jaimee Biggins production manager, Jonathan Dore project manager, Katharine Norman copy editor and the marketing department, Alison Fox, Margie Coughlin, and Laurie Sakura McNamee, lifted away the burden of the book's production and made it into an enjoyable experience.

Constructive criticism of the external reviewers helped me to sharpen, clarify, and improve the manuscript.

The Swiss National Science Foundation played a crucial role in providing me with the necessary resources for conducting my research and later for publishing the book.

Finally, the wholehearted support of my family, some of whom passed away during the making of this book, filled me with tremendous gratitude. Their encouragement was instrumental in shaping my determination. During long writing hours, my son Manojlo consistently reminded me of his presence. His distractions helped me to firmly remain on the ground and to not lose from sight a sense of purpose, wit and humour even during the most painstaking tasks. My husband, Saša, has been my most involved and inspiring intellectual sparring partner to whom I owe a great deal for this book.

1
The laissez-faire mentality: towards an understanding of peasant resilience, autonomy and institutional change

'Land never stays uncultivated, no matter the political and economic conditions.' So Ivan assured me, without even the faintest inkling that in this moment he had brought about the collapse of my whole working hypothesis of rural change. 'During the worst period of Serbian economic sanctions in the 1990s, people were selling a bull or a barrel of oil to enable tillage – and, surprisingly, not a single hectare lay uncultivated at that time.' He finished his thought, flicking away a fly that had rested briefly on his brow.

Ivan made me think about an issue that I had never considered before. Prior to my fieldwork, I was primarily driven by a neo-institutionalist logic embedded in development scholarship that sees in weak formal institutions harmful outcomes that disable progress, and vice versa. Given that systematic studies of post-socialist agricultural transformation in Serbia were lacking, my initial assumptions about the Serbian village were greatly influenced by the existing post-socialist rural literature.[1] Studies conducted in former socialist states in Eastern Europe tend to interpret recent developments in agriculture rather negatively and perceive the rural population merely as a collateral of new market–state relations. Post-socialist rural scholarship thus locates the problem of development of rural areas in weak states and institutions, corruption and clientelist networks that have grown over the course of neoliberal shift.[2] Similarly, in Serbian public discourse, peasants are seen as the victims of the post-socialist privatization of agriculture. I gradually started to realize that the rural population I observed and their behaviour defied mainstream explanations of post-socialist rural transformations. This is not to say that the Serbian village is greatly different from other post-socialist villages in Europe, or that institutional reforms have been more successful here than elsewhere. The example of Serbian agriculture well illustrates that continuous attempts by government to transform agriculture, which have persisted from the beginning of twentieth century to the present day, have not been particularly successful either in a demographic, agroeconomic or technological sense.[3] Yet the peasants have not disappeared. Moreover, gradually they have begun to thrive – but not because of formal institutional change. My several years of study of three villages in south-east Banat, Autonomous Province of Vojvodina (henceforth referred to as Vojvodina), clearly demonstrate that Ivan's attitude is not isolated. The realization that the relationship between peasants and the land is powerful, ethical and transformative, transcending political-economic conditions and determining life and thriving in the village more than state-planned change, was a major milestone in my research.

Even so, policymakers and many scholars continue to believe that planning and institutional change are the chief preconditions for any further transformations. Their emphasis on planning does not tell us *how* rural development occurs on the ground. Along the way, policymakers reproduce the wrong presumptions about change. They disregard the values of the very people they are attempting to change. Anthropologists have been drawing attention to the fact that neglect of the subjective dimension of value makes understanding of cultural reproduction and change inconclusive (Robbins and Sommerschuh 2016). People's values have a significant impact on their motivations and the pursuit of a desirable life, goals and compliance with the rules and regulations. Values are inseparable from people and their daily actions, as through people they become lodged in subjects and individuals (Keane 2016).[4]

The importance of values in determining social processes is not unknown, yet they have been treated only marginally in scholarship on rural development. Pondering the role of values in determining rural change inspired the broader set of questions that became my main intellectual occupation for several years. Why, despite so many reforms, did peasants in Serbia and elsewhere not disappear as a category? Why are they consistently portrayed as victims of state agendas, as if they did not have any impact on the reforms at all? How did the image of deprived and powerless peasants enter theoretical discourse and become representative of peasantry? The United Nations acknowledges that peasants still produce a third of the world's food and that their numbers have remained quite steady over the last four decades. If they had not been so resilient, surely this would be reflected in shrinking numbers of peasants on a global level. What is it that makes them so resilient? My conversation with Ivan triggered all these broader questions and set me the tricky task of trying to reconcile evidence from my research field with existing theoretical assumptions about the peasantry.

The resilient behaviour of Ivan and his fellow-villagers may only be explained to some extent through clustered historical, political and social rationales. The three most important points of Serbian agricultural politics – the first (1919–41) and second (1945–53) agrarian reforms, and the privatization of agriculture from the 1990s onwards – have made peasants wary and distrustful of the state. Decades-long failure by the authorities to prevent various levels of circumvention and violations of the rules have resulted in a situation where most of the common manifestations of disrespect for formal rules have become customary, broadly accepted and unproblematized. They are now simply a part of the culture. Recognizing this customary disrespect for formal institutions among peasants adds to our understanding of why alternative networks of exchange grow and flourish so quickly and why some institutional solutions hardly get implemented (cf. Ledeneva 2006; Giordano and Hayoz 2013). On the other hand, the established norm that peasants will never leave land uncultivated no matter the price of products, nor the political or economic conditions, offers them some room to manoeuvre in the context of constraints, through disregarding certain policy demands or plans. Furthermore, the sense that they live on the periphery has made most peasants feel as if they are of marginal importance to the state, both in spatial and political-economic terms. All these aspects favour an argument that low socio-economic stability seems to foster high resilience (Holling 1973).

But these factors only partially explain the resilience of peasants from my research field. I believe that their special resilience stems from their relationship with the land. It contains two fundamental components: the individual and the social. Land is critical for providing a sense of autonomy. Ownership is important for the dignity of the peasants, their accountability to the community and for maintaining their social standing in the village. Peasants that I studied are not solely utility maximizers; neither are they driven by completely instrumental reasons. They are equally dedicated to the preservation of their values and the village ethics. The individual and local values and responsibilities of peasants are, therefore, the main reference points that shape their attitudes and behaviour towards state and agricultural politics – not the other way around.

This book attempts to show that peasants from my study are not the victims of state politics but, rather, are the architects of their own and local wellbeing – conceptions of which are often opposed to Serbian state plans for agriculture. My ethnographic evidence reveals that the implementation of state plans for rural development in three villages in Vojvodina gets distorted and interrupted by autonomous actions and values of peasants. At the same time, they are responsible for generating spontaneous wellbeing.[5] The *first* argument of the book aims to explain through 'laissez-faire mentality' – the expressions of autonomous actions and values – the resilience of the peasants and their modification of agricultural policies.

The laissez-faire mentality

In around 1680, French statesman Jean-Baptiste Colbert asked François Legendre, a member of a merchant delegation, 'What should the government do in order to improve the conditions of merchants?', Legendre replied laconically 'laissez-nous faire' (leave it to us). French economist Vincent de Gournay (1712–59) used this anecdote and coined the most famous formulation 'Laissez-faire, laissez-passer', meaning 'let be and let pass' (Castelot 2015, 534–5). The phrase later became associated with a particular spirit, philosophy, and moral doctrine that appeared at the end of eighteenth century when ideas of an unhampered market dominated in Western Europe (Mises 2007). The online Cambridge Dictionary provides two definitions for 'laissez-faire' as used in the context of English language.[6] The first is the more general sense of an individual's 'unwillingness to get involved in or influence other people's activities', while the second pertains to a government that 'does not have many laws and rules that control the buying and selling of goods and services'.

The concept of laissez-faire in the second sense was popularized by the Austrian economist Ludwig von Mises in his magnum opus *Human Action: A Treatise on Economics*. Mises used the term in the original meaning, explaining the functioning of the market as a result of spontaneous human action that cannot be predicted and hence cannot be constrained and regulated by formal laws. Mises saw that it was precisely the inequality of people that harboured the driving force that could generate social cooperation and civilization (Mises 2007, 841). The principle of laissez-faire makes it possible for differences and inequalities to meet through voluntary, unhampered and non-violent cooperation. For Mises, the main question concerning laissez-faire was who should plan cooperation. Should it be the individual, every social actor who makes plans and decisions for themselves, or should it be a government that makes plans for all social actors? He believed that the answer lay in enabling more freedom for individuals and more spontaneous action among them. 'Laissez-faire means: Let the common man chose and act; do not force him to yield to a dictator' (732). Mises's use of 'laissez-faire' primarily implies the detrimental role of institutional constraints on the spontaneity of human action. In this book, I do not reduce laissez-faire solely to its economic definition, although that definition is relevant for peasants' understanding of trade and the economic activities of their households, and for compliance with institutional regulations. My use of the term rather entails peasants' laissez-faire as seen in the context of the manifestation of peasants' worldviews, where autonomy in decision-making, freedom of action, spontaneity and flexibility in everyday cooperation play a dominant role, and where individual and local values generate a self-regulating system that manages a range of economic, social and political relationships in the local setting.

The word 'mentality' on the other hand, while among those obscure and essentialist terms severely criticized in postcolonial anthropology and cultural studies (Said 1978; Appadurai 1986b), I acknowledge here as an emic term. When commenting on themselves or their fellow villagers, my interlocutors frequently ascribed their actions to a 'peasant' or 'Banat' mentality (*mentalitet*). Even though it is true that location does not necessarily determine social, cultural or economic behaviour, it would be incorrect to say that no causal connection whatsoever exists between location and certain types of behaviour – particularly in relatively small places such as villages, where most people work in agriculture and adhere to the same time cycles, work schedules and rituals. The *Banatski mentalitet* (Banat mentality) thus stands here for various personal characteristics, allegedly typical of this region, such as being hospitable, peaceful, calm, relaxed, humble and spontaneous. The *seljački mentalitet* (peasants' mentality) encompasses a group of personal and occupational characteristics and habits that refer to their autonomy, individualism, scepticism, peasant ethics, respect for local traditions, religion and superstitions. The way locals understand such mentalities may in fact be similar to how outsiders see them; nevertheless, observations and commonalities, and the generalizations that have been drawn out of them, do not presuppose value-oriented conclusions. Mentality, as I understand and apply it in this book, reflects the social climate of the three villages. The meaning that I employ is more akin to what Alexis de Tocqueville explained as the 'mores' and 'manners' of Americans (Tocqueville 1838).

Most of my ethnographic findings indicate that the important factors that shape peasants' attitudes and inspire their actions are *a sense of autonomy, village ethics, individualism, scepticism, distrust* and *life on the periphery*. The combination of these factors is what generates the peasants' laissez-faire mentality, but having a sense of autonomy forms its core. Peasants' autonomy determines individuals' understanding of themselves, their actions towards the state and others, and their attainment of goals and self-fulfilment. The laissez-faire mentality actualizes peasants' autonomy in the way that it enables a sense of full control over one's life and resources (as in 'to be your own boss') and creates comfort zones when making decisions that clash with state regulations. The laissez-faire mentality usually manifests in situations when peasants try to find their own, often informal, ways of doing things to access resources, or to cooperate without, or in spite of, state regulations.

The laissez-faire mentality, however, should not be understood as a manifestation of an anarchistic desire to not be controlled and governed either by the local or central, traditional, or state authorities – in other words, as a 'state of not being conditioned by anybody' (Van der Ploeg 2008, 32). The concept rather aims to explain how people in certain relational situations pursue or strive for their own, autonomous way of doing things, and how their undertakings can shape not only micro- but also sometimes macro-processes in Serbian agriculture. I do not claim by any means that the laissez-faire mentality exclusively determines the behaviour of the people I studied. Although this mentality may seem to be prevalent, it is not shared by all. The laissez-faire mentality is explored here as an explanatory concept that approaches most comprehensively peasants as creative and engaged actors in their own lives and businesses, who accommodate the state regulations to their own needs and, in doing so, also shape the rural social fabric through their own actions.

Laissez-faire mentality and land ownership

In my research field, the laissez-faire mentality is profoundly related to land ownership. The bond between the peasant and the land is direct and deeply transformative, which makes cultivation of land possible and necessary despite the price of produce or general political-economic conditions. Through farming, peasants develop their 'farming self' – a sense of autonomy that plays a major role in identifying, articulating, and conceptualizing how they see themselves, but is also key in navigating state constraints, expectations and tasks (Stock and Forney 2014). Peasants in Serbia were cultivating the land during socialist times when markets were controlled and their production was driven by the demands of the state; during the 1980s when they experienced relatively high profits, and state incentives such as subsidies did not exist; the 1990s (1992–4) with the highest hyperinflation in world history (19,810 per cent), when prices of goods doubled every 16 hours; and today, when state subsidies are provided and the market economy is being implemented. It is likely that peasants will continue cultivating the land once state subsidies have disappeared again, and even if the economic situation worsens once more. The land represents the symbolic and economic universe in which peasants act.

The land enables economic sovereignty, particularly in the domain of domestic food production. When wholesale prices are low or the state imposes constraints on the import and export of food, crops, or fertilizers, or when agribusinesses unexpectedly impose unfavourable conditions of cooperation, food as commodity opens avenues for alternative markets such as local markets, organized sale at family farms or slow-food chains. Experienced agro-engineers, knowledgeable journalists and entrepreneurial farmers assure us that there is no such thing as an oversupply of food. Any food that is produced is not a nuisance and will find its way to consumers. Knowing this, peasants hold to their land and production as their sovereignty token (Van der Ploeg 2010, 2014; Altieri and Toledo 2011).

The profound relationship between peasants and land is embedded through peasants' ethics and goes beyond food production and attachment to the natural environment or local traditions. For peasants, farming is not just about work, 'it is more than a job – it is a way of life' (Stock and Forney 2014, 162, Ward and Rawlinson 2017). The care of land and invested labour, commonly referred to as hard work, are intrinsically associated with ideals of personal worth (Redfield 1956). While hard work is both a symbolic and productive expression of a peasant's commitment to agriculture (Burton 2004, Emery 2014), dignity is held to be its result. In other words, dignity emerges from 'honest sweat', the time and effort invested in tillage (James 1899, cited in Burton 2004, 197). In the broader social context outside the family circle, such connotations of dignity are important in mutual evaluations of fellow-villagers and creating of affective connections. In an individual sense, on the other hand, dignity is closely connected with liberty – and these two things are hard to disentangle, as McCloskey rightly observes (McCloskey 2010, 11).

It is widely acknowledged that land and land ownership are fundamentally important for identity and personhood formation in rural settings (Burton 2004). In my research field, most people grasp the symbolic and economic dimensions of the land and ownership. For example, a missed opportunity to acquire land or to maintain and enlarge existing capital is commonly associated with failure. Land and its ownership are, therefore, not only important for materialistic and symbolic expressions of desirable values, but they also represent motivation for self-realization in a village micro-universe. From a broader economic perspective, being without property, or not having enough of it, motivates human action. As Mises argues, those perfectly content with the state of their affairs would have no incentive to change things – which constitutes a purposive action lying in the heart of the theory of human action. A sense of uneasiness, the image of a more satisfactory way of being, and the expectation that some purposeful actions will remove or alleviate that uneasiness is something which stimulates people to act and change their status (Mises 2007, 11–30).

Some scholars, though, would object to Mises's 'acting man'. His concern with an ultimate end overlooks the fact that people may not always be dedicated to fulfilment of a set goal. There are plenty of personal questions, doubts, ideas and other details or inner states that should be taken into consideration which may interfere with the main goal and even distract from activity towards that end. People are fluid and not always as stable and committed to their goals as economists tend to think (Heiss 2015). This is true, but despite being unequally successful in attaining similar goals – and even when they do not take action towards their fulfilment – people may continue to share the same affirmative perception of a particular action or set of values. And this is necessary for the creation of the ambience in which their realization becomes possible. Rich and poor Americans, for example, share an affirmative view of private housing. This does not mean that all Americans will eventually become house owners, but maintaining such a view enables markets to offer affordable credit for private housing, construction companies to keep operating and people to work hard to buy their house and attain this goal. Such an affirmative view of private housing in Pennsylvania alone, which is not among the wealthiest US states, resulted in 70 per cent of homeownership on average. In wealthy Switzerland, the rate of homeownership is 42.3 per cent. The Swiss prefer to rent.

The point is that a generally affirmative view of (land)ownership that I found in the villages where I conducted my research is not one confined to peasants. The Roma, too, most of whom are poor and landless, ground their aspirations for improvement of their livelihoods in the same values. While peasants with land are interested in maintaining, enlarging and protecting their autonomy, Roma strive for autonomy through attaining ownership and improving their social image in the village. In other words, having no property and a lack of means for desired livelihoods, motivates Roma to alleviate their uneasiness. Actions directed towards preserving the autonomy of peasants, or attaining it in the case of Roma, generate various sorts of formal and informal exchange, and open avenues for exploration of autonomous and flexible solutions. In the long run, achieving and seeking autonomy through the existing avenues in a local context enables sharing a laissez-faire mentality.

Laissez-faire mentality and institution-building

The laissez-faire mentality reveals the universe of local values and ethics. Local values that the laissez-faire mentality holds dear – that is, autonomy obtained through land ownership and food production – explain the motivation of peasants and the actions they are ready to undertake to protect or build their autonomy. Local ethics – for example, that land never stays uncultivated no matter the political and economic conditions – explain the constraints that are imposed on peasants and the community when reflecting upon duties, obligations and purposeful actions. Both local values and ethics are of fundamental importance for understanding the internalization of state policies, or the absence thereof. Externally imposed programmes, for instance rural development programmes that have been delegated by state agricultural departments for the past century in Serbia, have often not resonated well with local people. But instead of looking more closely at the source of the problem, policymakers and prominent agricultural scholars usually blame inefficient institutions in Serbia. This brings me to the *second* argument of the book: that the misconceived presumption of change makes rural development less likely. Pour in institutions, add new laws, change the bureaucrats, and stir – and everything will be all right (cf. McCloskey 2016a). Such a conception generates futile involvement of the state and leads to failed projects and wasted financial and human resources. Institutional expansion increases the chronic problem of corruption, as political networks throughout the agricultural sector in Serbia demonstrate with their widespread clientelism, cronyism and rent-seeking.

Lack of compliance with rural policies among peasants from my research field reveals, in essence, a broader problem. When people cannot identify with the imposed ideas of development, then the directives for creation of necessary institutions will be superficially implemented or will not be implemented at all. But external development programmes that resonate well with the values and ethics of local populations may even galvanize the atmosphere for their successful creation and operation. The laissez-faire mentality thus portrays how the local adoption of institutions around state policies of rural development evolves. The laissez-faire mentality, likewise, raises the broader question of how institutions emerge, and how change occurs.

Students of institutionalism advocate predominantly one of two approaches. According to one school of thought, institutions largely emerge because of conscious, tacit yet intentional and collective action that generates constraints on individual action on one hand and compliance with the rules on the other (Searle 1995, 2006; Commons 1990, Ensminger 1998). Another school of thought believes that institutions come into being in a spontaneous and unorganized fashion, as an unintended result of the actions of individuals who, by attaining their individual ends, contribute to their emergence (Menger 1892; Mises 2007; McCloskey 2010, 2016a). In explanations of the ontological character of institutions, John Searle (1995, 2006) argues that institutions exist because everyone acknowledges them, implying that collective intentionality represents the necessary precondition for their constitution. A founder of the Austrian School of Economics, Carl Menger (1892) contested for collective intentionality in his analyses of the establishment of money, arguing that it did not derive from an agreement or law. It was rather the result of a spontaneous system of barter where individuals – by meeting their personal needs in an exchange with other actors – did not know that their acts contributed to the emergence of the money system. When we put aside foundational arguments, we will soon see that these two schools in fact represent a methodological dispute between proponents of methodological collectivism on the one hand, and methodological individualism on the other.

The third, middle way, approach advocates an idea according to which individual, social and political-economic factors collaborate in the creation of institutions and suggests that the roots of institutions lie most likely in between the two approaches. Insisting on either a collectivistic (Searle) or individualistic (Menger) approach may, Tieffenbach rightly warns us, limit our potential for grasping a sense of the emergence of institutions in a comprehensive way (Tieffenbach 2010). Searle's approach, for example, overestimates the importance of consent and awareness of collective action in the process of institutional formation. Institutions are not as transparent as external observers like to think, and therefore people are not always aware of the collective action, nor do they most of the time feel they are contributing to the creation of institutions through their acts, thoughts and language (Tieffenbach 2010, 210). The collective action is therefore not really a satisfactory explanation of the emergence of an institution. Menger's theory, on the other hand, is unable to account for the normative (non-instrumental) dimension of institutions. In most cases, the instrumental goals of individuals are not motivated by achieving higher goals such as building a normative order, but by the sheer satisfaction of needs, where their mission usually ends.

Tieffenbach's critique of Menger, however, puts forward rather a formalistic understanding of the emergence of the normative dimension of institutions. Spontaneous, self-interested actions may also contribute to establishing normative frameworks, quite apart from consent or collective intentionality. In everyday life, when attaining their personal ends, and although they may act instrumentally, people do not simply put aside their ethos, attitudes and ethics. On the contrary, ethos, attitudes and ethics are already incorporated into every single act and piece of conduct of an individual, and they also determine the type of cooperation that takes place with other people, and consequently the normative dimension that may emerge out of it. The example of reputation – the social side of the dignity of peasants in the observed villages – will suffice. Reputation has an enormous effect on regulating behaviour, more than other formal requirements. In social exchanges, to maintain reputation people abide by agreements, keep their word and equally exclude those from cooperation who do not stick to the same unwritten rules. In the order that is created in a highly spontaneous and non-hierarchical way, reputation has the enforcement power – similar to the role of the law in a structured and hierarchical order (see Murtazashvili 2013, 37–47).

Tieffenbach, nevertheless, convincingly argues that institutions are neither fully spontaneous nor fully intentional creations of human acts; they emerge also as acts of force and power. World history records this well. Institutions were often introduced from the outside through oppression and lack of legitimacy, as in socialist countries, but were naturalized as given, and adopted as if they were spontaneously created, or as if they were a result of people's consent.

The laissez-faire mentality explains the relationships between institutions that are supposed to emerge through the set of state regulations in agriculture and individuals. The laissez-faire mentality and the ideas, ethics and values it embodies may hamper the development of institutions but can also create the atmosphere for their functional operation. By analysing manifestations of the laissez-faire mentality in three Vojvodina villages, we can learn about the emergence of informal norms and rules, local and individual preferences and village ethics that are necessary for understanding why some state agricultural institutions function better than others or why some have never come into being. The existing informality in Serbian villages further questions the implementation of agricultural policies and more broadly planned change, particularly when we have in mind that the informal setting usually does not lack operationality and a certain amount of order. The Serbian village often resembles Rushdie's vivid definition of India as 'functioning anarchy' (Rushdie 1991, 33).

In contemplating institutions, the laissez-faire mentality may thus point to two things. Firstly, the fact that spontaneity of actions and self-interested behaviour contribute to and generate normative order with stable prospects. Secondly, disregarding formal rules may happen when institutions are forcefully imposed, are perceived as a nuisance or are not in accord with local values and ethics. This leads us to the next fundamental problem of institution-building – finding the secret balance between collective commitment and pursuing individual interests.

Laissez-faire mentality and the free rider problem

Manifestations of the laissez-faire mentality contain some notable characteristics of what is called the free rider problem. On a methodological level, both the laissez-faire mentality and the free rider problem originate in an idea of methodological individualism. The free rider problem is often used to explain the failure of collective action, that is, why people in certain cases do not comply with the rules, or restrain themselves from doing something in the name of the collective good. It is an ever-topical philosophical, political and economic topic, with the exception of anthropology where it still does not receive significant attention (Acheson 2006).

There are at least two dominant perceptions of the free rider problem. The first approach to the problem originates in economics, the second in neo-institutionalism. The idea of laissez-faire, as explained at the beginning of the chapter, is adopted by the theory of the Austrian School of Economics that rejects the interference of government in commerce and advocates the unhampered and voluntary cooperation among men. Carl Menger believed in a spontaneous social order where, by maintaining their personal interests, people in fact unintentionally build and contribute to social structures. Self-interested actions may not be harmful to wider society, even though some may think differently. But long before Austrian economists, it was Adam Smith who was among the first to emphasize the positive effects of self-interested behaviour. In his conception, the sum of self-interested actions might be beneficial and might even better promote the interests of the whole society than when persons are obliged to do things or when they really intend to promote them (Smith [1776] 1976, 456). Maybe one of the most illustrative and recent examples of collectively beneficial free rider behaviour is the existence of Wikipedia.

> If you'd asked an economist in 1950, 1960, 1970, 1980, 1990, even 2000: 'could Wikipedia work?', most of them would say no. They'd say 'well it can't work, you see, because you get so little glory from this. There's no profit. Everyone's gonna free ride. They'd love to read Wikipedia if it existed, but no one's going to create it because there's a free-riding problem.' And those folks were wrong. (Russ Roberts, EconTalk Episode with Clay Shirky)

Or let us take, for instance, online free schooling materials, tutorials, books and education that is made accessible and affordable thanks to free riders (but also piracy and hackers) – that is, those who do not want to pay for authorization rights, nor wish to comply with the regulations around protected intellectual content. While breaching the rules, people who did such things have contributed to the collective good and the spreading of free knowledge, even though their initial motivation might have been just pure self-interest in obtaining information for themselves (Shirky 2008).

Neo-institutionalism, on the other hand, has analysed the free rider problem from a different angle. Proponents of this view believe that a free rider phenomenon is strongly motivated by the rational behaviour of individuals, who simply see contribution to the common good as irrational and a waste of energy. Rational behaviour drives individuals to do something that is not favourable for the group or community, something 'collectively disastrous' (Elster 1989, 17). At the heart of the free rider phenomenon lies the problem that individuals do not have to have socially beneficial incentives and, hence, are not interested in volunteering and cooperating for the common good, 'because they will have the benefit of it regardless of whether they help to produce it' (Acheson 2006, 119). Overcoming the problem between pursuing individual goals and contributing to collective benefits is one of the main concerns of the collective action dilemma (Haller 2010). According to neo-intuitionalists, this dilemma may possibly be resolved by the inauguration of certain institutions such as property rights and rules, although this is not a guarantee that the problem of the free ride will be solved successfully (Acheson 2006; Landolt and Haller 2015). The free ride has been particularly popularized and discussed in the context of property rights, environmentalism and nature conservation, thanks to Hardin (1968), who advocated the idea that the problem of overexploitation of commons can be stopped by enforcing private property rights and limiting access to those commons. Hardin, however, was proved wrong, because numerous scholars, such as Elinor Ostrom (1990), showed that in certain contexts without state enforcements and privatization of resources commons may function better than private property. In sum, from the neo-institutional point of view the free rider problem is seen as an obstacle to achieving collective wellbeing, but also as an institutional failure in harmonizing the whims and striving of individuals with the ideals of the collective.

The laissez-faire mentality observed in the three villages might in certain situations display the creative but also destructive features of the free rider problem. Acheson (1994) rightly notices that free riding and collective activities are not mutually exclusive: 'Humans clearly do devote much time and effort to collective activities such as charities, political parties, and efforts to secure collective goods for their community, profession, or other secondary group – even when they might be "free riders"' (25). As later chapters show, some of the examples such as subsidies, political activism in the village, access to common pastures, contributions to obligatory agricultural pensions insurance or evading land and local taxes can be regarded as collectively beneficial but destructive at the same time, and this predominantly depends on political and market incentives and holding to local values.

Why is laissez-faire not a form of resistance?

Functional institutions require compliance. When institution-building is imposed by force it plants seeds of social disharmony that, depending on how they are watered, rarely grow into direct social unrest but more often into an open or covert resistance. The laissez-faire mentality among the peasants observed in the villages may be understood as a form of resistance, but it is not this. Resistance implies behaviour 'on the part of some or all of the members of society, either passive or active, which is directed toward the rejection or circumvention of a social change' (Vander Zanden 1959, 312). It can entail local or widespread action. Resistance is generally understood as politically motivated, although some authors suggest it can be identity based as well (Hollander and Einwohner 2004). As a political action, resistance usually appears as a reaction to class and economic inequalities, and uneven distribution of power. Resistance, coming from different political spectrums, has the aim of levelling social differences, improving or maintaining living conditions and people's social position. Targets of resistance vary from case to case, and may be individuals, groups, organizations, institutions or entire social structures (Hollander and Einwohner 2004). Despite the strong political preconditions, resistance itself is not necessarily revolutionary, anti-state, or anarchist in nature (see White 1986). Most of the time, resistance is motivated by desired adjustments to the existing system, that is, correction of the system until it becomes more just and inclusive. Often, parties that resist may at the same time contribute to maintaining the system and indeed collaborate with parties with which they are in conflict.

Apart from being a vague and generic term, 'in many works, resistance seems to be as much a symbol of the writer's political stance as an analytical concept' (Hollander and Einwohner 2004, 547).[7] Perhaps for this reason, there are disagreements regarding its very conception. There are two crucial problems related to resistance: recognition and intent (Hollander and Einwohner 2004, 539). For some, resistance is overt, organized or spontaneous intentional action against someone or something. For others, resistance may be expressed through covert, subtle or unintentional sabotage, as well as through non-compliance with rules and expectations. The latter form has been greatly popularized in anthropology by Scott (1977, 1985, 1986, 1987; Scott and Kerkvliet 1986), who terms it 'everyday resistance' (see also Kerkvliet 1990, whose similar concept of everyday politics is broadly applied in peasant studies). Scott challenges the idea of resistance that is taken for granted as visible and recognizable, and instead emphasizes that powerless people do not have the capacity to openly confront those who are superior. Instead, they often apply more subtle and covert expressions of resistance such as foot-dragging, absenteeism or slander.[8]

The most comprehensive definition of resistance would be that it is an organized or spontaneous, overt or covert *political action* (broadly conceived), *against* someone or something, and *on behalf* of *common values*. For resistance (particularly that which concerns peasants) to qualify as such 'acts must be backed by a *consensus* among a significant sector of the local population – admittedly difficult to measure – *on the moral legitimacy* of certain social practices' (Korovkin 2000, 3).

When I said that laissez-faire is not resistance, I had the following distinctions in mind. The laissez-faire mentality is a *cause of certain behaviour*, while resistance is instead a *reaction*, sometimes a *means*. Peasants' actions spring from their sense of autonomy, ethics and uneasiness, regardless of what might be the definite end of their acts. The laissez-faire mentality and resistance also rest in two different methodological fields. The laissez-faire mentality stems from methodological individualism, where varieties of individual goals may not always drive people to comply with collective interests, the common good or political actions. On the other hand, resistance, even when it is in a form of individual conduct, usually emerges as a response to collective problems that affect the lives of people, which basically classifies it in the register of methodological collectivism. In Korovkin's words, this would mean that if people tacitly share a common understanding of inequalities and injustices in society, or if they have consensus on the moral legitimacy of resistance, then they contribute to collective actions even if they act as individuals (Korovkin 2000).

Put simply, the laissez-faire mentality manifests as self-interested behaviour that most of the time is not occupied with the interests of social justice or other political concerns. The preservation of peasants' autonomy which is a fundamental value in the moral universe of peasants, for example, often collides with commitment to common political goals. Even if some of the observed practices may look like resistance on the surface, they cannot be regarded as such, as long as they lack a shared political component. When peasants resist somebody or something, in most cases their acts are not motivated by political or social reasons in the sense that they want greater equality or more political rights. Their resistance is usually motivated by economic reasons, to gain more market opportunities or sometimes more protection from the market conditions. The predominant understanding of the concept, thus, classifies resistance as a primarily political and an ethical act. Manifestations of the laissez-faire mentality, on the other hand, although not political, are economically and ethically grounded in the local context.

Lastly, one dominant image about resistance prevails. Resistance is often presented as a homogeneous act, without paying much attention to the inner conflicts and personal disagreements on a number of issues that surround those who resist. By contrast, the laissez-faire mentality provides an insight into the numerous conflicts and needs of individuals that discourage collective action, organized or spontaneous resistance. The laissez-faire mentality explains why there is a lack of political interest and collective engagement.

§

Clarification of the complexity of the laissez-faire mentality should enable us now to draw several conclusions about what it stands for and what it is not. The laissez-faire mentality is an explanatory concept for human action, based on the free will of individuals and motivated by alleviating the uneasiness in their economic and social standing. It stems from a sense of autonomy that is profoundly intertwined with peasants' ethics, and which evolves around land ownership and food production. The laissez-faire mentality is an integrative element of institution-building, but it is also a factor that contributes to or prevents the changing and acceptance of externally imposed institutions. It is primarily concerned with individual interests and pursuing autonomous way of getting things done, which sometimes includes the circumvention of rules and avoiding collective participation that is often compared to free riding. But the laissez-faire mentality, like free riding, sometimes produces collectively beneficial outcomes. Laissez-faire actions are mostly not politically motivated, which is why they cannot be regarded as a form of resistance, despite many superficial commonalities between them. This book, in essence, brings closer the applied and ethical meaning of the laissez-faire actions and their influence on (a) the constitution of a good life in the local context, and (b) the compliance with the state agricultural policies aimed at strengthening rural development.

Where did this book emerge?

Gaj is the central village on the bank of the Danube River in south-east Banat, Vojvodina, around which two other neighbouring villages Malo Bavanište and Beli Breg orbit.[9] Gaj, with a population of around 3,000, is among the most populous villages in the area. Beli Breg and Malo Bavanište are significantly smaller, with approximately 400 people each. Gaj has continually existed in the same location since 1760 under the Austro-Hungarian empire, although before this period the old village (Staro Selo) used to be some four kilometres from its current centre (Pavković 2009, 21). Gaj displays urbanistic and aesthetic features of an undisrupted settlement. The streets, houses, public buildings and parks around the centre of the village are wide and spacious, mirroring the prototype of Austro-Hungarian urbanistic planning and the ethnic diversity of the old empire.[10] The families that live in the central village represent old and better-off domestic families of Serbian, Hungarian, Romanian and Czech origin. In contrast to the central village, significantly modest and less urbanized lower and upper parts of Gaj were recent additions to the village that emerged as a result of migration during the twentieth century, through either spontaneous or organized resettlement of people from the deprived regions.

Like upper and lower parts of Gaj, Beli Breg and Malo Bavanište emerged as recent settlements through intensive migration waves after the Second World War. Part of the population settled in the two villages during the second agrarian reform (1945–53) when there was also organized resettlement of the Orthodox Slav population from different regions of socialist Yugoslavia. The other part of the population spontaneously migrated from the poor mountainous regions of south-eastern Serbia, seeing in Bant and these villages a chance to improve their life. These two villages, although somewhat modest in comparison to Gaj, reflect a homogeneous ethnic and religious structure which was determined by the migration of predominantly Orthodox Serbs and Montenegrins. Gaj, on the other hand, because of its historic legacy has maintained a diverse ethnic and religious structure in which Orthodox Serbs form the majority, with Catholic Czechs, Orthodox Romanians, Catholic Hungarians and Orthodox and neo-Protestant Roma as minorities spread in central, lower and upper parts of the village (see Figure 1.1).

All three villages are predominantly agricultural, with approximately 45 per cent of the population dealing solely in agriculture. Some combine farming with other occupations, a small number are professionals who do not work the land, while the rest are pensioners or unemployed. Apart from the big agricultural enterprise in Gaj, there is a small amount of industry in nearby towns where some of the local population work full time and others work on an occasional or seasonal basis. Several entrepreneurs in the village run small or medium-sized businesses, usually based on providing services. The state, however, is seen as the biggest employer, where people work in diverse public sectors. Unemployment is one of the biggest challenges in the area, where according to unofficial data some 10 per cent of the population is considered to be unemployed. In Gaj, except in Roma families, every household has at least one member with a stable income, be it salary or pension, while other members work in agriculture or in other occupations, as either registered or unregistered workers. The rarest situation is households where all members are officially employed.

Figure 1.1 The Catholic church in Gaj. Source: Author.

Gaj's convenient location in relation to nearby towns (Kovin, Pančevo and Smederevo) has perhaps caused the outflow of people to be much lower than in other rural parts of Serbia. An additional reason for the low outflow of people from Gaj may lie in the fact that most families possess land which has been gaining value since 2000, which keeps people attached to the village despite their professional occupations. Unlike Gaj, in Beli Breg and Malo Bavanište one-third of the population lives and works abroad as temporary workers. The reason for this lies in the fact that families who spontaneously settled there after the Second World War did not have land; the only way for them to acquire it and satisfy the needs of growing families was through temporary work in foreign countries, which over time has converted into intergenerational practice.

How did this book emerge?

Back in 2013, I started my one-year fieldwork research in Gaj, Beli Breg and Malo Bavanište, with follow-up visits continuing until 2017. During this period, I studied primarily the active agricultural rural population and most of my ethnographic insights were obtained through numerous planned and spontaneous conversations and everyday socialization with peasants, during our joint visits to their pastures and fields, or while riding together on the tractors or combines, or while helping in small tasks that did not require agricultural knowledge. Weeding, mending garden paths or packing the meat were tasks that peasants were least afraid to delegate to me, and which also sometimes allowed the continuation of small and sometimes fascinating conversations about their lives, values or desires. Similarly, I gained many valuable insights from interviews with local professionals, entrepreneurs, clerks and the republic and local representatives of the Ministry of Agriculture.[11]

The peasants made up the core of my investigation (see Figure 1.2).[12] I decided to follow how my interlocutors addressed themselves in everyday life and so use terms that they were comfortable with. When talking about themselves, their fellow villagers and agricultural associations, my interlocutors predominantly used the Serbian term *seljak or paor*, meaning peasant, regardless of a person's sex or age.[13] In everyday speech, use of the term peasant seemed to present no issue, even though my interlocutors were well aware of its pejorative

Figure 1.2 Peasants at work threshing the wheat with a combine harvester.
Source: Author.

connotations.[14] Once, while walking with one of my female friends from the village, I asked her 'How did agricultural producers from Gaj react' to some or other state policy, wanting to express verbally my appreciation of their work by using a politically neutral term. She slowed down, turned her head towards me, and it seemed as if she was not used to the phrase. 'You mean peasants?', she asked. 'Yes, I mean peasants', I replied.

The core of my peasant interlocutors cultivated 5–20 ha each, while a somewhat smaller though significant group cultivated 30–60 ha. Only a few people cultivated more than 70 ha, and they represented the wealthiest peasants in the village. People who cultivated 5–10 ha combined agriculture with additional occupations and were not considered by other villagers as 'pure' peasants because they did not deal solely in agriculture. Those who cultivated 10–20 ha combined farming with livestock breeding, while those who cultivated more than 20 ha were devoted only to agriculture, with a few exceptions. The average peasant households, those that cultivated 15–20 ha according to my informal survey, usually possessed tractors and other necessary agricultural machinery that was generally 30–40 years old. Despite being outdated, their equipment was regularly maintained and in satisfactory condition, whereas only better-off peasants could afford to renew their machinery.

People who had less than 2 ha usually rented out their land because farming on such a small scale was considered unprofitable. In many cases, people who possessed less than 2 ha, did not have the necessary mechanization nor agricultural premises for stocking crops and housing machines, and so opted to rent out their land instead. Where this was not the case, people used these small areas for growing vegetables in greenhouses, gardening, producing watermelons or for orchards and sold their products directly at the village market or in the nearby towns.

The retired population of the village usually gardened a little and bred animals for household consumption. They also rented out their land and represented the main local supplier of additional land for cultivation. Apart from retired people, peasants could lease additional land from the municipality, which prioritized peasants who combined livestock breeding with agriculture, as a measure to support livestock producers.

The average household consisted of three generations living under the same roof. In Gaj, and in other villages, founding of separate households by younger family members was not yet the norm. There were a few examples where young couples had set up separate households, but this process was just beginning to emerge. This did not apply to

Roma, who generally have more family members living under the same roof and practise a different sort of household organization, separating easily to form new households.

Examination of social and economic aspects of village organization helped me to understand better the worldviews of peasants and other villagers that live from agriculture or contribute to the local economy and wellbeing in manyfold ways. Although Gaj, Beli Breg and Malo Bavanište are dominated by farming and peasants' ethics, they are not homogeneous settings, and the display of the laissez-faire mentality was especially instructive to point to different and inter-ethnic individual approaches for attaining of what constitutes a good life in the village. More importantly, the study of the three villages and the practices and values of the local population was essential for discovering the level of their agency and engagement in creating their own wellbeing, despite or without state interference.

The structure of the book

The book is organized into eight chapters. Following this chapter, Chapter 2, 'Peasants in theoretical and historical perspective', considers the theoretical development of the concept of peasants, and sets out the historical conditions of the peasantry and agriculture in Serbia. Through an overview of peasant studies literature, I show how the dominant perception of the peasantry as a disadvantaged group was constructed and how, by focusing mostly on the weakness of their position, such approaches neglect the potentials of peasant autonomy and ethics in adopting agricultural reforms. This theoretical overview is intertwined with the major political agrarian reforms in Serbia, from 1919 to the present day. The merging of scholarly and historical perspectives aims to demonstrate how historical events matter for the theoretical interpretation of the peasantry – as well as how theoretical interpretations draw on political-historical realities, but usually only to the extent that fits pre-existing scientific paradigms.

In Chapter 3, 'Nesting the laissez-faire mentality', I portray how laissez-faire emerges as a cultural matrix in which numerous elements overlap and coexist. Although the laissez-faire mentality cannot be reduced to bare historical, political, ideological or cultural contingencies, these aspects are, nevertheless, important for its more or less visible manifestations. Through ethnographic accounts I illustrate how peasants' sense of autonomy, village ethics, individualism, scepticism and distrust, and their life on the periphery come together and constitute formative elements of laissez-faire mentality.

The influence of laissez-faire mentality is most obvious in the everyday practices of peasants who accommodate state agricultural policies to their own needs and liking. In Chapter 4, 'Laissez-faire practices versus rural development policies', I discuss how, contrary to the predominant perception, state reforms have never been mechanically implemented, and how the local ways of thinking, practices and individual attitudes have distorted them. The chapter explores reasons why the state policies got trapped in the networks of voluntaristic, opportunistic and spontaneous actions of local recipients. Subsidies, regulation of the peasants' trade, crop insurance, compulsory pension insurance for peasants and village associations represent the major policies that were expected to bring prosperity to local people, but they all crumbled in the local context.

In Chapter 5, 'Local politics and rural development', I analyse how post-socialist institutional expansion in Serbia has affected state plans for rural development and the rural population. I consider the main byproduct of such institutional expansion on the local level – the rise of a new political culture and elites that are notably divorced from state ideals of rural development. I discuss why the narrative of state rural development has rather become a political mantra that serves clientelism and rent-seeking. The chapter also reflects on the role of the peasants in such circumstances and how the laissez-faire mentality greatly contributes to existing local arrangements and the understanding of local politics.

In the context of existing unfavourable political conditions, I examine 'Whose rural development?' in Chapter 6 and demonstrate that state policies are neither the drivers nor enablers of the gradual thriving of the local population. State policies, in effect, just make a tiny, favoured stratum of society richer and closer to sources of wealth. Conversely, endogenous development has proved to be the only possible route to thriving in a local context. This form of development emphasizes the genuine importance of local values, autonomy, role-models and social imitation for change. Endogenous development makes better-off individuals accountable for their success in the local community. The chapter demonstrates that such development spreads horizontally, unlike competing state-envisioned development. Likewise, it proves that a community strengthened through local networks of support and ethics is better able to endure political change and the whims of the state and the markets.

In Chapter 7, 'Roma and rural development', I turn the focus to Roma, who are largely excluded from state rural development policies, and examine the ways through which they attempt to improve their livelihoods. I continue to elaborate further on the meaning of endogenous development but in the context of Roma, who are among the poorest people in the villages. The chapter discovers how Roma make their own way towards ownership, autonomy and social recognition – the pillars of a good life in the village. Their attempts to do so often run contrary to state programmes of support for the Roma population. To avoid the transaction costs that they would incur by following state-controlled paths, Roma opt for flexible and laissez-faire solutions. I show that Roma do not passively accept the contingencies of daily life and that, through asylum-seeking, religious conversion and gleaning, they attempt to acquire property and restore dignity and social recognition.

The book concludes by reflecting on the processes of change in the context of the three villages and the meaning of development in the local context. Spontaneous development, which is often unrecognized and out of sight of the institutionally driven policymakers, may answer many riddles that have been haunting planners and scholars for a long time. I suggest that both scholars in rural development and policymakers should focus more on questions that can explain how local populations internalize the planners' values and ideas, why and to what extent, in order to understand how the cooperation between peasants and the state may be enhanced. As the laissez-faire mentality enables the atmosphere for fulfilling peasants' actions, thriving, and organizing local life, I question planning as the only means for achieving the change. Along the way, I shed new light on how peasants rise above victimization – an image that has followed them for many years.

Notes

1. When I started my research in 2013 there were no contemporary anthropological studies on the post-socialist transformations of Serbian villages. Since then the situation has barely changed, with only a few publications, which share a pessimistic view of the collapse of the socialist state and its negative effects on state social care and economy in rural areas (see Thelen et al. 2014; Thiemann 2014, 2017, 2023).
2. Thelen (2011) criticizes the reductionist approach of post-socialist studies that resulted in production of rather ambivalent conceptions of eastern and western types of political systems and economies instead of innovative theoretical conceptualizations.
3. Gaćeša (1995) in his book *Radovi iz agrarne istorije i demografije* documents the continuity of failures and problematic achievements of agricultural policies especially in Vojvodina Province throughout the twentieth century within two different political regimes: the Kingdom of Yugoslavia and later socialist Yugoslavia.

4   Numerous studies point to the fundamental role of values and cultural factors in a broad range of human activities, from voting (Cramer 2016), through economic calculation and commodity exchange (Appadurai 1986a, Ferguson 1992), to establishing institutions and especially property rights (Acheson 2002, 2015; Chibnik 2011; Ensminger and Knight 1997; Macfarlane 1978).
5   The concept of development in its most overarched meaning represents plans for improvement and political, ideological and economic emancipation of people usually conducted by the state and local centres of power. Another meaning of development refers to spontaneous intermingling of people and the local resources that generate conditions for attaining individual and local wellbeing. It is known variously as endogenous, domestic or development from within.
6   https://dictionary.cambridge.org/dictionary/english/laissez-faire?q=Laissez-faire.
7   Hollander and Einwohner (2004, 544–7) estimate that there are eight distinct types of resistance.
8   Scott's concept of resistance, apart from being positively accepted in social sciences, has at the same time attracted a good deal of critique. Brass (1991) charges Scott with neo-populism and anti-progressivism, because in his theory resistance is meant to preserve the status quo ante, and not to combat state capitalism. Furthermore, Scott's theory on everyday resistance has been criticized for exhibiting conceptual imprecision and analytical confusion (Brass (1991) and for undermining gender in analyses of peasant resistance, which would inevitably necessitate rethinking of the very concept. Joseph (1990), in a review of the literature on everyday peasant resistance, focuses on examples of covert and subtle self-interested behaviour of peasants that Scott and others equate with resistance, which in his opinion blurs analytical boundaries between resistance and delinquency.
9   Vojvodina Province (officially the Autonomous Province of Vojvodina) consists of three regions: Banat, Bačka and Srem.
10 After the collapse of Austro-Hungarian empire, Vojvodina Province became part of Kingdom of Serbs, Croats and Slovenes (SCS) in 1918, which in 1929 adopted the new name of the Kingdom of Yugoslavia which consisted of these three constitutive nationalities. After the Second World War, the kingdom was replaced by the Socialist Federal Republic of Yugoslavia which despite some territorial changes, represented territorial and ethnic continuity of the previous Kingdom of Yugoslavia.
11 The core of my fieldwork data comes from participant observation and semi-structured interviews. I conducted more than 90 interviews, most of which were with peasants, and other local people of different ages, sex, professional, social, political, economic and ethnic backgrounds from Gaj, Beli Breg and Malo Bavanište. Parallel to this, I conducted 11 in-depth interviews with policymakers, local and regional officials, in order to get a comprehensive understanding of the context of agricultural changes, policy paradigms and problems. Likewise, to document agricultural policy, strategies and outcomes, I used extensive quantitative data obtained from the Statistical Office of the Republic of Serbia and Ministry of Agriculture. In addition, for following different processes in agriculture and local politics, I used archive sources, such as the archives of daily local and national newspapers, official documents, laws and strategies, obtained from internet databases and the National Archives.
12 All my interlocutors are anonymized, apart from cases when I spoke to Republic officials and professionals who consented to disclosing their names for this book.
13 One of the biggest associations of agricultural producers in Vojvodina Province is named *Banatski paori* (Peasants of Banat), but there are also other associations such as *Novoseljanski paori* where the first part of the title refers to the name of the village Banatsko Novo Selo.
14 The use of the word 'peasant' as a disparaging term, implying backwardness and conservatism. Similar parallels can be found in other languages, for example the use of 'hick' in English.

2
Peasants in theoretical and historical perspective

Scholars have never quite reached consensus on the meaning of the terms 'peasant' and 'the peasantry'. The problem of the definition emerges, in fact, out of the heterogeneity of rural social organization around the world, diverse historical legacies, rural traditions and different economic practices. Sometimes scholars ask if peasants 'are a mode of production or economy or a class' (Shanin 1983, 79). Some think the term peasant is inappropriate in the context of a globalized world and the market economy, because it is obsolete and does not refer to the variety of livelihood practices and identities that rural populations are now experiencing (Kearney 1996). Others argue that the term peasant is imprecise because it confuses the 'persons and their roles' (Leeds 1977, 228). Some believe that the phenomenon of the peasantry is not even a universal one, arguing that Australia, New Zealand, Canada and North America, countries colonized by England, have never had a true peasantry (Macfarlane 1978, 201).

What are the common features of peasants, conceived as broadly as possible? Peasants are not a homogeneous group. They share some interrelated features, but also differ in many ways. Despite peasants all over the world having experienced significant transformations in the past few decades, the following two definitions of peasants are still relevant and quite accurate. Theodor Shanin argues that the peasantry is characterized by four intertwined facets. 'The family farm as the basic multi-functional unit of social organisation, land husbandry and usually animal rearing as the main means of livelihood, a specific traditional culture closely linked with the way of life of small rural communities and multi-directional subjection to powerful outsiders' (1973, 63–4). Frank Ellis bridges frequent problems in defining the peasantry that concern peasants' relations with the market and administrative state systems. 'Peasants [live on] farm households, with access to their means of livelihood in land, utilizing mainly family labor in farm production, always located in a larger economic system, but fundamentally characterized by partial engagement in the markets which tend to function with a high degree of imperfection' (1988, 12).

Two connotations of peasants seem to dominate today's perception of the peasantry. One is socio-political and refers to the rural poor; the other is economic and refers to subsistence production. Although peasants worldwide have been in the markets for centuries many scholars, including Wolf, hold that the aim of the peasant is subsistence not accumulation (1955, 454). Later, the subsistence image of the peasant economy was accompanied by the portrayal of the rural poor. Mintz rightly tried to point to the wrong identification of landless, wage-earning agricultural workers with peasants, because they are already involved in other economic relations (1973, 95). But his intervention did not influence the dominant perception of the peasantry. Such a trend can be explained as the result of Marxist legacy in peasant studies.

According to orthodox Marxism it is believed that the peasantry and agriculture suffered crucial transformations from being subjected to the capitalist mode of production, among which three forms were specifically stressed: differentiation, pauperization and marginalization (Shanin 1983, 69). Differentiation came as the result of the increasing accumulation of capital among a few rich people in agricultural production, while others inevitably became pauperized and marginalized in the unequal distribution of wealth. This theoretical presumption was reflected in numerous anthropological studies. It will suffice to name Geertz's (1968) analyses of agricultural relations in Indonesia during the centuries of Dutch rule, or Halpern and Brode's influential article on peasant society, in which the authors express concern about the peasantry because 'in historic times peasants were almost everyone, while during the past century they have been in the process of becoming no one' (1967, 46). In peasant studies, Marxist theoretical approaches seem to prevail and have continued to influence the production of the literature from agrarian economy to political and social aspects of the peasantry worldwide (see Bernstein and Byres 2001, Mencher 1983). *The Journal of Peasant Studies* has been the central point of reference since 1973. By acknowledging a variety of other approaches that have been contributing to discussion of the peasantry (Eastern European folklore school, the French school, the South-east Asian school and the Latin American school – to name a few), I focus only on the literature in English that has been formative for the portrayal of peasants as subjected class. I sketch out the leading ideas that have emerged in these works, aiming to present the development of the concept of peasantry.

From classical to contemporary perception of the peasantry: key theoretical concepts

Peasants' worldview

In peasant studies there has been a strong emphasis on peasants' specific worldview. In an attempt to comprehend how their particular worldview emerged, Redfield (1947) designed an ideal folk society. Redfield was influenced by the debate on urban–rural dichotomy that argued that both societies are characterized by specific occupational, cultural and social facets. The peasantry was seen as people who nurtured a lifestyle that had been lost in the urban areas, having a 'specific' culture and being a 'law unto themselves' (Buttel and Newby 1980, 7). Redfield argued that peasant societies have nurtured specific worldviews and ethics because of their relative isolation from urban centres, their strong collectivism and sense of autonomy, the subordination of a group to traditional institutions and norms, religion and magic, the absence of critical thinking, systematic organization of knowledge and individualism.

The specific 'peasant worldview' was furthered by Banfield's (1967) theory on the ethos of South Italian peasants, which he termed 'amoral familism'. It emerges out of sentiments such as strong distrust of non-family members. The ethos prevents collective action, because members of the society are exclusively interested in their own family members, and the broader community is seen as a threat. The ethos affects political incapacity to operate for the common good of the villagers, and consequently leads to a lack of economic progress and the 'backwardness' of rural societies in Southern Italy.[1]

Foster (1965), in a similar way, argued that peasant societies represent a relatively closed system with a strong integrating principle, which he terms *the image of limited good*. This principle operates as a cognitive category that nurtures a specific worldview. Since all resources, material and immaterial (including power, status, love, respect, friendship), exist in a limited quantity, if people want to improve their position it has to be at the expense of others from the village. Foster's image of limited good has been subject to long debates and critique in anthropology for its extravagance (see Bennett 1966; Kennedy 1966;

Du Boulay and Williams 1987), but it also opened new avenues in the interpretation of peasants' society and their ways of adjusting economic conditions.

Contemporary authors have also analysed the importance of the specific ethics, sense of autonomy and self-sufficiency of peasants. These originate in peasants' occupation, their specific relation toward land and farming practices, social and natural environment, landscapes and ecological concerns (Stock and Forney 2014; Stock et al. 2014; Emery 2014; Thompson 1995, Ellis 2000).

Peasant economy

The specific peasants' world view has been accompanied by approaches that focus on the peasant economy. The pioneering and distinctive work of Chayanov (Thorner et al. 1986, xi–xxiii), who developed the theory of family economy, has greatly influenced later scholars and debates. Chayanov believed that each peasant family is based on a principle of a *labour–consumer balance* between the degree of satisfaction of family needs and the degree of the drudgery of labour (xvii). Peasant family farms are driven by fundamentally different motives than capitalist farms, and it is not possible to apply principles of classical economics to them. Some of the crucial elements of classical economics that operate in close functional interdependence are wages, interest, rent and acquiring profit. Chayanov argues that if any of these four elements is missing, the whole theoretical pyramid will collapse. Because the peasant family farm relies on its own labour there is no need for hired labour and therefore there are no wages to pay. When wages are a missing element, the other three elements – rent, interest, and profit – are not sufficient to explain peasant family farm production by using classical economic theory (Thorner et al. 1986, xviii–xxi). Although Chayanov's theory of a peasant economy is static, he sees in peasant family farm production a particular advantage. Given that its underlying principle is a labour–consumer balance and not profit, he believes that the peasant economy has more survivability. In cases where the capitalist farm may go bankrupt, the peasant family farm may work longer hours, reduce consumption, sell its products at lower prices, and manage to survive (xviii). Chayanov's economic analyses of the peasantry were criticized chiefly by the Marxist scholars for not leaving space for the political action of peasants, nor for the explanation of changes in the village. The peasant, in Chayanov's view, is interested only in keeping his balance between the drudgery of labour and consumerism. For this reason, his theory is considered populist and anti-revolutionary by the Marxist vision of the peasantry (Brass 1991).

Wolf's (1955, 1966) approach is similar to Chayanov's, but with a slightly different emphasis. While Chayanov's method emerged from observing the occupation, production and lifecycle of peasants, Wolf's approach was holistic and concerned with the socio-political and economic organization of peasantry. Wolf primarily perceives peasants as an economic category and posits that non-cultivators cannot be identified as peasants. He sees in peasants' communities reflections of a larger whole. Wolf formulates three types of productive relations that characterize peasants. The first is between the peasant and the land, the second is between the peasant and the market and the third is between the peasant and the state. Wolf argues that economic organization of peasants mainly rests on their subordination to the outside world and relative dependence on external social and economic factors. In order to balance between family and outsiders' demands, peasants can choose one of two strategies. They can either intensify labour and increase production, or they can curtail consumption. This is, for Wolf, the main peasant dilemma (Wolf 1966, 12–18). Like Chayanov, Wolf dismisses the idea that peasants are static, even though their economy develops within a semi-closed context. They are rather engaged in the dynamic search for a solution, moving constantly between the two poles of their basic dilemma (Wolf 1966, 17).[2] In his later writings, Wolf became more interested in power relations that affect peasant communities, and saw economic and ecological processes simultaneously as relations of power (Silverman 1979, 64).

The peasant economy became a topic of interdisciplinary debate (mostly between economists, anthropologists, historians and sociologists), triggered by Karl Polanyi's book *The Great Transformation* in 1944. Polanyi argued that the emergence of the modern industrial society and market economy in Western Europe represents a distinct moment of human history – a breakthrough inspired by human invention, and a break with past times when the market was not embedded in the wider society. He holds that pre-industrial societies were primarily interested in maintaining reciprocity and redistribution that were, unlike markets, the two main integrating principles. The debate was advanced when Malinowski challenged the methods of classical economics as inapplicable to non-industrial, peasant and primitive societies (Cohen 1967). The 'battle over methods' (Hann and Hart 2011, 41) culminated in the 1960s and the 1970s, with two well-articulated positions: one represented by substantivists, and the other by formalists (Wilk 1996, 3–13; Hann and Hart 2011, 55–72). At the heart of the debate was the question of whether economic practices are universal or particular and embedded in different social institutions and types of society. The formalists contended that certain economic patterns appear in every society, regardless of its economic and social development, and that individual rationality is a universal phenomenon which directs economic behaviour accordingly. For example, the work of Macfarlane (1978), although not directly inspired by the debate, is an interesting support of a formalist view. By analysing English peasants from the thirteenth to eighteenth century, Macfarlane showed that these societies, although they were never peasant in the classical sense, practised some proto-capitalist forms of the economy such as the individualistic worldview that English peasants developed very early on, inclusive institutions of private property and hereditary rights that ensured women's equal rights to land and inheritance.

Substantivists, on the other hand, argued that there is a fundamental difference between industrial societies, on the one hand, and primitive or peasant societies, on the other, and that differences in the economies of these societies are of kind, not degree. The economies of non-industrial societies operate outside the principles of rationality and market. Fulfilling moral norms and obligations often appear as superior goals compared to profit maximization and individual gain. Thus, reciprocity and redistribution act as the most important integrating principles in such societies.

The formalist and substantivist approaches have further translated into the debate over the moral or rational peasant (or actors) and the nature of the peasant economy. In sum, scholars who advocate the substantivist view (Dalton 1969, Sahlins 1972, Scott 1977) hold that peasants prefer communitarianism to individualism, common to private property, and the welfare of the community that is provided through strong patron–client networks and mutual assistance. The economy is thus integrated into society through reciprocity and redistribution. The principles underlying these societies are a high level of solidarity and spontaneous or forced altruism. Yet it was Popkin's (1979) work which influenced rethinking pre-industrial peasant societies. He argued that peasant societies are to be seen as societies where coercion, and not solidarity, plays an important role.[3] Such societies were socially stratified even before implementation of the market economy because the whole set of relationships and access to resources were under the control of a patron or a landlord. Individual freedom and invention were subject to collective imperatives. 'In order to maintain dyadic ties and foreclose other options, the patron is often the one who prevents the spread of literacy, forcibly keeps peasants from direct involvement in markets, and rejects innovations for raising total production if the new methods have the potential to decrease peasant dependence' (Popkin 1979, 34). They were not less rational, but bounded.

Popkin and scholars who advocate the rational actor model (Chibnik 1980, Epstein 1967, Barth 1967, Finke 2003, 1995) present rather a marginal view which sees in the expansion of markets an opportunity that favours landless, poor or oppressed actors, given that markets provide mobility of labour and choice. And more importantly, the expansion of markets leads to the officialization and universalization of the rights of disadvantaged groups that were once exclusive and belonged to the authority of the landlord or patron.

Peasants as political category

As nation-state building projects and the market economy have spread over developing countries throughout the twentieth century, scholars have become increasingly interested in studying peasants as a political category. They are concerned with political origins and the forms of political development of peasants throughout history to the present. Likewise, special attention is given to the creation of the peasantry primarily as the result of political engineering of colonial authorities (see Vincent 1983).

One of the central themes in the political discourse on the peasantry is the subordination of peasants to broader social and power structures, with special emphasis on class struggle, resistance and inequality as burning issues for peasantry all around the world (see Bernstein and Byres 2001). Scholars often see in peasants' way of life and their occupation the essence of their inferiority and weak political capacity. In Hobsbawm's (1973) view

> [peasants'] weakness is based not only on social inferiority, on the lack of effective armed force, but on the nature of the peasant economy. For instance, peasant agitations must stop for the harvest […] But at bottom, peasants are and feel themselves to be subaltern. With rare exceptions, they envisage an adjustment in the social pyramid and not its destruction. (12)

As peasants' political uprisings have often turned unsuccessful because of lack of means for political and economic organization, scholars focused their attention on peasants' subtle ways of resistance and sabotage

(Scott 1985, Scott and Kerkvliet 1986) or, alternatively, new forms of production that are inspired by political motives of reducing peasants' dependency on market (Van der Ploeg 2010).

Contemporary views of the peasantry

Key perceptions concerning peasants' lack of economic and political capacities and their underrepresentation that emerged in peasant studies in the second half of the twentieth century have continued to exist through various development theories and policy discourse. These theoretical and political ideas have engaged in finding the ways to help peasants from less privileged parts of the world to attain industrial and technological development, improve their condition and overcome their semi-isolation, poverty, lack of education or economic and political deprivation. The ideological motivation for this evolved from the modernization paradigm.

Some of the first systematic development projects that emerged in the mid-twentieth century in essence contained an idea of the professionalization of peasants and their transformation, into either farmers, by means of intensified private or corporate agriculture, or workers, by means of state collectivization of agricultural production (see Kligman and Verdery 2011). However, in the 1960s many of these projects failed because it became clear that peasants were not going away, and in the meantime their numbers had even significantly increased. 'Whereas developmentalism, in both Western and Soviet forms, was designed to eliminate "the peasants" by developing them out of existence, postdevelopmentalism sought to stabilize them in the countryside' (Kearney 1996, 37–8). In continued development projects, the modernization paradigm, despite severe critiques, has never really ceased to be a central part of intellectual, state and international agricultural agenda. On the contrary, it is integrated within local, national and international policies, often under cover (Van der Ploeg 2008, 18).

Two significant processes have occurred in parallel with, or in spite of, development projects, which, depending on the point of view, have improved or deteriorated peasant conditions. These are *re-peasantization* and *de-peasantization*. De-peasantization is seen as a continuous weakening of peasantries and their livelihoods that eventually leads to their vanishing. De-peasantization emerges as a response to growing industrialization and urbanization, but also as a reaction to rural poverty, conflicts and wars. It is broadly accepted that peasants are one step closer to de-peasantization when they become solely dependent on wages in rural areas, and lose their own means of production. Re-peasantization, on the other hand, is a reverse process – returning the peasants to the countryside. Some see in re-peasantization a strengthening of peasant capacities and practices, and betterment of overall peasant conditions (see, for instance, Van der Ploeg 2008, 2010). The 'new peasants' tend to explore alternative and ecological ways of farming that help them to decrease their dependency on the market and resist agribusinesses. But scholars in general do not share such enthusiasm regarding re-peasantization. Their rather pessimistic vision of re-peasantization is explained as a decline of the welfare state, and shift to a market economy and privatization of state enterprises – which occurred in Eastern Europe after the collapse of socialism. Re-peasantization was caused by the poverty crises and high unemployment, social exclusion or the postwar situation (Bridger and Pine 1998; Burawoy and Verdery 1999; Hann 2002; Leonard and Kaneff 2002; Humphrey 2002; Cartwright 2001; Spoor 2012; Leutloff-Grandits 2006).

These and similar heterogeneous processes in the world paradoxically retained a simplified view of peasantry. Policy and theoretical discourses continued to sharply juxtapose the peasants to commercial farmers who are embedded in larger networks of intensive food production and agri-businesses (see Fox 2011). Peasants, the argument went, did not benefit as much from globalization and market economy and remained trapped in their coping strategies and subsistence production, struggling with manifold deprivation (Hivon 1998; Hann 2003; Verdery 2003; Shubin 2006). Only in recent years, the simplified views of the peasantry have been challenged by involving gender, activist and agrarian movements' interpretation of the peasantry, their rights, rural to urban migration or land grabs (Edelman 2013, Bernstein and Byres 2001). But looking at the whole, the trend remains unchallenged. Peasants are collaterals of the broader economic and political processes, while deprivation and struggles for autonomy continue to represent the main facets of today's peasantry (Van der Ploeg 2008, 2010, Hall et al. 2015; Narotzky 2016).

The historical perspective of the peasantry in Serbia

Throughout the twentieth and twenty-first centuries there were state attempts to connect peasants in Serbia with the political-economic trends of the world. Agricultural reforms contained the vision of peasants' modernization. In many ways, the reforms caused colossal changes in the peasant lives, especially in the property structure of the households and the organization of production.

Agrarian politics in interwar Yugoslavia (1919–41)

In interwar Yugoslavia (1919–41), the peasantry was the predominant part of the population, while agriculture was the main economic resource. Yugoslavia had a capitalist economy, and almost all agricultural land and production were in private hands. State investments in agriculture were not significant, although the state intervened, mostly indirectly, by imposing customs on foreign agricultural products, machines and through buyouts.

Yugoslavia's agriculture was severely affected by the world crisis in 1925. Although agriculture started to gradually recover as of 1935, general conditions were rather unfavourable. Peasants experienced low productivity, primarily due to the predominance of small private estates. They used outdated tools in cultivating the land and many of them regularly lacked modern machinery. Other salient problems were low competence and poor agricultural education among peasants, and a lack of health centres and road infrastructure. Unregulated property relations and voluntaristic taxation policies, usury and a poor system of agricultural loans were some of the additional factors that influenced low productivity. Post-crises state management attempted economic consolidation through increasing production, raising prices, spreading information about innovations in agriculture and promoting affordable insurance against floods and storms (Gaćeša 1995; Milošević 2016). Yet, one problem had constantly vexed the recovery and development of Yugoslavia's agriculture: the arbitrariness of political elites and the culture of clientelism. The dominant political parties lacked a genuine interest in the peasantry which, paradoxically, comprised 84 per cent of the total population at that time. Politicians from the two ruling parties (the Radicals and the Democrats) saw the peasantry only in a partisan capacity (Isić 1995, 229–47). The problems of the peasants were interesting to politicians until they won elections. Peasants, on the other hand, had never opted for the party programme, but for the ruling party, personal connections, powerful local and national candidates, hoping that by supporting them they will be spared from the whims and abuses of local bureaucrats (Isić 1995, 240).

The first agrarian reform (1919–41) emerged in the atmosphere of these and similar layered problems. It was a leading national economic project that was expected to improve the overall agricultural condition. The reform was inspired by three main rationales. The first was decreasing uneven property structure and strengthening small- and mid-scale peasants across the whole state. Central Serbia, for instance, did not have landless peasants and average private assets were about 10 ha. Vojvodina, in the north, had a disproportionate structure of a large number of landless peasants, on one hand, and big private estates of 500 ha and more, on the other. Kosovo, in the south, apart from a great number of landless peasants, also had the remains of an old feudal system that had to be dismantled and empower peasants as landowners.[4] The second motive for conducting agrarian reform was dismantling the remains of feudal relationships in Kosovo and big estates that belonged to the Habsburg dynasty or noble families in Vojvodina. The third motive was stronger integration of the newly founded Yugoslavia and its ethnically mixed areas such as Vojvodina and Kosovo through internal resettlement of people of Slav origin (Serbs, Croats, Slovenes, Montenegrins) to new territories. In Vojvodina, for instance, non-Slav people of Hungarian and German origin possessed the biggest estates while landless people made up 38.8 per cent of the overall population in 1910 (Erić 1958). On the eve of the first agrarian reform, out of 87 landowners in Banat who owned more than 1,000 cadastral acres, 81 were Hungarian and six were German. Of 3,456 landowners with more than 100 cadastral acres, 391 were Hungarian, 1,300 German, 160 Romanian, 148 Slovak, and 1,457 Serbs, alongside a few Croats, Russians and others (Erić 1958, 53).

In the first period of agrarian reform, the state determined the agrarian maximum depending on the type of land, region and the estate. The agrarian maximum ranged from 87 to 521 cadastral acres (Lekić 2002, 104–17). All land exceeding the maximum was allotted to the land fund, while the expropriated land was purchased from its previous owners at the market price. The beneficiaries of the agrarian reform were war veterans, army volunteers, resettled people (*kolonisti*), landless and poor. Planners of the first agrarian reform believed that smaller estates were more efficient than large ones due to the greater diligence of peasants working their own land in comparison to agricultural workers on big estates. In their opinion, the peasantization of agriculture would have unleashed hitherto dormant potential and led to a competitive atmosphere and more goods on the market. In the final phase of the reform, peasant-beneficiaries were supposed to purchase the land from the state through instalments and become the owners themselves. The process was supposed to end with registration of land ownership – that is, institutionalization of private property – without which, it was believed, competitive and modern agricultural production would not be possible.

The first agrarian reform in interwar Yugoslavia undoubtedly had a civil character, particularly because it eliminated remains of the feudal ownership structure on the one side, and it facilitated continuation of capitalist production relationships in agriculture on the other (Gaćeša 1995, 238). It changed the ownership structure in Vojvodina. A significant number of peasants became private property owners by 1941, which is an impressive fact considering that prior to the beginning of the reform they were only leaseholders. But there were unsatisfied people, especially among ethnic minorities, war veterans and army volunteers, who did not receive land, nor were they compensated – despite official agrarian law, according to which they had priority over others. Likewise, a significant number of people could not purchase obtained land because of the permanent crises in agriculture and personal debt. Some of the goals of the agrarian reform remained incomplete, while its implementation was accompanied by political controversies and scandal.[5]

Agrarian politics in socialist Yugoslavia (1945–91)

After the Second World War, the Federal People's Republic of Yugoslavia was declared on 29 November 1945. The name of the state was later changed to the Socialist Federal Republic of Yugoslavia, enduring until its dissolution in 1991. During the first period, from 1945 to 1949, the state tried to impose Soviet-style agrarian reforms. It was believed that the confiscation and distribution of yield and private property would erase the unequal share of surplus that emerged through capitalist production (Mises 2007, 800). The Yugoslav communists began enacting an agrarian reform that can be characterized as a radicalization of interwar agrarian reform and resettlement, but also as a radical break with the previous period (Dimić et al. 2009, 46–7). The new agrarian reform featured the same land-to-the-cultivator ideology as the previous reform. The first paragraph of the Law on the Agrarian Reform and Resettlement of August 1945 states: 'The land belongs to those who cultivate it' (Todorović 2001, 107; Gaćeša 1984, 140–50). The law was not specific about what ethnicities were entitled to obtain the land, but the Germans from Yugoslavia were targeted as those to be expropriated and expelled (Janjetović 2005). Moreover, those who fought on the side of the Yugoslav communists in the war had priority over others (Janjetović 2005).

The second agrarian reform and the internal resettlement of people (*kolonizacija*) were among the most important events in recent history, and completely changed the ethnic and economic structure, especially in Vojvodina. It had the biggest land fund, where over 600,000 ha was expropriated from Germans alone. Since 1945, approximately 250,000 people from all over Yugoslavia (Serbia, Montenegro, Bosnia and Herzegovina, Croatia, Slovenia, Macedonia and Kosovo) arrived in 'trains without order' in Vojvodina, to settle and replace the expelled Germans.[6]

For Yugoslav communists, the main goal of agrarian reform was a radical transformation of property relations. From 1945 to 1953, the reform aimed to resolve the problem of land ownership in villages, and it was eventually settled in this period (Milošević 2016, 154). The targets of land expropriation, apart from war enemies and collaborators, were big landowners, banks, joint-stock companies, churches and monasteries, wealthy peasants and small- and mid-scale landowners. Expropriated people were not compensated. Yet in the first years of agrarian reform, the state did not have a clear view about the role of the peasants in the new socialist state:

> The goal that the party set up was somewhat contradictory. The peasant was supposed to live better than before, but not better than an industrial worker, and not so good as to become indifferent toward the socialist reconstruction of agriculture, or to be against the building of socialism in villages. (Milošević 2016, 5)

The relationship between the communist party and the peasants had never been an easy one and was marked by deep distrust on both sides (see Bokovoy 1997).

From 1945 to 1953, the maximum area of private property for peasants was 36 ha. Any land exceeding this limit was included in the land fund and was later given to people who did not have enough. The Law on Agricultural Reform and Internal Resettlement of November 1945 stipulated in Article 36 that the distributed land should become the private property of peasants (Todorović 2001, 126). But peasants did not have much influence on the organization of production. The state was managing the economy and reorganized production in villages. It started with the foundation of peasant work cooperatives and compulsory delivery. The peasant work cooperatives were seen as the shortest path toward collectivization, but also as new leaders of myriad activities in rural areas. Peasant work cooperatives were supposed to have economic but also a political and educational role, through which peasants could become familiar with the main ideas of socialism and become its supporters. Peasants were forced to sell their products to peasant work cooperatives through compulsory delivery of agricultural products at low prices. Compulsory deliveries took on a humiliating form:

> [The] state buys wheat, meat and other agricultural products from peasants, the state decides on the type and the amount a peasant is supposed to deliver to the state at a certain time and in a certain place, and the state determines the price of the product, not the peasant. Such delivery was, in fact, a particular type of pillage and terror of the state over peasants. (Pavković 2009, 283)

Unfulfilled obligations qualified as a serious crime and were regarded as economic sabotage against the foundations of socialism (Pavković 2009, 284).

By 1948 the cooperatives combined predominately resettled people and poor peasants (Pavlović 1997). Peasants who became members, depending on the type of cooperative, either retained their ownership rights over the land and received rent for the land they handed to cooperatives, or they lost both ownership and related rights. The members of the cooperative could freely use and possess only their own personal property such as house and yard (*okućnica*) of up to 1 ha – which was considered sufficient for food production for family consumption. But collectivization and compulsory deliveries of agricultural products did not go as smoothly as planned, nor did peasants embrace them readily. The period was marked by unrest, peasants' resistance and state violence (Popov 2002). The following extracts describe how some of the elderly peasants remembered their family stories about collectivization in Gaj.

> My family always kept horses. We had eight horses, cows and poultry. In 1946 they took 9 ha from us. They took everything from us ... When they took everything from my grandfather, they invited him to join a dance party in *Janofa* [Center of Culture in Gaj], where those who had been expropriated were supposed to dance. When anyone asked whether they were angry with local party members because of the confiscations, nobody could complain or say anything. While these desperate folks were dancing, others [party members] would take photos of them. (Luka, July 2013, Gaj)

By 1949, a small number of cooperatives were created on a voluntary basis, but others were created through pure coercion (Milošević

2016, 442). The elderly peasants from Gaj, whose family members suffered during collectivization of agriculture, commonly associate cooperatives with coercion.

> In 1946 I was 12 years old. They didn't take the land from my father in 1946. But in 1949 the founding of cooperatives began. My father ended up in prison for a year and a half because he didn't meet compulsory delivery. If he had given all his machinery to the cooperatives, he wouldn't have ended up in prison. But he didn't want this, because in 1934 he left *zadruga* [extended family household] and divided the property with his brothers … During compulsory delivery, they tortured people a lot. They [party members] forced my grandfather to kneel and count stars. (Marko, February 2013, Gaj)

> They took 9 ha from my grandfather in 1946. He wasn't a member of the cooperative. He didn't want to become so. Nevertheless, he was obliged, under threat of penalty, to hand in his agricultural machinery in good shape within two days. (Petar, June 2013, Gaj)

Collectivization and compulsory deliveries in Yugoslavia did not fulfil their expected goals and, furthermore, they complicated the relationship with the peasants. It so happened that people preferred to consume or hide their crops instead of safeguarding it for the expropriators (Mises 2007, 801). By 1949, low productivity and sabotaging of cooperatives had become chronic problems of Yugoslavia's agriculture. Peasants had abandoned the cooperatives on a massive scale because selling their products at an enforced low price placed them in a disadvantaged position compared to individual producers. Cooperatives lacked work motivation, discipline and ethics, while their management was usually not transparent and democratic, despite claiming to be so. Specifically, the power remained in the hands of the directors who oversaw organizing the work and managing of surpluses (Tošić 2002).

The main characteristics of agrarian reform from 1945 to 1953 were compulsory deliveries, progressive taxation, disabling the trading of land, politics of cooperatives and collectivization. The consequences of agrarian politics in Vojvodina until 1953 were manifold. First, they eliminated a considerable number of interwar private agricultural producers who supplied markets both within the country and abroad. Second, the category of landless peasants ceased to exist due to the inauguration of three types of property: state, collective and private. Third, a significant number of people were resettled in Vojvodina. Fourth, the category of waged agricultural workers ceased to exist due to the abolition of the capitalist mode of production. Fifth, the state became the major owner of land, machinery, seeds and technical knowledge (Gaćeša 1984, 207; Tochitch 1959; Interview with Zaharije Trnavčević, July 4, 2014, Belgrade).

The Law on the Agrarian Land Fund of Common People's Property, passed in 1953, officially marked the beginning of the new phase in socialist agrarian policy that was in force until the restitution law enacted in 1991, and essentially until the end of socialist Yugoslavia.[7] In this phase, the new agrarian maximum of 10 ha for peasants and 5 ha for non-peasants (workers) was introduced. The party chose 10 ha as agrarian maximum because it was assumed that this amount of land could be cultivated by family members without using paid labour. Through this measure the state attempted to prevent individual producers from enriching themselves at the expense of poor peasants and hoped that all who aspired to expand their production would join cooperatives and contribute to the intensification of socialist production (Milošević 2016). This was clearly a naïve belief, given that after 1953 cooperatives never succeeded in transforming into an advanced organization for land cultivation, and until 1991 they predominately served only as suppliers of seeds, fertilizers, mechanization and services, and as mediators in trading agricultural products between peasants. Moreover, it was illusory to expect that peasants would prefer cooperatives over individual production, bearing in mind the state coercion and violence from 1945 to 1953.

The land exceeding the new agrarian maximum became the common people's property and was not distributed further to poor peasants. The Law on the Agrarian Land set out the possibility that expropriated land might be used for establishing state agricultural enterprises, cooperatives and farms. Likewise, the law enabled free trade of land within the set agrarian maximum (see Milošević 2016, 615–16; Slijepčević and Babić 2005, 32). The new phase in agriculture fostered the medium-sized peasant household, but also contributed to the growing numbers of peasant-worker households as the new category. The peasant-workers in Yugoslavia were broadly known as *polutani* (pl.), referring to peasant-workers having occupations engaged partly in agriculture, and partly in socialist factories. The peasant-worker living on his holding and commuting to a job outside his village became an important component of the Yugoslav labour force. According to a special agricultural census in 1960 in Serbia, it was estimated that there were some 1,306,000 peasant-workers in a total labour force of 2,985,000 (Halpern and Halpern 1972, 80).

From the perspective of peasants whose families were better-off before the second agrarian reform, the new agrarian maximum of 10 ha had drastic effects on their households and production, which consequently compelled them to seek various ways of coping with the new regulations and limitations. In Gaj, for example, several families that were again expropriated in 1953, could hardly maintain their household, as was the case for Petar and his family: 'This whole household was built in 1913 and was maintained thanks to 40 ha of land. One had to be a wizard to maintain it all with 10 ha alone' (Petar, June 2013, Gaj).

To maintain their households and cultivate more land than the prescribed maximum allowed, peasants often organized 'artificial' households. One household, for example, would split itself nominally into two or more, each of which could have 10 ha of land. A father and a son, say, living in the same household and cultivating the land together would split and buy additional land under their respective names. In addition, it often happened that families with members in both peasant and worker categories would list the whole household under the names of those who were agricultural producers, so that other members of the household working in industry could buy the land using their maximum quota for workers and in this way enlarge the family property fund (Diković 2015, 277).

I did not come across any cases either in the literature or in my field research of peasants' resistance against the new agrarian maximum of 10 ha. From the conversations with historians, I learned that this was most likely because until 1953, in Yugoslavia there were only 66,000 estates of above 10 ha, which is negligible. The private estates that became targeted for expropriation had up to 15 ha at most. One of the alternatives for those households that possessed land above the agrarian maximum was to sell the problematic amount of land, rather than let the authorities expropriate it. For example, domiciled peasants in Gaj and the neighbouring villages Malo Bavanište and Beli Breg, were selling off portions of land to people from mountainous and poor regions of southeastern Serbia (Pirot, Bela Planka, Vlasotince and Crna Trava) who had settled in these villages in the 1950s, in search of a better life.

Almost a decade after the introduction of an agrarian maximum of 10 ha, Yugoslavia's agriculture did not record any significant successes. Two agricultural censuses, one conducted in 1960 and the other in 1969, had shown a negative trend in agriculture and a decline in production.

The average agricultural household possessed approximately 4.2 ha of arable land at the time, and individual production was considered inefficient. Tractors in the possession of individual agricultural households were rare, which was also considered a negative sign.[8]

> Peasants could only dream of combine harvesters and similar mechanization. As a matter of fact, even state agricultural farms could not be proud of possessing advanced machinery: until the middle of the 1970s, when corn was harvested in the fields of state agricultural farms and cooperatives, soldiers of Yugoslav army as well as high school youth helped out on both voluntary and mandatory bases. Simply, there were not enough harvesters. The yield was a lot higher than were the capacities of the technology available. (Majdin 2012)

Because of these negative indicators, the state initiated a programme aimed at transformation and the liberalization of agriculture. Interestingly, the programme, known as 'the Green Plan' (1976–80) had individual producers as its primary focus. Households could buy necessary machinery such as tractors or harvesters by using affordable state credits. In the collective memory this period is usually remembered as the golden age of Yugoslavia, and it is similarly regarded among my informants in Gaj, Malo Bavanište and Beli Breg.

> From the 1980s until the 1990s, agriculture thrived. Many households cultivated sugar beet because there was sugar industry in the town of Kovin. Back then it fetched a good price. For 0.57 ha with sugar beet on it, one could buy a half hectare of land. For one fattened bull, within 2–3 years one could buy a half hectare. At that time, I built a house, bought a tractor, a picker, a car. (Mirko, August 2013, Malo Bavanište)

Although it is broadly accepted in my research field that the Green Plan contributed to significant improvement of peasants' standard of living, good harvests and private investments, it also caused social stratification and enriching of a few peasant families. The local distribution of the Green Plan loans, according to one of my informants, a middle peasant from Gaj, was considerably selective. The local authorities prioritized their loyal partners and friends and enabled a few families to stand out during this period. 'Many peasants from Gaj, as a result, had never received the necessary loan' (Petar, June 2013, Gaj).

During the late 1980s the conditions for agriculture were significantly improved. The state exerted less pressure on the peasants than before. The Green Plan coincided with the credit expansion of Yugoslavia, which in the 1980s was forced to take steps toward economic liberalization to reduce indebtedness. Table 2.1 demonstrates the trend in agricultural development after setting the agrarian maximum of 10 ha, and follows conditions from 1955 to 1990 with respect to cultivated land, number of tractors and general investment in agriculture both in the state (agricultural farms, enterprises and cooperatives) and the private sector (individual peasant households). It also shows significant changes in agriculture that have occurred since the Green Plan (1976–80).

The data indicate that the private agricultural sector was gradually growing and taking over production in the Socialist Federal Republic of Yugoslavia, as opposed to complex state-run agri-industrial systems that were supposed to form the cornerstone of agricultural production.

Agrarian politics in post-socialist Serbia

The crises of communist ideology led to the dissolution of the Socialist Federal Republic of Yugoslavia in 1991 and civil war (1992–5) between Serbs, Bosnians and Croatians. The state tried to solve the crises by implementing initial steps toward political and economic liberalization. In such an atmosphere, restitution took place and represented a symbolic indicator of structural changes. The law on restitution envisaged the abolition and restitution of so-called collective property (*društvena svojina*) that was taken from private owners during the period of collectivization from 1945–53.[9] The law anticipated the return of land to its former owners regardless of their occupation (Čurović 1998, 3–9). Until 2016, approximately 200,000 ha were returned, but the whole process of restitution of expropriated property of citizens from rural and urban areas has not yet been completed. For example, out of six families from Gaj that I interviewed, only three families whose land was expropriated in the period 1946–53 had got it back. The other three are still waiting. These people gave up on restitution because of the exhausting bureaucracy and complicated requests which they did not understand. Moreover, the deadline for completion of restitution has been constantly postponed, which infringes their trust in the state's readiness to finalize the process.

When the United Nations imposed economic sanctions on Serbia and Montenegro in 1992, due to war, the restitution was suspended

Table 2.1 General overview of agricultural development, 1955–90.

Year	1955	1965	1975	1984	1985	1986	1987	1988	1989	1990
Cultivated areas, thousands ha										
State agricultural farms and cooperatives	824	1,413	1,535	1,687	1,695	1,718	1,736	1,741	1,747	1,765
Individual households	9,276	8,840	8,466	8,171	8,146	8,136	8,098	8,077	8,059	8,039
Conditional heads of cattle, thousands										
State agricultural farms and cooperatives	279	497	458	866	863	910	935	924	929	915
Individual households	3,976	4,866	4,981	4,592	4,412	4,471	4,382	4,153	4,051	4,002
Tractors, thousands										
State agricultural farms and cooperatives	8.8	40.3	25.5	30.7	31.7	32.3	32.3	32.6	32.6	31.4
Individual households	2.8	5.1	200	778	850	923	985	1,033	1,075	1,061
Investments, thousand dinars										
State agricultural farms and cooperatives	98	263	322	440	395	337	295	275	205	…
Individual households	73	117	318	370	305	369	388	410	327	…

Source: *Statistical Yearbook of Yugoslavia* 1991, 241.

because of lack of financial means. The political isolation of the country and sanctions spurred the criminal activities and aggravated the condition in agriculture. The late renowned agricultural journalist Zaharije Trnavčević described the condition during the 1990s as follows:

> Agriculture in the last decade of the twentieth century became an economic branch very important for maintaining the regime in power that tried to prevent the rise of food prices, decrease in purchasing power and in the living standard of citizens. In those years agricultural producers were forced to sell an increasing quantity of wheat, corn, livestock, and other products for the same quantity of fertilizers and seeds. In those years, the peasant was really damaged – robbed, some would say – because the industry began to fall apart and collapse […] In order to maintain at least some standard […] politicians regulated low food prices at the expense of peasants […] That means politicians take from peasants, confiscate their profit because of development, survival, or to maintain the industry and other non-agricultural areas too. During that time […] hyperinflation additionally contributed to the robbing of peasants and the decrease of purchasing power. This was a time when the least tractors were bought, when the use of mineral fertilizers and other products necessary for highly profitable agrarian production decreased. We lost the market back then, exports stopped […] This was the period when we became even more dependent on weather conditions and the pattern of rains. Agricultural producers were weak and incapable of protecting themselves from this. (Zaharije Trnavčević, Belgrade, 4 July 2014)

During the 1990s the state undertook the project of shutting down the state cooperatives. This step was publicly justified as the abolishment of a collective property and its conversion into a state property until the end of the restitution. When cooperatives were closing during the 1990s, their property, where possible, was allotted to state farms or agricultural enterprises in the same or a nearby village. Through so-called insider privatization and 'strategical location of networks' (Ganev 2007, 19), people close to power were the first to become owners of former state estates. Shutting down cooperatives, and the introduction of new owners of the privatized farms, disrupted the existing relationships between services and local business.

> The state had serious problems with its budget, and it started to privatize those agricultural farms in order to improve the revenues [...] Our problem is not in the fact that privatization occurred, but rather something else. During privatization, big areas of land, complexes, farms, and estates came into the possession of ignorant people who had other goals, so-called money-laundering. They didn't want to extract profit from land and improve its production capacities. Agricultural stations, engineers, agronomists, counselling officers, they were all gone, discharged.
> (Zaharije Trnavčević, Belgrade, 4 July 2014)

Agricultural conditions and the active rural population, totalling 18 per cent, had somewhat stabilized as of 2000 (Subić 2005, 81–2). With the liberal-democratic changes, the opening of the market and a process of integration in the EU had started and continues until today. The Serbian Ministry of Agriculture imported a homogeneous body of EU agricultural and rural development policies, laws and trade agreements, with the aim of professionalizing the agricultural sector, based on the European model (Diković 2014). Enhancing production was the primary goal, since between 80 and 88 per cent of the total agricultural budget has been devoted to direct subsidy programmes for intensification of production, without reference to environmental protection or conservation (Ćurković 2013). Unlike other EU countries where subsidies make up more than half of farmers' income and whose behaviour and decisions largely depend on state support (Sutherland 2010, Medina et al. 2015), in Serbia, in 2012, when subsidies reached their financial peak, they made up only 8 per cent of gross income of middle-sized agricultural producers; today, that percentage is likely to be even lower, due to further reductions in subsidies.

Serbia, like other Balkan countries, has at its disposal some of the pre-accession funds for the development of agriculture (Volk 2010). Instrument for Pre-accession Assistance (IPA), and Instrument for Pre-accession Assistance for Rural Development (IPARD) are aimed at all types of agricultural households, but the application rates among producers are very low, because the funds require pre-investment and developed business plans, which many producers are not willing to make (Milovanović 2016). Serbian agriculture has not yet developed the culture and knowledge associated with the EU's Common Agricultural Policy (CAP), either from the state planners or end-users perspective (Papić and Bogdanov 2015). Pre-accession funds in Serbia are based on competitive platforms that favour better-off and advanced agricultural producers, unlike other EU programmes that have been initiating new agricultural and environmental schemes that, while also competitive, are more inclusive of different actors.

Along with many improvements in agriculture there remain some open issues. Significant state ownership in agriculture, for example, hampers privatization in the name of political goals and generates monopolies, clientelism and rent-seeking (Maksimović-Sekulić et al. 2018, Pejanović et al. 2017). A disparity in the ownership structure and productive units between the north, in Vojvodina, and the west, east and south of Serbia, where small-sized households of less than 5 ha prevail and remain the major issue (Strategija poljoprivrede 2014–2024, 10). Village infrastructure – major and local agricultural roads, irrigation and drainage systems, flood protection, access to electricity and water in pastures, and medical and educational services – is rudimentary and unsatisfactory. The number of livestock and the export of meat and other animal products are rapidly decreasing (see Arsić et al. 2012). There is a low rate of general investment in agriculture, particularly those investments that come from private savings or bank loans. Because of underdeveloped credit supply, the average producer in Serbia borrows seeds and fertilizers from private cooperatives. In most cases, such 'cooperatives' only borrow the name, but are not an organization of agricultural producers with shared interests and capital. They are private companies that call themselves cooperatives to take advantage of existing state benefits. They do not have joint capital, nor do they employ the inner structural organization of a cooperative. They do not serve to meet, protect and mediate the interests of a group of agricultural producers, but rather to fulfil the profit demands of their owners. Data show that approximately 1,200 cooperatives operate only nominally, while some 100 cooperatives are shut down annually (Ćurkovic 2013, 131). The absence of true cooperatives composed of agricultural producers presents a chronic problem in Serbian agriculture.

The current state in Serbian agriculture can be best described as 'inbetweenness'. The significant state control over agricultural capital does not align with peasants' visions of development, nor with EU standards. Market-oriented low subsidies maintain economic stagnation of one part of agricultural households on the one hand but also enable an ongoing small but important agricultural revolution at local levels on the other (SEEDEV 2017). Combined, these factors create a situation that has many positive and negative sides in respect to both agricultural and rural development. Most importantly, rising sale and rent prices for land indicates, unlike in previous decades, a shift toward a positive evaluation of agriculture as becoming once again a worthwhile business and lifestyle.

Reconsidering peasants' subordination

The dominant theoretical perceptions of the peasantry that opened the chapter, would find justification in an overview of agrarian reforms in Serbia throughout the twentieth and twenty-first centuries. Subordination of the peasants to the state, and later to the markets, would likely be understood as the main problem of the past and present agrarian conditions in Serbia. Yet a closer look at the agrarian reforms questions the peasants' subordination. Except for the period from 1945 to 1949, the state was experimenting with its own policies and adjusting them, trying to generate the minimum threshold of cooperation with peasants. As in the example of Gaj, peasants were joining cooperatives only by force; despite state attempts to limit private holding to 10 ha, many families found ways to enlarge their property and, most importantly, private production was always preferred over state production, displaying its full potential during the 1980s. Each time the reforms ignored the aspirations of peasants, they were less successful. This is the pattern that keeps repeating today, which the remainder of this book will reveal.

Some questions remain to be answered. If it is true that continuous unfavourable conditions in agriculture cause a decreasing number of peasants, why then do peasants still comprise 18 per cent of the overall population in Serbia? Some theoretical perspectives from the beginning of the chapter would argue that this is because of re-peasantization and pauperization, which did not leave people many liveable options but to remain in the village. But this argument is essentially wrong. The development and expansion of cities historically favoured bad economic conditions that caused severely affected peasants to move to cities whenever they lacked land or a means to invest in cultivation for the next season.

If we accept that the agrarian condition since 2000 has been unfavourable because of low subsidies, for example, or poor infrastructure, why did the cultivated areas with soy and sunflower increase by 23 per cent over the past 10 years, and why did wheat harvest increase by 18.6 per cent during the last 10 years (according to 2021 data from the Statistical Office of the Republic of Serbia)? Why are the prices for land sales and rents rising? Isn't the basic economic axiom relevant here: the attributed subjective value of an asset determines its demand? Such an indicator is often ignored by social scientists. But it reveals a substantial motivation that buttresses agricultural production, land market and the interests of peasants to keep farming. In another words, when agriculture is preferred by a significant number of peasants, despite periodical crises, it translates into the value of the land. Land ownership and its symbolic and economic properties are the binding strings that keep peasants in the village, maintain and raise the price of land and maintain an enthusiasm for production.

It is often assumed, nevertheless, that people living in villages are unhappy with the life they have and are just waiting for the opportunity to abandon farming. By diving into the manifestations of the laissez-faire mentality in the next two chapters, I provide a closer look at the range of relationships in the village that refute such assumptions. Moreover, the agencies of peasants motivated by land ownership, autonomy, local values and attitudes urge the reader to reconsider the assumption of peasants' subordination to the state or markets, and instead find in these agencies the answers to their resilience and fulfilment.

Notes

1 His hypothesis was questioned and criticized across disciplines, and in anthropology by Cancian (1961), who despite acknowledging the theoretical potentials of this theory believed that more thorough studies are needed before the behaviour of South Italian peasants can be interpreted in such a way. Cancian questioned the evaluating criteria that Banfield employed in his study, given that he conducted his own field research in South Italy and came up with different conclusions.
2 Wolf was criticized for similar reasons to Chayanov.
3 For a critique of the moral economy that comes from the political sciences, see also Brass (1991, 1997).
4 Kosovo was part of the Ottoman Empire until the First Balkan War (1912), when it became an integral part of the Kingdom of Serbia. As in Kosovo, the remains of feudal property relations had to be terminated in Bosnia and Herzegovina, Dalmatia and part of Macedonia that belonged to Yugoslavia.
5 Many controversies surrounded the reform itself such as selective conducting and interpretation of law on Agrarian Reform by state bureaucrats (Milošević 2008), and frequent political misuse and bribery aiming to increase the agrarian maximum for certain big estates (Lekić 2002).
6 See: https://www.politika.rs/scc/clanak/323340/Sedam-decenija-od-agrarne-reforme-i-kolo nizacije, accessed 23 February, 2017.
7 'Zakon o poljoprivrednom zemljišnom fondu opštenarodne imovine i dodeljivanju zemlje poljoprivrednim organizacijama,' Službeni list FNRJ, 22/1953.
8 See Majdin, 11 October 2012. Vreme. Pogled na smrdljivi sir i još bolje. https://vreme.com/vreme/pogled-na-smrdljivi-sir-i-jos-bolje/, accessed 1 March 2017.
9 See: 'Zakon o načinu i uslovima priznavanja prava i vraćanja zemljišta koje je prešlo u društvenu svojinu po osnovu poljoprivrednog zemljišnog fonda i konfiskacijom zbog neizvršenih obaveza iz obaveznog otkupa poljoprivrednih proizvoda,' Službeni glasnik RS, no. 18, 26. 03. 1991, no. 20, 10. 04. 1992, no. 42, 18. 11. 1998.

3
Nesting the laissez-faire mentality

The laissez-faire mentality emerges as a cultural amalgam. Peasants' sense of autonomy, village ethics, individualism, scepticism and distrust, but also of life on the periphery, are factors that predominantly determine its development. The factors combined help us to understand better the framework, or more precisely social climate, in which the laissez-faire mentality gets nested in the local community and in local population.[1] They provide an inner view of social and economic interactions, and the habits of local people.

A sense of autonomy

Peasants cannot be ruined. They can only have more or less.
(Sava, August 2014, Gaj)

For the peasants I encountered in my field research, psychological and sociological senses of autonomy were intrinsically related to land and ownership. They usually understood autonomy as the liberty to govern their own time and life, as in the vivid phrase, 'to be one's own boss' (see also Stock and Forney 2014). Peasants drew parallels with jobs in companies to emphasize the advantages of their position, and the disadvantages of having 'the boss over their head' watching their employees' every move, and measuring their time spent at work or on lunch breaks. Supplementary qualities such as having a relaxed lifestyle, production of home-made healthy food, the proximity of nature, a healthier environment and rich social interactions additionally strengthened the peasants' sense of autonomy and made them more attached to the village, their work and the community. Nikola, a middle-aged peasant, who had been actively working on his family farm since high school explained what it meant to be the master of his own time.

> The working hours are important here. In companies no one knows their working time. I create my own work schedule. I work whenever I want, and as much as I want. I am my own boss. (Nikola, July 2017, Gaj)

Toma, Nikola's fellow villager and a peer-peasant, similarly explained the core of his autonomy. He had experience as a factory worker and occasionally experimented with jobs outside agriculture, but eventually found himself entirely in farming.

> I love land, animals. I love agriculture. I don't have a boss over my head to tell me what I should or should not be doing. I don't have to finish something within an hour or a day. I know these things because I worked for five years in a company. I can slaughter a pig, eat as much and when I want. I can coordinate my life as I want. I can sell the corn when I want. For instance, I sold corn in bags in front of my house on the street for 1,000 RSD more than was the commercial price back then. (Toma, July 2017, Gaj)

The assumed psychological benefits of working in agriculture and on one's own land, without pressure and stress, had motivated several people from Gaj to leave their jobs in state companies in nearby cities. A few had resigned willingly and others decided to take severance pay, leaving companies when that were about to privatize, in the 2000s. As an example, a sense of autonomy, strong bonds to the land, agriculture and the village lifestyle were the main reasons that had motivated Janko to return to Serbia after almost a decade spent in Austria as a guest worker. He took his whole family and settled in Dubovac on a family farm where in addition to crop agriculture they started to breed an autochthonous small, short-horned cattle *buša (busha)*. He vividly summarized his decision to return from Austria: 'I didn't have oxygen' (Janko, July 2013, Dubovac).

Professional and personal satisfaction are aspects that are strongly embodied in a sense of autonomy. Autonomy and personal liberty have proved in different contexts to be equally if not more important than income (see Helliwell et al. 2012, 58–79). In an informal neighbourly conversation with Iva, an elderly peasant who had spent his entire life in Gaj, raising his children and farming his own land, I asked him how it felt to be in the fields. Iva swiftly retorted, 'I feel great!'. His instinctive answer led me to realize that land ownership alone is not sufficient for a developed sense of autonomy. There must also be an emotional attachment to the land and a professional satisfaction in taking care of land, crops and the harvest for a sense of autonomy to be felt worth preserving. Peasants' dedication to land and agriculture was also recognized by a local doctor who was born and raised in Gaj and whose entire career was tightly related to this village.

> When patients go home from hospital, they first go to visit the fields, to check the quality of corn, wheat. It is their life, and more. It is their very love for the land. (Marija, July 2013, Gaj)

For most of the peasants I met during the fieldwork research, farming came up as a direct, unquestioned and natural choice (Figure 3.1). But for others the struggle to become a peasant had meant leaving a conformist position and entering into open conflict with their family.

For instance, Franc, now forty, revealed how the appeal of peasants' autonomy and farming prevailed over his family's plans for him. Franc was raised in Gaj, with his extended family. While his grandfather and

Figure 3.1 The generations work together; a great-grandfather and his great-grandson stand proudly in front of the family's grain trucks, 2013. Source: Author.

father owned a few acres, they did not work on the land themselves. Franc could not wait to graduate from high school and commit fully to agriculture. Franc's father was against his choice and tried to dissuade him from becoming a peasant and cattleman in various ways – which sometimes involved beatings. Once, when Franc got his pocket money, he had bought a goat. He continued saving his pocket money and bought cattle secretly, while still in high school. At age 14 he earned his first 800 German Marks (DM) from the sale of cattle. Franc then again bought a cow and a calf, keeping them in a neighbour's stall without his father's knowledge. He would wake up at 5 a.m. to feed the animals and clean the neighbour's stall and then he would go to school. Franc's father finally found out, and reluctantly accepted his son's secret hobby. Today he is Franc's reliant helper, and together they work daily with the cattle and crops. For Franc, the choice was simple: farming was the realization of his love, not only for the land and animals but also for autonomy.

In contrast, several peasants had grasped the potential of farming and peasant's autonomy only *post festum*, after years of work in agriculture. This was most likely because farming was never their first choice. The shift of perception is associated with the growth of agriculture and better prices of products that came after liberal democratic transformations in 2000. These factors had positive impacts on some – their work motivation, perception of agriculture, and their autonomy. Nađa, a middle-aged public officer who rented out inherited land after the death of her parents, understood the trend as the result of overall improvement of the economic situation in Serbia.

> During the 1990s no one saw himself in agriculture, even though many of us went picking in the fields during summers for pocket money, but no one seriously considered agriculture as a job nor was the demand for land as high as it is today. Moreover, leaving high school early was unthinkable. In my generation, all who have stayed in Gaj graduated from high school. In the meantime, I don't know what exactly happened, but high school has devalued, and agriculture has risen. This happened from 2000 onwards. Nowadays you can live decently from agriculture, own your land, and be your own boss. (Nađa, July 2015, Gaj)

In a similar way, Ana, a middle-aged nurse who combined a job in the city hospital with growing strawberries on her family farm in Gaj experienced the shift of perception of land and farming that occurred after the 2000s.

> In the mid-1990s our grandfather wanted to buy [a] half hectare close to our house. But we were all against this, and we put too much pressure on him not to buy the land. He eventually gave up on buying the land. Today we don't dare to even mention this to him because this is the biggest mistake we have ever made and we regret it a lot, particularly now when we are developing a business with greenhouses and strawberries. (Ana, July 2015, Gaj)

The increasingly diversified market opportunities that emerged after 2000 boosted the work motivation of peasants. Financial gains were a reward for the productivism that plays a special role in peasants' autonomy. Most of the peasants proudly stressed the productive and sustainable capacities of their households. Almost every house in the village has its own courtyard (*okućnica*) that consists of the front yard, a back yard for animals and a garden with vegetables, fruits and flowers. The area of the courtyard varies from a couple to 50 or 60 acres and everything needed for daily consumption is produced there. The ability to produce their own food was perceived by peasants as providing a more direct control of their life through the process of food production, control of quality and healthy intakes. Peasants emphasized this as one of the chief aspects of their autonomy in comparison to city dwellers, who must buy food and are unaware of the general conditions under which the food was produced and kept (cf. Caldwell 2009). Most of them believed their autonomy afforded them a healthier lifestyle, and significantly reduced their dependency on the markets and shielded them from price hikes in everyday purchases.

But when it comes to trade, peasants' autonomy can be estimated by their capacity to store their agricultural products. If the capacities of barns are bigger, peasants' autonomy is greater too. It is seen as the most reliable way to maintain farmers' autonomy and financial solvency, and it is usually practised by mid-sized and bigger farms (15–60 ha). Although expanding storage capacity has been initiated by better-off peasants with mid-sized farms, local agricultural engineers confirmed that expanding storage capacity has slowly become an imperative for peasants with small farms, too, but as yet its effect cannot by gauged. By storing grains, peasants allow themselves to retreat from investing (in labour, production, premises) and selling when they face higher risks, but they can also assume more risk when the risk premiums fall and prices get better. Those who are not in such a position are forced to sell grains immediately after the harvest, and to borrow seeds and fertilizers from private cooperatives. An ability to finance the entirety of their production independently is considered in the local context to be a matter of dignity for a peasant. Rista, a peasant with a mid-sized farm from the neighbouring village Beli Breg summarized the predominant attitude among the peasants: 'If I am not capable to buy the essentials such as seeds and fertilizers with my own money, then I should not be working the land' (July 2013, Beli Breg). An agricultural engineer from the municipality of Kovin confirmed the trend, saying, 'many agricultural producers now opt for self-financed production, while only a minority has continued to borrow from cooperatives. This trend was initiated by better-off peasants and is now followed by medium-sized and perhaps a few small households' (July 2014, Kovin).

Protecting the boundaries of peasants' autonomy by enlarging storage space and self-financed production is not a novelty and goes back to the past. *Žitnice* (pl. storehouses) were usually built within the household for keeping wheat and crops and were designed to store larger amounts of grain. They were built as floor storage, or sometimes an attic served for keeping smaller amounts of grain. Before the communist revolution, building of *žitnice* was the usual practice among mid-level and better-off peasants because they traded their products on the market. When the communist government abolished the market economy this practice disappeared. Isa, a local observer and self-proclaimed chronicler of the village life, explained the revival of the past practices in terms of time cycles:

> [The] time came when all products return to and are stored in individual households, like it used to be in the past when people built *žitnice* (storehouses). Whoever can does so, and keeps his wheat and corn. This is what most people do.' (Isa, July 2017, Banatski Brestovac)

Although some peasants struggle more than others with markets and financial conditions, Sava, an elderly peasant and one of the few remaining cattle breeders in Gaj sees in the autonomy of peasants the core of their resilience: 'Peasants cannot be ruined. They can only have more or less' (August 2014, Gaj).

Sometimes peasants expressed a more abstract understanding of the autonomy embodied in land ownership. Although many may have instinctively felt it, Edi, a middle-aged peasant raised in a family that for generations had exclusively working in agriculture, was able to articulate a correlation between private property and liberty. 'Private property and liberty are the most important things. Thomas Jefferson said this a long time ago. I have only eight grades of elementary school, but I know history' (Edi, July 2017, Gaj). Local understanding of private property in some ways resembled Jefferson and Locke's understanding of private property as a pillar of liberty and life (Locke 1999). Locke's elaborated understanding of property was not constrained only to material things, such as real estates, fields, books or jewellery. In fact, his understanding of material property comes from a deeper appreciation of self-ownership as a precondition for all other sorts of properties. As such, property also encompasses our life, our self, our freedom, and also the ideas that we govern respecting agreed boundaries (don't kill, don't steal, don't infringe, don't usurp – to name just a few) that protect us from the unrighteous actions of others, and in turn prevent us from undermining those same rights for other people (Pešić and Novaković 2008). These are the basic principles of freedom and private property embedded in the rule of law. It is a common view among peasants in my research field that private property rests on the exclusive right of the holder to choose to use, control, sell, rent out, profit or alienate (dispose of). The crucial aspect of private property is *control*; not only over one's own resources, time and activities but also over one's life – even though property may be a liability and a burden at the same time (see comparative studies Sikor 2006; Sikor and Lund 2010).

A sense of autonomy, as we see by now, encompasses personal liberty, the feeling of control and governing one's own land resources and life. Such bonds create a necessary boldness in situations when rules are circumvented or openly disregarded. A sense of autonomy, apart from providing 'room to manoeuvre in a context made of constraints' (Stock and Forney 2014, 161), represents the core element of the personal identity of peasants in their everyday life and work environments. This is not to say that all peasants share such a sense of autonomy. Although it is a dominant feature, there are certainly peasants who possess land but who, for various reasons, lack a sense of autonomy. In some cases, the lack of motivation for farming and lack of autonomy correlates with various personal, family, economic or political circumstances and evolves as an overwhelming feeling of dissatisfaction and limitation. A few such peasants who I met during my fieldwork research saw farming and land ownership as a burden that they carried in the absence of other opportunities for occupation and self-fulfilment. But even in the cases of those peasants, land ownership was perceived as a certainty that, according to Jelena, a widow and small-farm peasant, represents a 'sort of saving and life insurance. What keeps me doing this [farming] is that even in the worst-case land provides me at least a bare minimum of subsistence' (Jelena, July 2017, Gaj). In other cases, land ownership and farming seemed to transcend existential pragmatism and form a sense of autonomy, and of social and occupational satisfaction.

Village ethics

> *If peasants look after the village, the village will look after them. (Sava, February 2013, Gaj)*

Village ethics are the ethical core of the peasants' laissez-faire mentality: they help us in understanding better the ethical grounds on which local people undertake their actions and their motivation for prioritizing local solutions over state recommendations or plans. Village ethics as a concerted set of beliefs, attitudes and behaviours that have spontaneously emerged from village customs and traditions, labour and local values provide guidance about what is right and wrong and discourage unwelcome behaviour in the local context. The ideal function of village ethics is to harmonize relationships among the local population and maintain order. Village ethics transcend individuals, who derive from them a sense of community, environment and desirable behaviour, and accept them as common wisdom or knowledge. Given the predominant occupation in rural areas, most village ethics derive directly from labour and farming.

> For centuries, the entire life of a peasant went by in labour thus scheduled. His habits were formed according to this schedule. Every task, when it became due, was urgent. Every task and every deadline was vital. Not by coercion of another man, but under the discipline imposed by nature and put on him directly. Such necessity always gives a high moral sense to the drudgery of the peasantry. Never is a peasant so ethical as in his work. The qualities thus gained by each generation are bequeathed to the next generation, who enrich the heritage. Rich funds of certain working qualities were thus accumulated and settled in the rural population. (Vukosavljević 1983, 418, author's translation)

Agricultural labour, through the cycle of nature and work habits that have been developed accordingly, has created a system of values that distinguishes and categorizes labour, laziness, appropriate and inappropriate treatment of land, a dignified householder, and appropriate behaviour in public or in relationships toward the poor (see Vukosavljević 1983; Kostić 1969; Vlajinac 1929, Diković 2017). Village celebrations, for example, serve as public exhibitions of set values. The main festival in Serbian villages is *seoska zavetina* or *slava* (the celebration of the village patron saint), dedicated to the fields and farming. It is always celebrated either in spring when nature reawakens, or in summer when the plants grow tallest. Gaj celebrates Spasovdan, which falls on the 40th day after Orthodox Easter. On this day, the celebration starts in the early afternoon with the oldest traditional manifestation in the village *Fijakerijada* (festival of horse carriages) (see Figure 3.2). Most of the population including Catholics celebrate Spasovdan, while Orthodox families commonly refer to this day as their second *slava*.[2] The collective spirit and sense of belonging among locals intensifies with each of such village celebrations. Spasovdan brings together existential, social and spiritual aspects of life in the community. Žarko, a young worker from Gaj, talked about local enthusiasm about Spasovdan and its importance for different generations and the village.

> Many people live for this day. Everyone dresses nicely and comes to the event in the centre of the village. People from neighbouring villages Beli Breg, Malo Bavanište, Dubovac, Deliblato come as well. Many invite their families from elsewhere. People usually have a nice feast at home first, and then they go out to the centre to see fairs and have fun. (Žarko, June 2013, Gaj)

Figure 3.2 *Fijakerijada*, a festival of horse carriage riding that takes place in Gaj. Source: © Vasa Petrov, used by kind permission of the Library of Gaj.

The same enthusiasm takes over the village during summer when village people organize *Gajački kotlić*, the contest of fish stew. The event gathers contesters from Gaj and other villages. In the past several years it has grown into one of the biggest manifestations in the region, of which people from Gaj are proud. Many told me that after village *slava*, it is certainly the second most important event in Gaj (see Figures 3.3 and 3.4).

Figure 3.3 *Gajački kotlić*, the contest of fish stew-making that takes place in Gaj during the summer months. Source: Author.

Figure 3.4 A celebratory atmosphere at *Gajački kotlić*. Source: Author.

Village ethics manage the sense of community by binding every member in an invisible network of duties and expectations, be that village *slava* Spasovdan, *Gajački kotlić*, shared work (*moba*) or charitable activities (helping poor, sick and disabled people). Apart from their role in attaining order and relative harmony, village ethics also work toward enabling the wellbeing of different categories of population and provide them with a sense of purpose. This is best seen through the following examples of hard work and thriftiness, dignity of ownership, *veresija* (credit to trust), relationship toward the poor and practices when buying and selling.

Hard work and thriftiness

Hard work and thriftiness are considered the most important virtues among peasants in Gaj and neighbouring villages. As in farming communities elsewhere, the label 'hardworking' endorses the peasant as being good and dedicated (Emery 2010, 135). The reward for hard work is often symbolic and not financial, because hard work finds its expression in the proper looking after of both the land and the household. As it is often the case, the best farms are not always the most profitable (Emery 2010, 135; see also Cohen 1979). Hard work emerges in a combination of religious motivations, symbolic rewards, material achievements and ecological consciousness, but also as in the psychological feeling of happiness and satisfaction that comes from a job well done (on the work ethic, see Weber 1930; Thompson 1995; Emery 2010, 132–8; Silvasti 2003). Thriftiness, on the other hand, is a virtue that derives from hard work and environmental ethics, which have taught peasants through generations to be considerate in the conservation of nature, land, air, water and the environment in general, and to act against waste by developing various waste management techniques (Thompson 1995, 71–93).

The only case when hard work and thriftiness, even being desirable virtues, are not appreciated among peasants in Gaj and neighbouring villages is when they are the goal in themselves. Such people are subjected to mockery because they are seen as antisocial and unable to better integrate in the community, share, and develop. Common expressions usually ridiculed thriftiness and hard work for its own sake: 'he knows only of hard work' or 'he has a snake in his pocket'. Mirko, an elderly peasant, who had moved to Malo Bavanište from Eastern Serbia in the early 1950s in search for land and work, understood the expressions as a kind of communal sarcasm, directed at 'newcomers': families from poor and mountainous regions that had settled in Gaj and neighbouring villages in the second half of the twentieth century. Being a newcomer himself, he knew that for those people hard work and thriftiness were the only escape from dire living conditions.

> In this and neighbouring villages people used to prepare for Sunday on Saturday afternoon. On Saturday afternoon all work would be stopped, and people wouldn't do anything. In the evening they would go out in the village. If there was some music they would dance and enjoy themselves. Sunday was a time for rest. But when the newcomers came here in the 1950s, hungry and barefooted, this custom disappeared because they were working all the time. (Mirko, August 2013, Malo Bavanište)

Criticizing or mocking those who prioritized work over communal events did not mean that general devotion and care for the household was less appreciated. Social expectations for thriftiness and hard work remained strong and this was especially evident in village attitudes toward leisure and holidays. Until recently, going on holiday was considered by the majority an unnecessary luxury that mimicked the behaviour of city dwellers. Leisure, except on Sunday, religious and national holidays, was perceived as a bourgeoisie habit reserved for people with no 'serious work' or 'better things to do in their life'. Today, the perception of holidays has somewhat changed. It is still usually only the younger population, not necessarily associated with farming, the better-off peasants and professionals such as doctors, teachers and lawyers who take holidays. For the remaining peasant population, holidays are what they sacrifice first when it comes to investment in land, property or machinery. Danica, a local shopkeeper, confirms that the trend of going on holiday is just emerging, but still not practised by many.

> The village discovered the seaside only four years ago. Many have still never been to the seaside or have been on holiday only once or twice. (Danica, August 2013, Gaj)

Thriftiness and hard work characterize peasants throughout their whole lives, and continues as a feature even in their funeral customs. The tractor is in the local context also a symbol of the peasant, his hard work and modesty. It serves to show what peasants' hands and this machine achieved during his lifetime. The tractor is a sign of a modest beginning, in other words. And it is a sign of a modest ending, when a peasant's coffin is driven on the tractor to the cemetery. Several times I witnessed a tractor carrying the coffin from the house of the deceased to the cemetery, passing the whole village and making stops on the crossroads and by the church at the centre of the village. In all cases, it was a male peasant in his late sixties who had died. The use of a tractor in funerals is so deeply rooted among the local population that even contemporary ways of coffin transportation could not replace the tradition. The owner of a funeral shop in Gaj who bought a hearse had soon regretted such a business undertaking.

> Only 20 per cent of people in the village use this service, while others prefer tractors for transport of a coffin in the procession to the cemetery, because they respect tradition. We do not even charge the costs of this service to those who opt for it, in order to stimulate a slow shift from practice with tractors to a funeral car. (Siniša, August 2013, Gaj)

Hard work and thriftiness are socially binding virtues. As we can see, they not only shape a community's atitudes towards invested labour, spare time, holidays and economic decisions but also serve as a life-long marker of people's identities that accompanies them even in their death. Hard work and thriftiness are, likewise, an intrinsic part of the broader package. They are vital for the practical and symbolic preservation of the social image of the dignity of ownership.

Dignity of ownership

Gaj, as in perhaps most other villages that live chiefly on agriculture, developed an ethic according to which the land never stays uncultivated, regardless of political and economic circumstances. Such ethics shape the local images of the dignified householder – a reputation that is built up for generations, and if it is ruined one pays a high social price (Cohen 1979).

In Gaj nothing can compare to the intensity with which laziness is despised, and conversely the admiration for a hardworking householder, either on the farm or in the home. Such local perceptions have created a spontaneous self-regulating system, with elements of competition and admiration, in which neighbours tried to be the same, if not better than each other. The properties in Gaj, Malo Bavanište and Beli Breg exemplified a 'household beautifying competition' that was hard to miss. Peasants also take on an element of competition with their neighbours when they cultivate the fields, apply new agrotechnical measures, use new seeds or compare livestock. To earn dignity and a reputation as a good householder one should not go below a set local minimum. What this minimum was exactly was disputable, but my findings suggested that it primarily referred to achieving the average harvest, getting agricultural jobs done within proscribed deadlines, keeping fields free from weeds so that neighbouring fields did not get contaminated, and keeping stalls clean and livestock fit. See Figure 3.5.

The dignity of ownership imposes the responsibility of tending the household and a sense of liability, not only toward oneself and one's family but also toward the village community. Maintaining dignity is a hard job which poses constant challenges to peasants. In Keane's view:

> [These challenges] depend on the ways in which people are emotionally attached to their own 'face' – that is, to how they see themselves through the eyes of others – and the vulnerability that ensues from the dependence of face on being affirmed by others. (Keane 2016, 109)

Figure 3.5 A view of the backyard of a household in Gaj. Source: Author.

THE LAISSEZ-FAIRE PEASANT

The peasants had a common understanding of what it means to be a good *gazda* or *domaćin* (householder/landowner), terms that are used interchangeably.[3] A *Gazda* or *domaćin* is a person who is not neglectful, and who gets jobs done in the household and fields in due time; someone who is a good planner and whose household is tidy and neat and has all that is needed; who is a good and generous host at celebrations; who respects local tradition and people in the community; and who is honourable and content with the work. Yet, the two labels are not identical: one can be a good *domaćin* even without having any land, but one cannot be a *gazda* without land.

Becoming a *gazda*, or maintaining this label, was certainly one of the most important goals for peasants. Katarina, a retired teacher from Gaj, shed light on peasants' attachment to land from a different but important perspective. Namely, she saw this attachment as the biggest problem in the poor education of their children.

> In the past two decades there were only a few people from Gaj who graduated from the university. It is not only the political and economic situation to be blamed for this. It is their parents, who could not separate them from their land. (Katarina, April 2013, Gaj)

Katarina's perspective provides an insight into what land stands for in the local context. Failing to maintain property structure is clearly related to fears of losing land, or peasants' losing their established image of *gazde* (cf. Berg 1975). But the perception of failure is also deeply entrenched in the phenomenon of loss aversion that two psychologists Daniel Kahneman and Amos Tversky detected in economic behaviour. Loss aversion makes people extremely worried about any risks, even small, that are consequential for their active choices. People, thus, rather opt for the status quo and restrain from any potential changes that can jeopardize even the slightest structures of their lives (Kahneman and Tversky, as described in Banerjee and Duflo 2019, 40). In the example of peasants, that means that they usually try to either maintain the existing scope of land and image of *gazde*, or safely enlarge their household without taking too many risks, since land and household make a person fulfilled in the village hierarchy of things. Once these are lost, people know it is hard to regain them. The two excerpts demonstrate such local perception quite closely.

> Agrarian reforms [during communist time] turned *gazde* into bums (*slepce*) when land and machines were taken from them and when they were left with only 10 ha. (Jovan, July 2017, Gaj)

> Every time I bought a piece of land, I had to fast for a whole year to pay off the debt, but one motive has always kept me going – that one poor man earns capital, because my parents did not have a gram of land. (Ivica, February 2013, Gaj)

The first excerpt above demonstrates how communist curtailing of private property jeopardized the sense of ownership and social image of many peasants in Gaj. The second excerpt demonstrates that becoming a landowner is perceived as a goal in personal and professional self-realization. Mere land ownership, however, gives a person dignity only in a limited sense. Land ownership in combination with hard work and responsible care for the household enables a full sense of dignity. This probably explains why people do not leave land uncultivated, despite prices of products and political situation. My conversation with Jovan, a retired peasant from Gaj, powerfully illustrated the essence of the relationship between land ownership and dignity.

> Jovan: During the 1990s I paid 400 DM for a barrel of oil for cultivation of the land.
> J. D.: Oh! Isn't it too expensive for one barrel? I mean, why would you pay so much for a single barrel of oil?
> Jovan: Well, a person who has grown up here cannot leave the land uncultivated. You watch it every day. You can't let it go. It's in the genes. Either you love it or you don't. And yes, it cost me like Greece [a common Serbian expression when someone runs into debt], but, well, we are used to living like this. I was working at a loss back then, but at least my children weren't hungry, and we didn't lack anything in the household. (July 2017, Gaj)

I heard many times in consecutive interviews that people did not leave land, despite the political and economic situation, working hours or having other occupations. Even households that did not have unemployed members and where farming was not a necessity still worked the land (Figures 3.6 and 3.7). The level of education and type of profession in general did not appear to be an obstacle for doing agriculture in parallel with regular jobs in cities. An agricultural engineer in Kovin statistically confirmed the tendency of not leaving the land uncultivated. In 2014 in the whole territory of Kovin municipality only 0.2 per cent of land remained uncultivated.[4]

The dignity of ownership mattered in the local context because it tacitly imposes duties on people to diligently tend their land and

Figure 3.6 A field of sunflowers in bloom, ready to harvest. Source: Author.

Figure 3.7 A large field of wheat, ready to harvest. Source: Author.

household, and develop sensitivity for the preservation of their own and family farm reputation, and for the values that the village holds dear. A broader village community yields many benefits from such a self-regulating system. The benefits are best observed in economic relationships in the village such as *veresija* (credit on trust), gleaning, and buying and selling practices. These and related practices test the reliability and endurance of social ties that hold the village together.

Veresija (credit on trust)

Veresija is a spontaneously emerging form of delayed payment that is realized later, usually at the end or beginning of the month, when people receive salaries, pensions or other income. English equivalents would be 'credit to trust', or 'putting something on the slate'. It is a form of social transaction that is predominantly based on trust. There is no contractual nor formal confirmation of it, and a customer who asks for veresija invests his dignity in this arrangement. The shop owner is not obliged to give it to everyone. Humorous vignettes hanging on the wall above the cashier in small shops in city quarters nicely indicate that veresija is not possible where there are no trust bonds. 'Veresija died. We accept condolences only in cash', 'Great respect to everybody, but veresija to nobody', 'Veresija is allowed only to persons from 70 on, in presence of both parents'. (An American equivalent is the sign I saw at a restaurant in New York, 'In God We Trust. All others pay cash'.) Veresija is not a sustainable custom in expanding urban quarters with constant shifts of population – the cost is too high. Trust should not be given to someone about whom the shop owner knows nothing. Unlike in the villages, city populations are in flux and residents come and go; it is not possible to build stable local ethics that will oblige customers to keep their word.

Almost all owners of grocery stores in Gaj accept veresija as a means of delayed payment. They select trustees of veresija by their reputation. Veresija is based on the goodwill and sense of dignity of both customers and grocery owners. By giving veresija to the locals, grocery owners, as *gazde*, initiate such economic and social arrangements. But they also invest their own generosity and commitment to the community.

Veresija is a long-surviving custom that probably dates from the first appearance of private grocery stores. Today it represents one of the basic modes of shopping in villages or small towns, where people know each other well. People go to a daily shop and take necessary goods that they pay for later in due time. The owner of the shop keeps a written record of all who buy on veresija, the amount they owe, and their due date for payment. There were numerous state attempts to terminate veresija, but this practice appeared to be vital in the villages. Strictly speaking, veresija is nowadays an illegal practice that goes against official requirements of the Serbian Ministry of Commerce. Every item sold must be confirmed by a receipt slip that is issued by the cashier to the customer, and directly recorded in accounting software. This is not possible when people buy some items on veresija. That would imply a need for double bookkeeping, which is an illegal practice too. The fact that veresija is not legally recognized makes the owners of shops vulnerable in situations where they cannot charge for goods they have sold. 'Credit is a festering sore on the body of commerce', a favourite phrase among merchants in Vaucluse, France, would be relevant in such cases (Wylie 1964, 181). Trust is the only guarantee of payment. Given that trust is not sufficient proof in court, shop owners usually do not prosecute people who betray their trust so, as a rule, end up empty-handed.

Even though veresija may seem to be a risky and fragile arrangement, it is in fact based on much stronger and durable social pillars that are not obvious at first glance. Veresija cannot be explained simply as a necessity that exists because of the unfavourable economic situation in Serbia, although this is an important factor. In fact, people have cooperated and functioned like this for decades, in both good times and bad. It demands a high degree of social trust and accountability, which explains its survival even in the times of harsh crises and poor economy. One might assume that in bad circumstances people would have more incentive to act immorally. But this has not happened in Gaj, either now or in the past.

What makes veresija strong is village ethics. One invests not only trust in this arrangement, but also the dignity of the household, one's good name and reputation. Betrayal of veresija on a more obvious level brings loss of respect for a person, a bad reputation and shame on the household. In the long run, it threatens the existence of the practice by the breakdown of social ties that keep it going. Likewise, it deprives other members from the local community of the chance to practise it when they need it most. People, therefore, feel obliged both on a personal and community level to be respectful of veresija, as was powerfully encapsulated in Sava's words: 'if peasants look after the village, the village will look after them' (Sava, February 2013, Gaj).

In the local bakery in Gaj, for example, people every morning would bring along a small notebook in which a baker made a tick for one loaf of bread, or two ticks for two loaves, and so on. The baker himself kept his own record of purchase amounts. At the end of the month, baker and customer compare notebooks, and if everything adds up the payment can be realized. Likewise, in stores a cashier is in charge of keeping a record of daily purchase amounts in a special notebook used only for veresija. After every purchase a customer must put his signature next to the purchase amount. This ensures that both parties are agreed, avoids the possibility of fraud and maintains mutual trustworthiness.

In Gaj, veresija for some represented an existential strategy, particularly so for Roma and pensioners, while in other cases it was both an existential strategy and also a local way of purchasing goods, not necessarily associated with poor income. Sometimes it was about shortage of the means of payment. Credit was a way of not having to have cash all the time, and people could settle monthly. Veresija was vital for the local economy and as such could hardly be abolished.

> If I abolished veresija, I would have to shut down my shop. I can't work any other way. Every shop in Gaj works like this. Debt collection is hard sometimes and mostly depends on the sale of crops. Whoever succeeds in getting a good price pays his debts immediately, but if the price is not satisfactory, we feel this during collection of debts. Then people come and ask for a prolongation of a deadline. I can't even prosecute those with unpaid debt because I don't have any proof, we didn't make a contract, there is no bill, confirmation […] So, these debts remain unpaid. At the end of the day, everything rests on trust, and I believe in the honesty of people who buy from me. So far, pensioners are the most regular payers since only their income is secure. (Sanja, August 2013, Gaj)

Another store owner explained the functioning of veresija in a similar vein:

> We rely on trust exclusively. We have worked like this from the very first day, although this has always been the case in the village. If the harvests are good we collect debts, but if not then it is easier for me to forgive the debt. (Bogdan, August 2013, Gaj)

In only one case in Gaj, in 2006, veresija, along with accumulated debts, unpaid taxes and the high costs of running the business, had been the reason for shutting down a shop. But this one example did not affect the practice.

Veresija is seemingly a fragile arrangement, but the longer it exists, the more strongly it confirms village cohesion and the resilience of village ethics. Veresija acknowledges Granovetter's argument, that 'trust, the confidence that others will do the "right" thing despite a clear balance of incentives to do the contrary' emerges in the context of smaller communities with dense social ties where the enforcement of norms is easier (Granovetter 2005, 33). Building affective connections among villagers through the social laws of versija demonstrates the validity of Haidt's thesis that the environmental conditions of being small, isolated or morally homogeneous increase the moral capital of the community (Haidt 2013, 337–43).

Relationship toward the poor

In Gaj there is a custom that regulates the relationship toward the poor, known as gleaning (*pabirčenje*). Gleaning means that landowner allows the poor to gather any fallen stalks of grain after the first harvest. The institution of gleaning most likely emerged as an obligation that landowners held toward their social environment. The right to glean was thus regulated by customary law and served as a mechanism for attaining social equilibrium when poverty and landlessness were widespread. Probably for the same reason, almost every agricultural society has been familiar with similar practices. Gleaning can be seen as one of many existing facets of collective property or, more accurately, temporary collective rights to private property.

> When the harvest is reaped on arable land, it temporarily becomes common. Everyone has the right to bring cattle to graze on it, or to glean it, i.e. to collect grains of wheat, clips of corn, or grapes in a harvested vineyard. From this originated the old proverb: To find oneself in a non-harvested vineyard ['Naći se u neobranom grožđu'], i.e. in a legally or morally impermissible act or situation. The message is clear: you can glean in a harvested vineyard, but should not find yourself in a non-harvested one! (Pavković 2014, 287, author's translation)

While in south Slavic countries collective property was primarily related to grazing areas, the arable lands were, in contrast, exclusively in private or family ownership (Pavković 2014, 284–96). In the first case, collective property entitlements automatically evolve from common territorial, kinship or tribal belonging. In the case of arable land, consent is necessary to authorize gleaners' rights. Consent may be either explicitly gained from the landowner or shared implicitly, mostly through custom. The lack of consent is also verbally or symbolically communicated. In Gaj, for example, there is an old symbol of the *čova*, an improvised scarecrow made of wood with a birch broom, which personifies guardianship. *Čova* may have different functions and one of them is to prohibit gleaning. When the owner puts a *čova* at the entrance to a harvested field with the broom handle facing down that means that there is no consent; even though the field is harvested, the landowners often need the straw that remains for baling. Otherwise, gleaning is allowed and is understood as a customary welfare for the poor.

In Gaj and neighbouring villages, this practice has changed to some extent over time and is occasionally used as a euphemism for field theft (Diković 2016). It is considered theft when people who glean abuse their rights and steal the crops from neighbouring non-harvested fields. For those who glean appropriately, the practice is a source of livelihood diversification, while for those who violate the custom, it is a way to make a profit without the investment of hard work and money in the production. Such shifts in customary forms demonstrate that they are not static and are sensitive to social changes and the influence of human agency (Turner 2015, 382; see also Von Benda-Beckmann 2002; Von Benda-Beckmann and Von Benda-Beckmann 2006; Von Benda-Beckmann et al. 2009).

Like gleaning, village ethics are not static. They are responsive to the social and political predicaments, when it is necessary to amortize urgent problems, prevent potential conflicts or adjust to the circumstances. The adaptability of village ethics is perhaps best illustrated in this example of the occupation of pastures on the territory of a neighbouring village. A livestock breeder from Gaj had placed his *salaš* (summer ranch) on the actual territory of Šumarak, the neighbouring village. The shepherd he hired to look after his cattle was a Roma from Šumarak. The council of Šumarak did not want to evict the livestock breeder from Gaj and his summer ranch. He was not even asked to pay the rent for the pastures, as prescribed by the municipality of Kovin. The council had known the shepherd for a long time. He had four children and was a welfare beneficiary at the time. By offering such a solution, the council of Šumarak disregarded the municipality's requirement to generate profit from leasing the village pastures. Yet the council's rationale was that the community of Šumarak would be better off with at least one Roma with reliable income. They placed community wellbeing and village ethics before the municipality's formal requirements.

Buying and selling relationships

The buying and selling practices in villages are influenced by local ethics in situations when people prioritize solidarity, reciprocity, social norms or kinship obligations over obtaining profit and enlarging personal wealth. Economic relationships that are primarily embodied in the ethics of the local community are thoroughly studied in anthropological literature and are usually referred to as the moral economy, a term inaugurated by E. P. Thompson (1971) and further developed by Scott (1977).[5]

Buying and selling relationships that are adjusted to the principles of local ethics represent one of many facets of life in Gaj. Buying and selling relationships are not always transactional. Sometimes, they are constrained by the anticipation of the social costs necessary for attaining expected order in the community. There are many examples where villagers will not take advantage of others to expand their assets or profits even though the opportunity may be challenging. In Gaj and neighbouring villages peasants do not buy land from people who sell property because they are in debt. Peasants consider their attitude to be ethical because no one wants to enlarge their own capital using someone else's bad fortune. A couple of posters advertising six hectares for sale remained on the information board in the centre of Gaj for about three years. No one from the village wanted to buy the land. Everyone knew the family concerned faced bankruptcy. I observed a similar situation in another Banat village. In that village peasants usually do not buy land from Slovaks who because of their strong attachments to land seldom or almost never sell land. So, if Slovaks opt to sell land that must mean they either face bankruptcy or some other serious problem (or that the land is of very poor quality in which case it is not worth buying) (Diković 2016, 281). Peasants prudently refrain from taking such an opportunity because social costs may be too high. Gossiping or defamation of a family that bought such land is one of the common reactions. Many peasants are not ready to withstand it. In all other situations, peasants will buy land at any point in time, but sell it rarely and only under very special circumstances.

§

Village ethics, as we can see, encompass a broad scope of relationships, ranging from individual aspirations for gaining a reputation as a respected and hardworking peasant; to collective aspirations of maintaining trust thresholds and wellbeing networks, in the case of *veresija*; gleaning and other relationships toward the poor; and in buying and selling practices. Village ethics come first when people consider what is beneficial for the community's wellbeing. Their function is sovereign, even when state policies try to govern the local environment.

Individualism

Individualism is one of the most salient characteristics of peasants and the laissez-faire mentality.[6] Peasants I interviewed in my fieldwork saw individualism as one of the main obstacles to the more harmonized functioning of the village and blamed it for the lack of unified political and economic organization. Individualism might indeed be responsible for a lack of cooperation, but it was not always an obstacle. Peasants in the villages cooperated on activities that can be associated with traditional wellbeing of the community such as veresija, funerals, weddings and village slava, but rarely or almost never cooperated when it came to joint production or forming cooperatives. They usually explained the lack of cooperation among themselves by invoking the Banat mentality, individualism of peasants, envy, lack of solidarity and unity. An agrarian technician from Gaj hopelessly attempted to present to peasants the advantages of cooperation and concerted action. They didn't listen.

> Cooperatives and associations in the village do not function because of the mentality of people. All of them think they can function alone. In Gaj there are, I think, around 40 mechanical harvesters for 400 ha of wheat. One harvester can harvest 10 ha per day. The machine that costs 100,000 euros works only one day a year. In comparison, in Holland there is one harvester for 300 ha of wheat. A lot of people [from Gaj] bought a harvester in order to become *gazde*, although it works only one day or two a year. In the remaining period these machines don't work and lose their value. Instead of joining together and having at most two harvesters in the whole village – which would be busy every day for two months in a season – peasants waste their money and lose on the potential sale price of the harvesters. (Agrarian technician, July 2017, Gaj)

Goran, a peasant from Gaj with a larger amount of land, knew of more efficient ways of protecting grains through the correct application of pesticides, but peasants' individualism, in his view, was one reason why these were not used.

> We all would be way better off if corn, wheat and other grains were sprayed directly from an agricultural aircraft and larger areas would be treated at one stroke. But this is not possible in Gaj, because there is no unity. Other reasons matter as well, for example several peasants have different-sized land plots in the same area … one doesn't want it, for the other it is too expensive, the third one has another reason, and so on. (Goran, August 2013, Gaj)

When I asked a small breeder of rabbits why he and his peers from the village did not unite in an agricultural cooperative he almost apologetically explained that their cooperative fell apart even before it was founded, because everyone had different interests and ideas. Jovan, a small vegetable producer from Gaj, thought that peasants' incapacity to unite stemmed from their individualistic consciousness. 'It is in the consciousness of people from Gaj not to unite into cooperatives. During socialism, cooperatives were founded by taking private property of people' (Jovan, July 2017, Gaj). Jovan basically said that peasants accept cooperatives only by force, while their founding under different circumstances is very rare. The failure of peasants to join up in cooperatives remains one of the longstanding problems in the village. A survey that the Ministry of Agriculture conducted in 2013 is indicative: 94.7 per cent agricultural householders in Serbia were not members of any agricultural association, and 97 per cent believed there is no representative agricultural association that would protect and advocate for peasants' interests.[7] Unlike bigger households, small and medium-sized households showed less interest in joining cooperatives even though, ideally, they would have more chance to reap better prices for their products, have the benefits of bulk purchase or negotiate contractual production for retailers. The state incentive to generously subsidize newly formed peasant cooperatives was not helpful either.[8]

Individualism and lack of cooperation are common topics in laments about the alienation of the people and disinterest in the community. Rade, a retired worker from Gaj, poetically explained the problem of cooperation in terms of moral decline. 'I fear the erosion of morals. In previous times, people were afraid of God, then they feared the party and nowadays they fear neither' (Rade, July 2013, Gaj). Envy also appears as a hampering factor. Envy was one of the reasons for dysfunctional cultural, civil or sports associations in the village that only formally existed as associations but in practice were run by one or at most two people.

> *Gajački kotlić* [festival of fish stew in Gaj] should have been named 'Milovan's kotlić'. I organize everything and pay all costs myself. Villagers do not contribute, not even those who are better off. There is no collective spirit at all. Me and my wife organize the whole event, while every shop, restaurant, or cafe in the village makes a great profit on that day. Then, [ironical smile] people talk, you know, as if I earn money from the association and they don't want to step in because they think they would just make me rich. (Milovan, August 2014, Gaj)

Jovan saw the envy of his immediate neighbours as an explanation for why they do not buy watermelons from him, even though they were on good terms. When I wondered what the reason for that may be, Jovan retorted, 'they don't want me to get rich' (July 2017, Gaj). Local observations indicated people's strong tendency to act individually. I heard many times people saying words to the effect of 'they hate you anyway. When you're rich, they despise you because you work, and you got rich. And when you're poor, they despise you for being lazy and poor.'

One question, however, remains: why do peasants cooperate on matters regarding the traditional wellbeing of the community but not on common agricultural matters which are equally vital for their existence? Why does veresija work but agricultural cooperatives do not? Social conventions maintain veresija, and if the convention is broken people may face potential sanctions and embarrassment. In the case of veresija, for example, altruistic punishment, a concept that Fehr and Gächter (2002) developed, may be one of the explanations for its successful functioning. Veresija, thus, can be seen as a practice that strengthens the constructive behaviour of individuals toward a common goal – maintaining trust and functionally discourages breaking its rules (cf. Henrich and Henrich 2007). Yet, Blanton and Fargher (2016) refute the assumption that culturally modelled altruism or fear of punishment is a trigger for cooperation. They believe that cooperation is based on the mutual dependency of people which arises as the result of highly rational assessment of the information at hand and the gains and losses of the potential cooperation. Yet, although it would be quite rational under these terms that peasants with small and middle-sized households in Gaj cooperated within agricultural cooperatives, in practice this was not happening. Preserving peasants' autonomy (being one's own boss) in a rural household presupposes that the responsibility for different undertakings, successes and failures remains within the household, thereby reducing the possibility of social exposure.

The individualism of peasants determines the type and level of cooperation in the village. The cooperation is spontaneous, transactional and sometimes counterintuitive. Peasants cooperate in domains where there is a high social awareness of the consequences of non-cooperation, such as in traditional arrangements (village slava, funerals, veresija, etc.). On these occasions the village hardly resembles the unit made of atomized individuals. It highlights its social side, which Predrag, a peasant with a small-sized holding from Gaj, explained as follows: 'we argue among ourselves, but we get things done' (July 2017). Yet they avoided cooperating on matters that could have a potentially negative impact on their private property, decision-making process or social exposure. In such cases, attempts to cooperate are to a great extent destined to fail.

Scepticism

Scepticism is an attitude of doubt and reluctance. Scepticism is relational and emerges as a reaction to a concrete set of beliefs or events. Over time, with new information, experiences and knowledge about a certain matter, a sceptical attitude may lean toward a more positive, faithful attitude. Or, on the other hand, it may turn into a negative attitude, in which case it falls under the domain of distrust. Scepticism related to state-imposed agricultural education and to crop insurance is a familiar attitude among peasants. It is also one of the formative elements of their laissez-faire mentality.

In the book *Moralizing the Environment*, Lowe et al. (1997, 173–80) make a distinction between radical and sceptical farmers. Radical farmers accept emerging environmental morality and the new superior discourse on the impact of agricultural pollution. Sceptical farmers are closer to the old environmental morality and traditional way of farming, seeing in their work a manifestation of the virtuous and thoughtful care for land. Most of the peasants I talked to would lean toward Lowe et al.'s categorization of sceptical farmers. Their knowledge and experience in agriculture made them sceptical toward new *methods* of spreading knowledge about agriculture. This is not to say that they were reluctant in accepting ideas that might significantly improve their production, although among older peasants this might still be the case. Their scepticism was not associated with agrotechnology, but with the *ways* in which new knowledge and experiences are shared.

Peasants themselves were aware of their scepticism, but they accepted it as a given part of their mentality and identity. They were commonly sceptical about actors who promote agrotechnology improvements. The Ministry of Agriculture, agricultural associations, NGOs or agrotechnology companies organized lectures and courses for peasants that were officially obligatory for registered agricultural producers, who would get licensed after attendance. But most of the peasants admitted that they rarely or almost never attended these courses. They were sceptical about the genuine interest of the lecturers and the relevance of the seminars in the era of the internet. For Predrag, a mid-size landowner from Gaj, traditional knowledge transfer through seminars was useless for peasants: 'The main problem is that these presenters are always the same people who constantly rotate the same topics. We can update our knowledge on a few novelties through the internet. Why bother with lectures?' (Predrag, July 2017, Gaj).

Peasants believed that the internet provided more useful knowledge than standard forms of education. The internet allowed for the rapid and direct information they sought, and free of charge. They socialized in online forums and exchanged their experiences and thoughts. The time flexibility and availability of online content and tutorials was something peasants appreciated. Peasants saw the internet as a substitute for formal education and training, which explained their reluctance to attend and sometimes pay for the seminars. Likewise, peer recommendations were highly respected in the peasant community and were more impactful than formal seminars or lectures because peasants were more prone to learn from people they knew and trusted. An agricultural engineer from Kovin municipality noticed that peasants look at those among them who are better off and try to follow in their footsteps, listen carefully to their advice and accept suggestions. 'Better off peasants represent a role model to other peasants, and they are an important factor in the transfer of knowledge' (Engineer, July 2014, Kovin municipality).

Peasants' acceptance of new agrotechnology is greatly determined by their own assessment of risk, peer recommendation and their experience. In the case of testing new seeds, peasants for example applied new varieties carefully and always in combination with attested old seeds. The generational difference also matters in accepting novelties. Older peasants predominantly preferred cheaper domestic seeds even though these bring lower yields. Predrag estimated that most younger and middle-aged peasants 'are prone to accepting novelties', but they do so carefully. 'I, for instance, am seeding 50 per cent new and 50 per cent old sorts of crops' (Predrag, July 2017, Gaj).

Peasants' scepticism was especially visible in the sphere of crop insurance against weather risks. Results from an informal survey I conducted among peasants were surprising. The better-off peasants (around 8 to 10 households) regularly insured their crops, while most of the small and medium-sized households rarely or never did so (around 50 to 60 households). These data seemed even more confusing given that the state provides significant financial support to peasants for insuring their crops. In my daily conversations with peasants, I realized that one of the reasons for their low insurance might be a lack of trust in insurance companies.

> Better-off peasants usually take out insurance, but small- and mid-scale peasants are sceptical. If you are a small-scale peasant, insurance companies look down on you, while they look completely differently at those who are better off. [short contemplation] Even if you take insurance, who is going to pay you for this damage and drought. (Predrag, July 2017, Gaj)

Peasants compensated for their lack of insurance by the skilful combining of types of seeds that can bring satisfactory yields despite hazardous weather. In the case of better-off peasants, it seemed that their trust in insurance companies grew in proportion to the growth of their businesses. In their case, crop insurance appeared as a necessity for the protection of their investment, and sometimes even as a condition for joining bigger national agricultural associations or unions. Scepticism, although being one of the important motivators of peasants' actions, is a dynamic feature. The same cannot be said for peasants' distrust, which is rather more of a constant.

Distrust

Distrust has been one of the prominent topics in peasant studies. The disunity of peasants that originates in individualism, envy and distrust, makes peasants vulnerable and prone to control and manipulation by various interest groups, including the state. Some scholars argue that peasants are apolitical in general (Adie and Poitras 1974, 49). Peasants' passivity stems sometimes from the lack of means for political action. In other cases, it may be their social isolation and the type of economy they deal with, or simply a lack of confidence in their own ability to change society (Hobsbawm 1973). Classical anthropological and peasant studies see in distrust a cultural pattern of rural-peasant communities (Lewis 1951; Foster 1965; Banfield 1967; Cancian 1961; Stavriani et al. 2014). Some scholars suggest that peasants' distrust is exaggerated and that they are capable of self-organization and political action (Booth and Seligson 1979; Scott 2009). The nuanced view of peasants' distrust, as Seligson and Salazar (1979) view it, is often lost because scholars do not differentiate between political and interpersonal distrust, which is why peasants' distrust exists as a generic concept. I tested this assumption and distinguished between peasants' distrust of the state and distrust of their fellow villagers, but I could not find any evidence to indicate a crucial difference between the two, nor I was able to grasp what such a methodological nuancing would mean for the theory of peasants' distrust.

Peasants' distrust of the state

The peasantry in Serbia has for decades been distrustful of the intentions of the state. The second agrarian reform (1945–53), had turned their fears into plain reality. A strong sense of autonomy, individualism and scepticism set the foundations for peasants' deep distrust of the state. Likewise, turbulent political-economic conditions in the past couple of decades created an atmosphere in which a 'culture of distrust' flourishes (Nef 2003). Peasants are concerned that their property, work and products will be undermined by state intervention. These beliefs have been fed by the older generations, as was the case with Suzana, a middle peasant from Gaj.

> My grandfather used to tell us that, when it was supposed to go to war, the state first called and mobilized peasants. When taxes were levied, the state first took it from the peasants. The peasants feed the whole of Serbia, but the state still takes and demands most from them. (Suzana, July 2017, Gaj)

Distrust has made peasants cautious and wary of the state and it has consequently motivated them to deal without the state whenever possible. The most common examples of peasants' evasion of the state are land consolidation and the founding of agricultural associations and cooperatives.

Land consolidation emerged from a necessity to rearrange scattered privately owned land plots, and enable conditions for larger land holdings and more efficient agricultural production, improvement of rural infrastructure and environmental policies. Land consolidation started in the 1990s in Eastern Europe, when nationalized private land holdings were given back to the original owners through the restitution processes. In Yugoslavia, land consolidation happened somewhat earlier. The director of the cadastre of the municipality of Kovin (the body that documents land boundaries) confirmed to me that land consolidation in the municipality began in the 1980s with the mapping of the fields and the making of new land plans. Where conditions allowed, the land was consolidated, but where it was not possible the situation had been recorded but no further action was undertaken. The director of the cadastre admitted that people within the municipality reacted differently to land consolidation, but did not specify the situation for Gaj. The director's diplomatic answer prompted me to further investigate land consolidation in Gaj. Most of the older and middle-aged people recalled the policy in fragments. They reckoned that it was mainly only people who did not live in the village anymore, or who did not work in agriculture, who had accepted offered land consolidation plans. There were several exceptional cases of peasants from the village who had agreed with the plans. Others were reluctant. They did not trust the authorities and doubted that the land they were supposed to get in compensation would be of satisfactory quality and in the preferred area, anticipating that they would be financially damaged. It seems as if peasants had not wanted to face transaction risks that they could not control themselves.

The current land structure of most of the holdings in Gaj questions the success of land consolidation in Gaj. During seasonal work on their land, the great majority of peasants cannot physically visit and cultivate all their land parcels within three to four days because their plots are scattered all around the village area. Such land organization, peasants agreed, may be inconvenient in terms of time management, or because of risks of trespassing or lower yields. Yet the scattered fields offer a compensating advantage that provides the rationale for the continuation of the practice. Scattered fields represent a form of insurance. 'When a peasant has, say, five land plots scattered around the village, if the hail hits, it will hit only one plot, but the other four will be unharmed' (Bojan, May 2013, Malo Bavanište). In this way, peasants prudently insure the crop against failure and weather hazards. Scattering also has the symbolic function of maintaining the autonomy of the peasants and distrust toward the state. By keeping their fields scattered, peasants keep a low profile, and in such a way avoid being subjected to state agricultural and environmental surveillance, that can result in increased taxation and unnecessary costs that land consolidation brings along (Vasiljević et al. 2018).

Another example of peasants' distrust of the state can be seen in the founding of cooperatives and associations. The state encourages peasants by various means to organize and join cooperatives and associations. It provides affordable loans, subsidies and support for obtaining new machinery and building storage spaces. Yet, in Gaj there is no agricultural cooperative, apart from several private companies that represent themselves falsely. There is also no functional agricultural association. Since the second agrarian reform the cooperatives have predominantly had a negative connotation. Most peasants I interviewed saw cooperatives today as the means for the state to take control of the work and the organization of peasants.

> I think the main intention behind the state recommendations for peasants to join the cooperatives and associations is easier control over them and manipulation through these associations. Presidents of the associations are as a rule always from the dominant party. The goal of state politics is to decrease the rural sector to 12–13 per cent, and those who are within would control the whole land and livestock fund. (Dušan, June 2013, Gaj)

Peasants like Dušan, who cultivated an average land holding (15–20 ha) and whose production was mostly self-reliant, saw cooperatives and associations as political organizations that did not have the aim of improving economic conditions for peasants. Thus, they believed that they would be better off alone than within these organizations, which may compromise their property, dignity and decision-making processes. Legal uncertainty added to the peasant's distrust and discouraged the founding of cooperatives and associations. The following event from 2014 illustrates this in detail.

The collapse of a local private cooperative

'What are we peasants to do now when everyone is playing with us as they please?' shouted one man at the tense meeting with the local businessman, a co-founder of the local agricultural cooperative (in fact a private company, which had adopted the term cooperative in order to gain taxation reliefs and agricultural subsidies). The people had come together to find a solution to the problem of the cooperative's non-payment for crops from the last season. Some peasants did not have the means to cover costs for the season, or to pay upcoming loan instalments. One had 17 wagons of wheat trapped in the cooperative. Another had been forced to sell a press to buy fuel for threshing. The cooperative owed hundreds of thousands of euros to the peasants but also as a company had around the same amount owed to them by their own debtors. After several consecutive meetings in August 2014 and many unsuccessful negotiations, one fact appeared certain: the cooperative was at a dead-end, facing collapse.

The atmosphere at the meetings was sometimes hectic, filled with the dull, repetitive and naïve speeches of the local businessman.

Peasants would listen, confront him, shouting in despair, mocking and joking – but, essentially, they hoped to find a solution. They regularly attended the meetings, each time in increasing numbers, even though no solution was on the horizon. Several people succeeded in getting their money back, while the majority ended up empty-handed. In summer 2015, the cooperative was taken over by new management and only five peasants filed a lawsuit against the old cooperative's management. They won their case at court, but since the cooperative was in an insolvency process, the parties could not be paid for the loss. They then decided to initiate a criminal charge against the businessman, but their lawsuit was rejected for the second time by the higher court without right to appeal. The decision was made on the basis that peasants were damaged by a corporate body and not by a private person. It demotivated other peasants to initiate a lawsuit against the cooperative as most of them did not believe the law would protect them. Snežana, one of the damaged peasants' party, summarized the problem of the legal vulnerability of peasants.

> There is neither economic nor legal certainty. When we sell our products to the middlemen, i.e. cooperative, we don't sign any contract. We only get a piece of paper, an unofficial receipt, where it is noted when we delivered the crops, how much, and who confirmed the delivery, without any stamp on it nor any other official mark. This functions on the basis of trust and everyone just hopes that bad things will not happen. Everyone can cheat the peasants, and we don't have any mechanisms to claim our rights at the court. That's why many people didn't prosecute him [the businessman]. Because, apart from being damaged, we must pay for the court costs and a lawyer. Many are not ready to take these steps and they don't have the means to do so either. He [the businessman] knows this mindset of the peasants very well, that's why he cheats them easily. (Snežana, July 2017, Gaj)

To this day, it remains unclear whether the collapse of the cooperative was deliberate or not, and the local rumours hold it was an intentional closure. A couple of years ago the businessman, as the rumour goes, had cheated people from another village in a similar way. In the first years, he was successfully working and developing trust among peasants, and then one season he took the crops from the peasants, and he declared bankruptcy. The cooperative became insolvent and the whole case ended without any legal consequence.

This vignette about the businessman illustrates the conditions in which legal and political macro-predicaments manifest in the daily life of peasants, where the lack of enforcement of the rule of law creates a conducive atmosphere for the flourishing of similar frauds. The weak state, on the one hand, motivates spontaneous and informal arrangements between people, their direct negotiations and businesses, which are in most cases based on trust. On the other hand, there are the clear limitations of the weak state which is not capable of sanctioning frauds. A weak state thus favours the development of the laissez-faire mentality and a growing distrust of the state.

Interpersonal distrust

The peasants' interpersonal distrust drags them away from the ideals of collective economic actions and representation promoted by such bodies as the World Farmers' Organization, the CAP agenda of the European Commission and the Serbian Ministry of Agriculture. The biggest agricultural association in Gaj collapsed because of interpersonal distrust. The association, with over 60 members, was founded in 2012. According to its founder, it emerged out of the necessity to unite against the local businessmen who had taken most of the state land on lease. One of them had bought a state farm and co-founded the problematic cooperative described in the story above, on which basis he was then able to the lease the state land. The common goal of the members of the association had been to pressure the local municipality into enabling fair distribution and access to state land and to prevent the businessman from expanding further. The association grew over time and became an influential political factor in the village. Many peasant-members were proud to be part of an association which, they believed, protected their interests and enabled their visibility both at the local and regional level. There were also some more sceptical members of the association. They believed that the association rather served the interests of its founders and not the common goal of the peasants. It turned out that the sceptics were right. With one of those ironies that often seems to occur in life, the association fell apart in 2015 because of the local businessman.

When the businessman started to delay payments for crops in 2014, most of the affected peasants did not take any action but waited. Three founders of the association were among the first who got their money back. Their excuse for having been first in line was that other members had been too passive. That is, they had tried to persuade members of the association to protest in front of the businessman's cooperative, and even suggested they undertake more severe action. But other members feared the businessman's reaction or his potential revenge. The rest of members, thus, had decided not to take any action. The founders of the association eventually gave up persuading. They could not comprehend that their fellows were not ready to face the businessman and ask for their own money. In the meantime, three of the founders had met with the businessman, who promised that he would transfer a certain amount of money every week to the financially damaged peasants according to a list of priorities. The promise was short-lived. He soon stopped making payments, and the three founders of the association were among just a few peasants from the entire village who got their money back. One of the founders of the association reckoned that the businessman did this on purpose as it was his strategy to create division among members of the association, causing its final dissolution. 'He has been long enough in the company of various people, and he exactly knows when and how he should speak with someone. He made the split easily' (Kolja, August 2014, Gaj). By dismantling the association, the businessman defeated his main competitor and destroyed its influence in the village. After this event, the association did not meet for more than two years, and now it exists only formally, while the founders of the association have lost their previous reputation in the village. Peasants commonly commented on the dissolution of the association and agreed on the main factors that caused its collapse.

> Envy and venality are the main reasons why the association does not exist anymore. Likewise, all our previous associations were short-lived because they were driven by personal interest. (Edi, July 2017, Gaj)

> The association collapsed after the events with the businessman. The leaders of the association took their money and they have had neither influence or dignity ever since. People don't trust them anymore. Dishonesty, distrust, and mentality are the main reasons why we do not unite in the associations. (Predrag, July 2017, Gaj)

Sava's view, that '[T]he peasants are an easy target for manipulation because there is no rule of law' (Sava, August 2015, Gaj) only partly explains the peasants' situation. Such a situation is indeed a product of a weak rule of law, on the one hand, and peasants' inability to unite as a strong counterpart of powerful actors on the other. But if we slightly shift the perspective, their poor organization is not all bad. As will be shown in Chapter 4, it opens new avenues for doing things in an individualistic, efficient and laissez-faire manner, which would not be possible within a cooperative or association composed of different people and often colliding visions and ideologies.

Life on the periphery

The periphery determines people's lives in terms of physical space, expectations and provision of services. Discrepancies between the expectations of people and existing state provisions often cause problems in the relationship between citizens and the state. In some cases, it may develop into resentments with significant political repercussions (Cramer 2016), and sometimes, as in Gaj, it may buttress the laissez-faire mentality.

In Serbian villages, generally, a lack or complete absence of services and infrastructure is common, which strengthens the sense of marginalization from urban centres. Gaj is no different, although it is in much better condition than the neighbouring villages. There are numerous examples that demonstrate what Cramer calls 'unfairness in terms of geography' that is based on the belief that village people always pay higher social costs and higher prices for a range of things than people in the cities (Cramer 2016, 59). Some of the most salient problems are an inadequate health service, a lack of medical staff and an ambulance, the absence of public transport to the city, a lack of kindergartens and bad agricultural and road infrastructure. Gaj residents commonly described their position in relation to the city with the humorous comment, 'We are the appendix in the system of priorities of the republic of Serbia.' Things may appear different only during elections, when rural areas become a political battlefield. Yet, after the elections the burning issues mostly remain unsolved.

Life on the periphery is best described through this example of the functioning of public medical services in the village. Slobodan, a middle-aged small entrepreneur from Gaj, explained its consequences for the local population.

> We pay the same amount for health and social insurance as those who live in Kovin and other cities, but we don't have the same treatment nor the same conditions. The village health centre doesn't work in the afternoons, a dentist works every second day, an ambulance doesn't come to Gaj, except in rare cases. If someone gets sick on Tuesday afternoon, for example, he cannot go to the

health centre in the village to see a doctor, because a doctor doesn't work in the afternoon. On Wednesday, if he is lucky to get through the queue to see a doctor, he gets an official referral for blood tests. Since it is already late to take blood tests in Kovin, he has to postpone taking tests until the next day. But Thursday is the day reserved for diabetics and only they can do blood and other tests in the health centre in Kovin. So, Friday remains for doing blood tests, yet he can't get results before Monday at 1 pm. Then, he can't go straight to a doctor in the village with the results because a doctor doesn't work in the afternoons. Finally, he ends up on Tuesday seeing his doctor who analyses his results seven days after he got sick. This may vary from 20 days up to several months if a person has to undertake a treatment in Pančevo or Belgrade. (Slobodan, August 2013, Gaj)

A similar problem arises with public transportation. The residents of Gaj do not have public transportation to the nearest town Kovin. The bus route was cancelled some years ago because it was not profitable, and since then only private taxi transport operates between the village and the town. Likewise, in Malo Bavanište, the school bus that was transporting the students to the town was cancelled for the same reason, and now children either rely on their parents to drive them to school or they share a taxi. Such problems physically and mentally influence the sense of segregation between the rural and urban population and hamper their synchronized functioning.

The condition of life on the periphery became a metaphor for an unequal share, services, attention and care. In such an atmosphere, people in the village do not care too much, nor do they think that state bureaucrats are interested in them. The minor presence of the state creates more room for laissez-faire manoeuvring. The local sayings 'who cares?' or 'who's asking?' are particularly indicative and refer to a lack of state presence and interest in life in rural areas, and are used as justification for actions that often run contrary to the law, state recommendations and plans. Land-leasing contracts, subsidies, selling of products beyond official channels and tax avoidance are examples that demonstrate the dialectical position of the villagers. While they may lament the lack of attention from the state, they use it to their advantage, in fact, to bridge the gaps themselves, and to build and grow their own spontaneous mechanism of trade and cooperation. As Arce and Long rightly observe, 'despite their geographical and institutional "marginality"', peasants 'nevertheless know how to live with their "isolation" and extract some benefits from it' (Arce and Long 1993, 194).

Nesting is a precondition for manifesting laissez-faire mentality

The discussion concerning the formative elements of the laissez-faire mentality aimed to present how local ethos, attitudes and practices have evolved and nested through a long social process. On the one hand, it is generated by the external political-economic conditions which the village population faces every day. On the other, it is moulded by an internal mixture of customs, habits and values, embedded in the local social fabric. External and internal factors merge in the peasants' attitudes about what they regard as important for individual and village wellbeing and existence; what are the possible but also less likely modes of cooperation with the co-villagers themselves and with the state; and how individual and collective aspirations of villagers should synchronize in governing the social order in the village. In the next chapter, we will see how the laissez-faire mentality manifests further and reveals its full capacity in relation to agricultural and rural development policies.

Notes

1 Milica Bakić-Hayden invented the concept 'nesting orientalisms' to explain the gradation of otherness and backwardness among the Balkan countries and peoples (see Bakić-Hayden 1995). In this chapter, I borrow the term to explain causal development of the laissez-faire mentality and its embedding in people and local culture. Except rhetorical similarity, nesting laissez-faire mentality does not share the conceptual understanding Bakić-Hayden applies in her work.
2 First *slava* is aimed to celebrate the saint protector of the family.
3 *Gazda* (sing.) in the local context usually refers to people who run small private businesses, such as a grocery store, mechanical shop, restaurants, beauty salon, or similar, or who have more land than average and bigger households. *Gazde* (pl.) may also be people who do not have a lot of land (up to 10 ha at most), but who are distinguished in the village by their good reputation. During the second agrarian reform (1949–53), those who owned more than 10 ha were perceived by the communist party as a threat to the system and were derogatively called *gazde* or *kulaks*.
4 Those who have land (usually from 1–2 ha) but do not work it, such as a tiny group of university-educated professionals and craftspeople, rent it out to others from the village because they do not have time, or cannot afford farming, or do not have the necessary machinery, or the required knowledge. In cases where the land they possess is less than 0.5 ha, farming is not profitable and is suitable only for the garden, which provides for household consumption.
5 Moral economy, for example, appears as a relevant concept in studies on kinship (Yalcin-Heckmann 2010, 133–65), or as a substitute for broken institutional ties in post-socialist states (Morris and Polese 2014). The concept is, however, controversial as it holds that most market-driven and self-interested economic activities are immoral or unprincipled in nature. It is sharply juxtaposed to market economy, presupposing that a common good is possible to maintain only through the moral economy. In the literature, it is broadly accepted as a necessary informal corrective of a market economy.
6 Classical anthropological and peasant studies literature discuss individualism and independence as essential characteristics of the peasantry and pastoralists and argue this phenomenon

emerged as a product of ecological adaptation (Goldschmidt 1971), ethos (Banfield 1967), limited material resources peasants need to cope with (Foster 1965), or psychological and social factors that strengthen their self-reliance (Dumont 1986; Stock and Forney 2014; Stock et al. 2014; Emery 2014, 2015).

7   See: https://tinyurl.com/ybts38wk, accessed 30 December 2016.

8   Studies of peasants' cooperation reflect various reasons that may lead to cooperation or to its absence (Wynne-Jones 2017). Some studies also suggest ways for overcoming peasants' individualism and strengthening their position globally (Van der Ploeg 2008; Cogeca 2010; Emery and Franks 2012).

4
Laissez-faire practices versus rural development policies

After the Second World War, world governments adopted the concept of development to promote and attain a range of ideological, political, economic and national aims and secure new alliances in the emerging post-war landscape.[1] It gradually evolved from agendas into projects of global dimensions and importance. Despite the different ideologies embodied in the concept of development in much of the Western, Soviet Union or post-colonial countries, there were two main blueprints that governments followed in their attempts to overcome economic discrepancies and poverty. The first preferred industrialization to agriculture and was prevalent until the 1970s, while the second preferred agriculture to industrialization and was gaining on importance especially by the 1970s (Kay 2009). Bringing rural areas back to focus was partially inspired by Michael Lipton and his influential thesis on urban bias (Lipton 1977). Lipton revealed that less than 20 per cent of all investments ended up in rural areas, even though most of the people in the poorest countries are dependent on the countryside and farming. Investments in agricultural infrastructure and production were not only insufficient but also inefficient in contrast to urban areas. Even favouring larger over small farms and investing in them did not enable growth in rural areas. Lipton asserted that development in rural areas should be governed as an encompassing package of solutions that would ensure economic, social and environmental wellbeing of the rural communities.

After the collapse of communism in Eastern Europe, state-policies focused special attention on rural areas. Intensified industrialization had devastating effects on the agricultural sector which served primarily to underpin, delegate a new labour force, and transfer surpluses into the industrial sector. Likewise, the state investments in state farms and cooperatives negatively affected the development of private households and their means of production. In most of these countries, thus, consensus was that investments should be re-transferred to agriculture, small and middle households, and that governments, international organizations and NGOs should be the main supporters of rural development (Forsyth 2005). Since then, rural development plans have combined elements of market and social policy and envision the improvement of economic and social wellbeing of the rural population.

Development planners (national governments and international organizations such as the European Commission), often 'exhibit a degree of ambiguity towards neo-liberal principles' incorporated in the rural development visions (Swain 2016, 577). While some advocate the role of the state in pursuing rural development projects, others believe that the state should have minimal authority and leave it to the market economy and competitive incentives to lead rural development. Such visions of rural development, except perhaps in New Zealand, have remained to a large degree unpopular and seldom applied in practice (Stock and Peoples 2012). Most of the rural development projects in Europe and perhaps beyond are, thus, governed, supported, and promoted by the state and its local and regional departments. As of 2000, the Serbian Ministry of Agriculture embraced such management of rural development and has been its major promoter and an ideologue since (Diković 2014).

The prevalent top-to-bottom approach in rural development projects was criticized in *Beyond Modernization* (Van der Ploeg and Van Dijk 1995). Top-down narratives of modernization and rural development undermine the local as the most relevant point of reference in the projects and see it just as another setting where development models should be implemented (vii–xiii). Through the concept 'local as resource', Van der Ploeg and Van Dijk emphasize theoretical and empirical value of an endogenous path to development. Endogenous development should be an alternative to top-bottom development models and 'local as resource' should be a channel through which the locals speak and introduce their visions of development. By focusing on the local as a resource, we add to our rich knowledge about leading concepts of modernization, the alternatives to dominant modernization paradigms, which are insufficiently known (Van der Ploeg and Van Dijk 1995, x). 'Local as resource' primarily refers to technological and practical solutions in agriculture that have emerged spontaneously in local settings, but it is also a useful concept for understanding how the local practices, economic and social arrangements, can mould, influence and direct state rural development plans and agricultural policies. This chapter reveals that state policies designed to improve rural areas are far from being mechanically and linearly implemented in Gaj and nearby villages. It lays out how agricultural and rural development policies related to subsidies, trading the products, agricultural insurance, agricultural pensions and village associations have been moulded by local laissez-faire practices. Unlike state policies, the laissez-faire practices are sensitive to local conditions, they are informed by the local rationales and serve both individual and local aspirations and wellbeing.

Subsidies

As of 2000, the Serbian Ministry of Agriculture has implemented a set of legal and economic reforms to synchronize with EU agricultural policy. Although Serbian policies are officially committed to the Common Agricultural Policy (CAP), the ministry often struggles to carry out CAP's principles systematically because it is under pressure of low and unequal economic activity across the agricultural sectors. The selection of agricultural policies and priorities has usually been made ad hoc, driven more by pragmatic interests toward enhancing production than by the needs of the rural population, improving services and tackling inequalities in rural areas (Martinovska-Stojcheska et al. 2016; Papić and Bogdanov 2015; Volk et al. 2014; Bogdanov 2007). The Ministry of Agriculture and other state agencies, thus, see in subsidies the main resource for improving life in rural areas.

Peasants in Gaj and neighbouring villages exhibit ambiguous attitudes to subsidies. They appreciate subsidies and consider them to be an important measure, but they also reckon that they have created more problems and accelerated social stratification in their community, instead of preventing it. Until 2016, agricultural subsidies were aimed at those peasants who cultivated from 0.5 to 99 ha. I was told that during this period subsidies aided the better-off peasants in Gaj, who enormously enlarged their private resources and assets. Those who cultivated more than 50 ha had already adjusted to market economy and did not need subsidies to facilitate their own agricultural production. Meanwhile, subsidies granted to peasants who cultivated up to 10–15 ha hardly covered their investments in production. In 2016 the Ministry of Agriculture modified the subsidy legislation because of large-scale misuse. Only households that cultivated between 0.5 and 20 ha were entitled to subsidies. In the meantime, the amount of the subsidy per hectare went down from the previous 90 EUR to 30 EUR.

Such low subsidies were not an economic support, but rather act as a social measure with the aim of levelling social discrepancies among peasants. In our numerous conversations, many peasants stressed that the agricultural subsidies represent a 'pittance', 'social help' or 'charity'. Yet, although they might agree that the subsidies are low, they disagree about their effect. Their disagreements in fact reflect a broader dispute over whether subsidies cause more harm than good. The core problem for some is that subsidies artificially decrease global prices of crops, disable small farmers and eliminate them from competition. In the long run, subsidies may cause producers to become less inventive or competitive, and more reliant on the government, which is the case in some European countries where peasants produce less or average amounts for an increasing financial support. On the whole, peasants from Gaj with mid- or large-sized holdings tend to share such attitudes and think that they do not need subsidies to improve their production.

> It is disputable whether subsidies are a positive change after all. Better-off peasants have already stood out by 2006 [when the subsidies were implemented] and subsidies were just wind in their sails. It's better not to give us this pittance but to enable good prices. (Mirko, August 2013, Malo Bavanište)

> Peasants don't need subsidies. If they [state bureaucrats] let the market economy work, peasants would find their own way. Subsidies don't mean anything to us when we lose on the price of wheat or corn. (Goran, August 2013, Gaj)

> Peasants should not be given subsidies. They lived well even without them. They just need stable prices and the market. (Toma, July 2013, Beli Breg)

> Peasants who cultivate above 30 ha do not need subsidies. But the state was mistaken. Instead of money, it should give only fertilizers. (Bogoljub, July 2017, Gaj)

> I don't need subsidies, but instead the state ought to let the prices be as they should be, and not try to control them. (Predrag, July 2017, Gaj)

In summary, peasants from Gaj with mid- or large-sized holdings share an understanding according to which subsidies in Serbia are not designed to foster production but rather to keep the heads of small peasants above water. Unsurprisingly, peasants who exhibit a wholly positive view on subsidies are small producers cultivating 5–7 ha at most. They see in subsidies a way to ensure themselves in the agri-business and continue to work in agriculture, without being thrown under the feet of better-off and rich peasants. In contrast to their middle and bigger peers, small peasants tend to exhibit greater reliance on the government: 'I would work easily if the state tells me what I am supposed to do' (Nikola, July 2015, Gaj). Subsidies for them are the grain of certainty that ensures their survival and organization of their production.

The importance of subsidies in the context of Gaj and neighbouring villages, nevertheless, goes beyond their effect on agricultural production. Subsidies reveal the larger picture of how the laissez-faire networks subordinated this state policy to local ends that are not related to agriculture. And how, ironically, the non-agricultural population has become the main beneficiary of subsidies.

Subsidies and spontaneous social order

Once subsidies came into force, from 2006, they soon been accommodated in the local network of spontaneous social order. In the local context, subsidies attracted people from various professions, affinities, both poor and rich, and also their interests, who by attaining their personal goals (getting subsides usually through informal and sometimes illegal ways), also generated the wellbeing of others.

Since 2016, subsidies have been aimed at peasants who cultivate up to 20 ha. But households from Gaj that cultivate more than 20 ha use them as well. They apply several strategies to show themselves as eligible beneficiaries. One of the common strategies is that adult members of the same household do not register under the same address although they generate income from land under the same roof. The land titles are passed down to a few family members who register only nominally as a separate household and, in that way, request subsidies for what is nominally their own cultivated land.

Before 2016, strategies for getting subsidies for the land that was beyond the prescribed maximum (0.5–99 ha) demanded more effort and sophistication. Some couples from the village had divorced nominally to present themselves as if they lived in separate households and cultivated the land separately. Some younger couples did not want to get married for this reason, and usually the wife would remain registered at her parents' address. If the household did not have enough eligible mature members, they made agreements with friends or cousins who had little land, or did not have any at all. The friend or cousin then registered as a cultivator of the land in question, while in exchange the household shared the subsidies with them. Marko, for example, made an agreement with his old unemployed friend from the village, who registered nominally and applied for subsidies for Marko's land. In exchange, Marko paid his friend social and pension insurance, since he had a few years to go until full retirement. Consequently, these strategies contributed to the rising number of registered agricultural households in Gaj, while the actual number of agricultural producers has in fact remained the same.

Accessing subsidies in cases of those who are not eligible sometimes requires support from external networks. Administrative employees in authorized institutions that keep records of all changes related to land, have an overview of the land plots for which subsidies have not been claimed in the last couple of years. The employees sell the information to interested parties and instruct them to wait until the day of the application deadline. The parties submit an application on the last possible day, requesting subsidies for those exact land parcels as if they are cultivating them. I learned that such delicate operations are less common in Gaj and neighbouring villages because of negative transaction costs that both sides may incur if trust and reliability between them are not strong. Unlike external networks, close circles of family and friends prove to be bolder and more resistant to potential risks in conducting similar operations. For instance, one of the relatively recent measures introduced by the Serbian Ministry of Agriculture reimburses livestock breeders 80 per cent the price of cattle per head. The measure incentivized some peasants to apply similar strategies to those for subsidies for land. I met a couple who registered at different addresses and the wife (in some other cases it may be someone else loyal to the family) appeared as the salesperson from whom the livestock breeder (husband) officially bought cattle. No new cattle were, in fact, brought to the farm, because the wife was selling her husband the cattle they already had. The trade was thus just a cover, while the household continued to have the same number of cattle it did before this transaction.

In informal conversations with the peasants who applied these or similar strategies, I found out that the money acquired through subsidies and reimbursements for cattle purchasing had, in most of cases, been used for non-agricultural purposes, such as building houses or renovations, buying cars, financing summer holidays, organization of weddings or birthday celebrations. The money, in other words, was invested in sustaining the image of the good household and *gazde*.

Likewise, other local actors such as builders, musicians and rentiers of venues kept their businesses in operation partly due to the allocation of money acquired through subsidies.

Subsidies and similar state programmes for facilitating agricultural production have generated on the local level a black market of services that intertwine different people and networks. Peasants and livestock breeders, for example, get refunded by the Ministry of Agriculture for fuel, seeds and fertilizers and are required to submit confirmation of purchase of these items. Most peasants submit receipts for fuel without, in reality, having bought it from registered gas stations. Gas stations in fact supply peasants with official receipts, selling them for 0.01 euro cent per litre. Likewise, there are several dealers in nearby villages who collect various receipts for fertilizers or seeds and sell them on request. Peasants usually emphasize that anything that the village needs can be found on the local black market. And indeed, it seems to be so. Peasants are thrifty and they prefer buying what they need more cheaply at the black market, including fuel, seeds and fertilizers. Through buying official receipts from the dealers they formally satisfy the criteria of the Ministry of Agriculture for getting reimbursement.

Many peasants buy fuel from cheaper suppliers, so-called fishermen who smuggle fuel from ships that sail the Danube. The fishermen arrange in advance with the captain and helmsman of the ship to intercept it on the Danube, near to Gaj. The operation takes place late at night. At the appointed time, the helmsman shifts one of two engines onto silent mode, saving significant amounts of oil. The smugglers get notice through trusted channels of when the ship will be near the appointed place. At the agreed time, the ship shifts course slightly and gets closer to the coast. The smugglers approach the ship in their boats with tanks, and the captain or someone from the crew passes them the refuelling hose. Since the ship is not allowed to stop, smugglers must skilfully approach the moving ship and cling to its fuel tank. Many accidents and deaths have happened exactly at this moment because the whole operation is conducted in complete darkness. If the operation goes as expected, smugglers usually obtain up to 90 gallons of fuel from a ship and transport their tanks to their final destinations.

Fuel smuggling was not triggered by agricultural subsidies. The proximity of the River Danube established smuggling routes between Romania and Serbia that have been in use for decades, particularly during socialism when smuggling cigarettes, fuel, goods and even people was common (Archer and Rácz 2012; Cosmin 2009). The examples of fuel smuggling, access to subsidies and the black market for agricultural receipts illustrate how a state policy that ought to target only one group of people – that is, agricultural producers – becomes trapped in the local, spontaneous ways of social organization. Existing local arrangements that skewed the use of subsidies are not necessarily a result of complicated official procedures. On the contrary, bureaucratic procedures for claiming agricultural subsidies are clear and simple, according to peasants. The reason rather lies in something else. In small communities, information concerning shortage and supply of demanded goods circulates more quickly than usual. Supply competition in such places is much stronger and more obvious, which drives one group of people to impose themselves as reliable suppliers of alternative, cheaper and better services. Spontaneous, local solutions thus get priority because formal supply networks often lag and do not respond fast enough to meet the local needs.

The power of local arrangements is also evident in their ability to subordinate subsidies to land-leasing contracts. After 2000, with the opening of the market, the price and demand for land increased significantly. Peasants from Gaj have been taking additional land on lease for decades, and in many cases the leased land usually makes up between a third and half of the total area they cultivate. The growing cost of land leases did not favour small- and mid-scale peasants who often must pay 200–250 euros for a lease of 0.5 ha, and compete for access to land with bigger producers. Yet the increased prices favoured small landowners whose land before 2000 was devalued. The most vulnerable villagers, such as retired peasants and widows, gained the most from the new circumstances, as did those who had recently decided to withdraw from agriculture because they possessed less than 2 ha. Small landowners, most of whom have low income, thus found a way to benefit from subsidies through new leasing contracts.

Landowners had continued to rent out land for cash or crops, as was the case before 2000, but now they also demanded a share of the subsidies received by their tenants. Tenants and landowners might share subsidies in the ratio 60:40, and sometimes even 50:50, determined, in economic terms, by the unique selling points of the leased land, such as its quality, the proximity of irrigational and road infrastructure and the village. Such arrangements might not be ideal for tenants, but if they did not agree with the terms of the lease they could easily be replaced by new tenants. As of 2016, with the shrinking amount of subsidies, small landowners started to register themselves as agricultural households on a huge scale, in order to claim for themselves the full subsidies, for land they did not cultivate and actually leased, so preventing their tenants the same right. The market economy in Serbia had an affirmative effect on land ownership and on the rising price and demand for land. Landowners from Gaj have explored the ways through which their land revenues can be perpetuated and stabilized. Subsidies have only expanded new possibilities in land transactions. Landowners and local arrangements have eventually shifted the aim of subsidies. Instead of rewarding production in the local context, subsidies have become a reward for land ownership.

Subsidies are flawed, but they continue. Why?

Viewed from the broader perspective, subsidies in Serbia did not meet the expected goals for improved investment in agriculture and mechanization. The Ministry of Agriculture has never clearly communicated what are the expected goals, either to the peasants or to the public. Moreover, it did not set benchmarks that would determine the expected growth. Presumably the Ministry expected that such a policy would simply bring obvious betterment in production. When the Ministry decided to reduce the subsidies in 2016, the decision was delivered in response to subsidies-misuse by some producers who 'parcelized their households to get more subsidies'.[2] In another earlier media outlet, the minister of agriculture stated that subsidies were failed policies that did not give the expected results.[3] The agricultural experts and the former ministers of agriculture I interviewed agreed that the purpose of subsidies remains problematic in the long run.

> The right question is whether subsidies in their current form (paying per ha, subsidized fertilizers, fuel, etc.) resolve any problem either on the level of agricultural producers or on the state level. Then, my answer is that on the level of agricultural producers they do not resolve anything, while on the level of the state, they represent only expenditure. (Interview with Dr Ivana Dulić-Marković, June 2013, Belgrade)

> Since this measure [subsidies] has been introduced, we do not have any indicators of the growth of production. Which means that money has not been used for the right purposes, but for some other things and unproductive affairs. (Interview with Zaharije Trnavčević, July 2014, Belgrade)

> Money given for subsidizing investments and employment in agriculture […] did not get results because it simply did not increase either investments or employment. (Interview with Milojko Arsić, December 2013, Belgrade)

Although agricultural subsidies in Serbia are low compared to EU countries (Swain 2016; Martinovska-Stojcheska et al. 2016) this cannot be the sole explanation for their failure. One of the core problems in the failure of this policy that I see is that local arrangements have significantly influenced the flow of funds, redirecting their investment toward non-agricultural activities and changing their purpose so much that the agriculturally inactive population has become a significant beneficiary of subsidies.

So, why does the policy continue, despite clear state and local (mine, for instance) evidence of its ineffectiveness? Some scholars argue that the subsidies, being more than economic policy, represent an important political means for enhancing government control over the peasantry (Krasznai-Kovacs 2019). True, but the deeper analysis of the findings from my field site reveals a more dynamic exchange of power between the peasants and the state. Subsidies are a power game where the assumed positions often change the prospects of gain. Current and previous governments sense well that the rural population, peasants especially, remains the most stable and coherent electoral resource. Peasants, usually on the eve of the elections, demand either higher subsidies (even when they do not use them for production), state protection against price hikes or loosening of regulations regarding import and export of their products.[4] Sometimes they threaten strikes, sometimes they physically block the roads, discard milk or destroy cabbages or raspberries. The range of their demands swiftly changes from those that are pro-regulation to pro-market and back, depending on their assessment of the risks or benefits of the forthcoming season. Such occasional demands are also common for the peasants in Gaj and neighbouring villages. Although it may look contradictory to the laissez-faire practices, in fact it is not. Namely, such demands do not limit peasants' autonomous behaviour, especially in the informal spheres of trade, deals and negotiation, as this chapter will reveal in detail. Nor do subsidies determine their growth, as I already indicated, and again demonstrate in Chapter 6. Peasants' demands should be understood in the light of trade-offs between peasants and the state. Not always confronting the peasants, and meeting some of their requests, is a wise strategy from the government's point of view. Peasants, on the other hand, compensate by ensuring the political status quo in return for less state control in the countryside and over their informal activities. From this perspective, maintaining low subsidies, instead of abolishing them, with flexible adjustments of import-export terms is a win-win situation.

Trading of products

Direct trade represents one of the notable characteristics of peasants in Gaj, Beli Breg and Malo Bavanište. Because most peasants belong to a category of small and middle producers, they are familiar only with the local and regional markets. They almost never engage in transnational trade (cf. Yalcin-Heckmann 2014). The global markets seem too abstract and unreachable to them. On the one hand, the distrust of the state demotivates peasants to engage in any official trade channels beyond the regional borders. On the other hand, most peasants share the opinion that only the biggest among them have the privilege to trade internationally because of their connections and close ties with the state, by which they mean the ruling party. Luka, a middle peasant from Gaj, summed up a common rationale of peasants like him who refrain from international trade on the stock market.

> If peasants are willing to sell their crops on the stock exchange they must meet many demanding criteria. First of all, they have to become members of the stock exchange, which costs 90 euros for six months. They have to obtain certificates issued by a state institution for quality control and public store houses. Peasants should have their storehouses which also fulfil some conditions such as being away from residential areas, having their own electricity etc. Then if they meet all these criteria, peasants sign a contract with the stock exchange and agree to respect the delivery and payment deadlines. The problem is that many reject this path, even if they meet the conditions. It's not a secret that public storehouses take 10 per cent of the total value of crops to issue certificates. A lot of peasants avoid the stock exchange because of their racketeering and complicated procedures. (Luka, June 2013, Gaj)

International trade goes beyond peasants' control and they perceive it as being too risky, bureaucratic and unfavourable. The more direct the trade gets, the better. 'Direct' here means informal trade. Siniša, a small-scale peasant from Malo Bavanište who is an active vegetable supplier of the local market, estimates that '80 per cent of all economic activities in the village take place on the black market' (July 2017, Malo Bavanište). The Serbian government has made numerous attempts to implement measures that would curtail the unreported economy, including peasants' trading activities. The letter of the law officially forbids peasants to sell their homemade products such as meat, milk products, honey, alcoholic drinks and canned food (*zimnica*) because of various hygiene and quality standards that the Serbian ministries have adopted. Yet, peasants continue to trade them at the marketplaces or from home.

Peasants sell their products for cash and mostly at the local marketplace or right in front of their houses. They advertise products on improvised billboards clearly visible to the outsiders who pull over and make a purchase. The regional road to the Romanian border goes through Gaj, and those living near this road make part of their income from home. A great range of products such as pigs, rabbits, corn, vegetables, beans, poppy seeds, eggs, worms for fishing, wheat, hay, straw, home crafts and local arts, are sold in such a way. There are several households in Gaj that produce and live entirely from the sale of seasonal fruits and vegetables. Depending on the trade dynamic, they sell their products in carts, either in front of their houses or in the centre of the village, in the early morning and late afternoon. Switching between two selling places during the day is designed to maximize on the busyness of the regional road and the working hours of people who commute between the villages and nearby cities. During the summer months, the intensity of the traffic is higher because of Romanian citizens who pass through Gaj on the way to the Greek seaside. In these busier periods, usually all household members work in shifts and keep two instead of one cart full of products, one in front of their house and the other in the centre of the village.

Women mainly trade their products from home or in the marketplace in Gaj and Kovin. Saturdays are reserved for the village market that is open to all vendors who trade various goods (see Figure 4.1). The stalls are reserved for those who regularly pay rent to the village council. In the case that they do not show up, it is common that anyone else can occupy their stalls. Sophisticated forms of trade take place through the internet and especially Facebook. Peasants invest time in creating appealing images and advertisements. For example, they post a few photos which show the process of preparation of canned food (*zimnica*) to assure their buyers of what they buy – carefully prepared high-quality food.

Zimnica is made from vegetables such as paprika, tomato, cauliflower and pickles. It is a traditional canned food prepared in the form of a sauce or stew, or sour vegetables. *Ajvar*, as the most famous addition to autumn and winter dishes made of paprika and tomato, is the most desirable product that is always in high demand. Most women from Gaj, find the internet the easiest way to offer their *zimnica* to the market. In my repeated visit to Gaj in 2017, I learned that the households

Figure 4.1 The informal outdoor Saturday market in Gaj. Source: Author.

working with *zimnica* are getting most of their orders through Facebook. For both female and male peasants the internet is close to the ideal way of trade because it facilitates swift, simple and comfortable trade from home with fast payment. 'Today peasants can have direct contact with markets without a middleman, thanks to the internet, but it limits them to Serbia only. Nevertheless, all goes; literally, we can trade anything' (Mirko, August, 2013, Malo Bavanište).

Trading on the spot, but beyond the common marketplaces, also brings lucrative trading arrangements for local and regional buyers. Until recently, Gaj and nearby villages had traded a lot with Albanians from Kosovo because of the proximity of the highway that connects Serbia to the south and north. Milijan, one of the peasants from Gaj who traded regionally, vividly illustrated that 'there were hundreds of trucks arriving in the village and loading tons of products, corn, cows, pigs, hay, and transporting them back to Kosovo' (August 2014, Gaj). Beli Breg was known for selling its products to Kosovo Albanians and buyers from south-western part of Serba (Region of Sandžak). The entire trade was direct and for cash. Although private cooperatives in the villages have taken over mass purchase in the last decade, they could not influence the vanishing of such practices. Likewise, trade with Kosovo has somewhat slowed down because of the political circumstances. Yet trade continues rather through more subtle forms.

Trade on the spot is cash only, and if it is trade of cattle, for example, the transactions are in euros. The network of buyers ranges from reliable buyers to the new customers who are willing to come to the village and transport cattle that have been sold under the radar. Livestock breeders usually sell their animals to so-called 'brokers' who further trade them through the official channels. The function of brokers is, hence, to 'make informal (and sometimes illegal) deals possible within formal organisational boundaries' (Jancsics 2018, 208). Arrangements between peasants and brokers exist on a large scale, presumably because there is no common marketplace nearby Gaj where livestock breeders can sell their cattle, pigs or sheep. Brokers buy animals from livestock breeders who keep them in summer ranches, a few kilometres away from the villages, hidden from the main road that passes through Gaj (Figures 4.2 and 4.3). The brokers have registration as agricultural households, which is important, as we will see, for the transportation of animals from the summer ranches. When a livestock breeder informally sells cattle, he informs a local veterinarian that he slaughtered cattle and asks to write them off from the record, so that their marks become invalid. Then the broker takes the marks from his own cattle (for which he has proper documentation) and puts them on the bought heads. With the loaded trucks the brokers go to their

Figure 4.2 The dirt track leading up to the summer ranches. Source: Author.

Figure 4.3 A summer ranch, set against the hillside. Source: Author.

destination, and in case the police intercept them, their registration as agricultural producers is used as a cover, to indicate that they are simply transporting their own animals.

Like brokers, the livestock breeders with whom I spoke from the area were all registered as agricultural households and not as livestock farms. The reasons are plenty for such a decision. By classifying themselves as an agricultural household, they evade unnecessary surveillance of the state. Such registration gives them more room to manoeuvre, especially in cases of the informal trading of cattle. Registering as a livestock farm would mean meeting many high standards and special conditions for animals. Since they are not interested in expanding their cattle business, for the reasons I explain in detail in 'Unsustainable livestock breeding: a problem caused by the state', they prefer to 'keep it simple'. When I asked one of the livestock breeders to explain to me what is meant by this, his answer was revealingly intuitive. People like him are uneducated and unskilled in 'nice' talks; most of the day they live with their cattle on the ranches, dirty and smelly, so they avoid unnecessary contact with people unless they are brokers, similar people to them, with whom the trade is direct and without complicated bureaucracy.

Existing state measures do not much affect peasants' understanding of trade. The state supports livestock breeders in selling their cattle to the slaughterhouses and adds 30 per cent to the price the slaughterhouse pays to them, to establish a firm production chain between slaughterhouses and livestock breeders. Yet peasant's refraining from

Table 4.1 Reported number of slaughtered cattle for 2013, 2014 and 2015 (thousands).

	Number at beginning of year	Slaughtered in households	Slaughtered at abbatoirs
2013	921	318	147
2014	913	320	151
2015	920	302	161

Source: *Statistical Yearbook of Republic of Serbia* 2016, 235–6. https://www.stat.gov.rs/en-US/opsti-uslovi. © Copyright SORS, used by permission.

such an arrangement is a mixture of both distrust, that has grown with previous negative experiences peasants from the area had with the dairy industries that still owe them thousands of euros for milk, and avoiding unnecessary bureaucratic work. Should they agree to supply the slaughterhouse, they would need to provide legal, current and correct documentation of animals, and the payment instalments would need to go through the accounts of registered livestock farms. In other words, they would need to formalize their status through the livestock farm. Not a single livestock breeder I interviewed has planned nor attempted to do this. The livestock balance statistics for the period 2013–15 indicate the trend that livestock is predominantly kept and slaughtered in the household (see Table 4.1). The data show that more than half the total number of slaughtered cattle on average is slaughtered in household settings. By the official interpretation of the data, this number of slaughtered cattle is in an economic sense wasted because it ended up in household consumption instead in the meat processing industry and export. But this is not really the case, as my findings indicate. A significant percentage of this reported number of slaughtered cattle in the households in fact ends up in informal trade.

Direct trade and informal markets: what do they reveal about peasants and the state?

As we see, a great deal of peasants' trading activities in Gaj, Malo Bavnište and Beli Breg, takes place in the so-called informal economy – a world of economic activities outside the organized labour force and markets (Hart 1973). The informal economy and unwritten rules of 'getting things done' exist everywhere, yet there is a tendency to describe some countries as more informal than others, and post-socialist countries are among these. One question that intrigued scholars was what are the institutional factors that trigger informal economy and illicit practices in the first place. Many agree that informal practices emerged as a functional substitute for the over-bureaucratization of the economy, prohibition or shortage of goods and services, which was, for example, typical of the socialist economies (Kornai 1992; see also Cole 1985). The galvanization of the informal economies in many post-socialist countries, however, gradually ceased to be interpreted as a transitional phenomenon (Wallace and Latcheva 2006), but rather as an endemic feature of the capitalist-market economy that was emerging in the region (Morris and Polese 2014). In Chapter 2, I discussed the historical development of the political and economic conditions of the Serbian peasantry in the twentieth and twenty-first centuries, which contextualized their preference for informal practices within a broader set of causes: as a response to their distrust of the state, bureaucratic coercion or shortage, or through their customary disrespect of formal institutions.

Whatever might be its real cause, the everyday reliance on informal ways to 'get things done' – either as a coping strategy, shortcut or a customary norm – reveals the general embeddedness of the informal economy and informality in Serbia, as in other post-socialist countries. It signals that in the lives of ordinary people 'there is no clearly defined gap between formal rules and informal practices' and that 'the boundaries are blurred' (Barsukova and Ledeneva 2018, 487). In case of peasants from Gaj and neighbouring villages the informal trade is understood as an ordinary practice, that carries no legal or moralizing connotations in the local context. The common expression 'everybody does this or that' (something informal) among the local people spreads the internalization of the practices to the extent that they lose sense that it is formally impermissible or at least problematic. Informal trade in the village points to a deeper discrepancy in understanding the same practices between the state and peasants, because peasants see them as unproblematic or, in the worst case, as part of the grey zone, while the state sees it as legally wrong and impermissible. Just remember *veresija*.

A great deal of trading practices in Gaj, Malo Bavanište and Beli Breg are guided by a laissez-faire understanding of commerce, which should be fast and direct with the least possible transaction costs and greatest gain. Likewise, the factor of living on the periphery away from cities enables peasants to organize their lives and trading activities in an autonomous way, often contrary to existing regulations. They have been familiar with and inherently dependent on the market and its impulses for decades. They perceive the right to trade as an integral part of their autonomy and productivist mindset. Denying or curtailing them this right, most peasants understand, is an attempt to jeopardize their existence. But there is something more to it. Direct trade is one of the pillars of peasants' resilience (Diković 2023). During hyperinflation in the 1990s in Serbia, many peasants from Gaj practised direct trade and barter interchangeably. In such a way, they bridged the gap in destabilized exchange which was manifested through food shortages. Peasants were an invaluable factor in the relaxation of market tensions. Their food and product supply reduced the deficit and expanded consumer choice in the market, but also sustained their value in a trade chain. All these facets of direct trade, thus, make it hard for peasants to see anything harmful about it.

State policies, on the other hand, often have a stricter view and understand formal and informal practices as clearly separated and confronting ends. The purpose of the state policies is, thus, to ensure the separation and eradication of informal practices or to convert informal practices into formal flows (see de Soto 2001, Marx 2018). In principle, the Serbian government proclaims to put informality in the countryside 'under control', but this fails in practice. The Farm Accountancy Data Network (FADN), for example, was introduced as a new instrument for evaluating the income of agricultural households and the impacts of CAP. It was an attempt to trace peasants' income given that their trade is mostly unreported without paid VAT on the sold goods. Peasants in Gaj have told me that many people avoid paying VAT in everyday trade but also in the event of bigger purchases/sales. The common way to evade tax is when both parties, seller and buyer, do not report the transaction. In cases of bigger transactions, it is usually someone loyal who nominally sells products for the peasant. The person 'launders' the cash and returns it to the peasant. With FADN, which started as a pilot project in 2013, the aim of the Ministry of Agriculture was to surveil and assess income from the producers and adjust agricultural policies accordingly. For peasants, it would mean trading only in official channels and making neat reports of purchases and their investments. It would also involve paying VAT. On the one hand, the lack of peasants' cooperation hampers full implementation of FADN. Peasants from Gaj do not seem concerned about potential consequences, presumably because they sense that the state authorities are not capable of implementing the policy. The Ministry of Agriculture, on the other hand, lags in enforcing its own rules because it is not politically profitable to ask peasants about their income. Eventually, such an unspoken understanding between the state and peasants creates an atmosphere where informal practices perpetuate in the countryside and become a norm.

Livestock breeding

The numbers of livestock and the export of meat in Serbia are both rapidly decreasing. On an annual basis the export of veal, for instance, is below 2,000 tonnes, while in 1989 it was 100,000 tonnes.[5] Two factors are decisive. First, the livestock sector has been neglected for a long time (Arsić et al. 2012), and many contemporary agricultural policies and investments have attempted to recover the situation and give it new momentum. Second, the traditional, customary ways of livestock breeding that are predominantly practised are slowly vanishing, despite being the most economic and environmentally friendly.

Unsustainable livestock breeding: a problem caused by the state

The growth of livestock farming relies on increased production of milk and meat, which Serbia has not achieved for over a decade. Most of the agricultural experts I interviewed agreed that harmful state policies and poor law enforcement together jeopardized the whole sector. Zaharije Trnavčević summed up the commercial side of the collapse that small- and mid-scale livestock breeders face every day.

> Serbia has the smallest number of cows in its history, and they are not even particularly productive. On an annual basis, they produce on average 3,500 l [of milk] instead of 8,000 l as in Denmark, Switzerland, or Germany. The retail price of milk is level with European prices, and there is no space to increase it anymore. Milk is expensive. If we have expensive milk, how much will milk products cost? (Zaharije Trnavčević, Belgrade, July 4, 2014)

The premiums for milk, on the other hand, have constantly been too low, which does not incentivize livestock breeders to expand production. Moreover, over the past decade half of the total number of cattle was not in the subsidies system, which recognized only purebred calves, while all other high-quality calves remained unregistered and so, in an economic sense, were wasted. This discouraged livestock breeders, and many of them gave up, sold off their cattle and turned to other branches of farming. Zaharije Trnavčević explained how it affected the whole chain of later events. It first affected the production of organic fertilizers, placing Serbia almost in last place in Europe in their production and use. The lack of organic fertilizers causes a problem with yields which, despite good hybrids, are still at the average level.

Average yields in turn affect the constant drop in the numbers of livestock. The longer the cattle stay within the household, the more the supply of food decreases, so peasants are forced to sell the cattle as soon as possible. Urgent selling of cattle holds their low price on the market. In contrast, when yields are above average, this increases the price of cattle because it is fed for longer. The low cattle supply has affected export activities. In Serbia, as Zaharije Trnavčević stated, there exist at most two slaughterhouses that meet all the standards of the European Union for meat export. Others do not. A similar situation exists with pigs and other animals, which increases the need for the import of both animals and meat.

The weak enforcement of the law is an additional institutional reason that draws peasants away from livestock breeding. Milan, veterinarian from Gaj, reckoned that 'livestock breeders were the most cheated of all, mainly by the dairy industry. In the 1990s and the beginning of the 2000s, the industry owed individual peasants thousands of euros and the state did nothing to protect them' (Gaj, July 2017). These were mostly state dairy industries that were declared insolvent and then privatized, while the debts have never been paid.

Those who remained in the business, Milan further elaborated, face paradoxical challenges. They are required to meet the highest sanitary and quality standards even if sometimes they do not have the basic conditions for farming. The dairy industry, for example, does not invest in livestock breeders nor in their training, and lets them cope alone with the requirements. On the other hand, the livestock breeders are left alone when it comes to disposal of animal corpses, which is not managed according to the highest sanitation standards. Unlike in previous decades when it was organized by the municipality branches, today the livestock breeders from the region must individually manage disposal of corpses at illegal animal cemeteries. Such and similar conditions prolong dissatisfaction among livestock breeders and forced many to give up the business.

Not surprisingly, the livestock fund in Gaj and neighbouring villages has shrunk dramatically. Three to four decades ago, Milan recalled, there were 50,000 head of livestock in the territory of the municipality of Kovin, while in Gaj alone there were 2,000–3,000. Today there are only 150 head of livestock in Gaj (Figure 4.4). In the past, peasants could lease pastures that were drained, cleared and fertilized. But today the municipality does not invest in the fertilizing of pastures, so livestock breeders do it at their own expense. Likewise, pastures, where livestock breeders settle their summer ranches do not have even basic utilities. They do not

Figure 4.4 Cows grazing beneath electricity pylons at the summer ranch pastures. Source: Author.

have water, electricity or road infrastructure, meaning the dairy industry cannot buy milk directly from remote and inaccessible ranches. Livestock breeders instead transport the milk to the village to accommodate the request of the dairy industry. Such breeding becomes too costly and time-consuming, keeping only a few enthusiasts in business. In Gaj alone, relatively older people withstand the difficulties of livestock farming, while the young are not interested because it requires full-time dedication, without the possibility of going on holidays or enjoying leisure. In Gaj, only one person has 60 cattle and people consider him to be the biggest livestock breeder. He is over 60 years old, and there is no one below 40 who wants to dedicate themself to livestock.

The state has inaugurated several measures to regenerate livestock breeding. One is to give priority to livestock breeders over other peasants in leasing state land. Each breeder has the right to lease 1 ha of state land per cow from the local municipality under favourable conditions and price. Likewise, the new scheme of livestock subsidies now recognizes a variety of livestock, and includes non-purebred heads as well as purebred animals. Yet, despite the changes, Marta, one of the few remaining livestock breeders, commenting on the overall atmosphere in which livestock breeders have been working, bitterly concluded: 'We are among the last who are still in the business. No one has returned to cows who left it once. No one is crazy anymore' (July 2017, Gaj).

Unsustainable livestock breeding: a problem caused by traditional arrangements

Peasants from Gaj and neighbouring villages practise the traditional, customary way of livestock breeding which is in the local context known as *bačija* or *supon*. This custom dates to the medieval period and the local variations have been known across South-eastern Europe (Pavković 2014). It represents an oral contract agreement between livestock breeder(s) and a shepherd. A shepherd is a hereditary and contractual job, and shepherds usually come from families that have worked with animals and have been familiar with pasture landscapes for generations. Shepherds mostly live in a hut next to the summer ranch where sheep, cattle or other animals are kept during the grazing season from early April until late November.

Livestock breeders from Gaj combine their herds, usually sheep and occasionally pigs, and jointly hire a shepherd who looks after their animals day and night. The shepherd is paid in money and in kind, therewith livestock breeders have an obligation to provide him with meals, cigarettes and beverages. The shepherd also keeps a portion of the milk and wool for himself, with livestock breeders sharing these products in accordance with the number of animals they have. Livestock breeders provide the shepherd with food and other supplies in shifts in the following order. A livestock breeder who collects milk is obliged to prepare and bring meals to the shepherd for two consecutive days. After the second day, he passes a milk churn to a peer who takes care of the shepherd for the next two days until they all rotate. When sheep are not milked, the shepherd gets more food, which should compensate for the lack of milk (see Figure 4.5).

Livestock breeders who have cattle do not combine their herds and make individual agreements with a shepherd, yet their obligations toward the shepherd remain the same as in the case of the combined herds. People from Gaj often complained that it was very hard to find a reliable and responsible shepherd. Those who knew how to look after the cattle were aging, while there were not many younger replacements who were interested in taking over this demanding job. As a rule, most of the shepherds had a problem with alcohol and neglected the animals. Arrangements with shepherds were often very fragile, insecure and sometimes even risky for the physical condition of animals.

Figure 4.5 Milk canister used to collect milk from the shepherd at the summer ranch. Source: Author.

This is why livestock breeders often looked after their own cattle, but during the season it was difficult to combine farming with taking care of animals on remote summer ranches. A few livestock breeders from Gaj emphasized it as an essential problem when they considered abandoning this work.

The pastures around summer ranches are also organized according to traditional arrangements (see Figures 4.6 and 4.7). Livestock breeders do not pay a lease because this land is village property and dwellers from Gaj have the right to use only the area that belongs to the village, where they are allowed to build temporary summer ranches. The number of summer ranches has oscillated between five and six, while in previous decades there were many more. Keeping animals on summer ranches is the cheaper, environmentally friendly and most profitable way, in contrast to when they are kept in the household. When cattle are grazing this is reflected in a better quality of milk and meat, and finally in the higher price of the cattle at market. All the livestock breeders reckoned they made pure profit when they kept herds in summer ranches. When they kept cattle in the household, they had to provide food, hay and straw which was too costly, and these costs were not compensated for by the selling price of the milk or meat.

Figure 4.6 A shepherd tending pigs (shepherds tend not only sheep but also pigs and cattle). Source: Author.

Figure 4.7 An improvised watering place for cattle at the summer ranch pastures. Source: Author.

Even though there are many advantages of pasture-grazing and keeping herds in summer ranches away from the village, fragile relationships between the livestock breeders and the shepherds interrupt successful development of the business. It pressures many of them to give up livestock breeding because they cannot easily find a substitute for the loss of a good shepherd. Unstable traditional arrangements are thus the core problem, which even the most favourable agricultural policies for livestock breeders or increased direct payments cannot repair and motivate breeders to continue with their business.

Agricultural insurance

According to the Serbian Ministry of Agriculture there are currently 450,000 registered households that make a living from farming. Statistics show, however, that 8 per cent of arable land is insured in total, which is only 3 per cent of agricultural households. In countries of the European Union, for example in Denmark, Finland, Austria and Cyprus, the insurance covers from 60 per cent to 85 per cent of total arable land, and 65 per cent to 90 per cent of the total number of cattle.[6] In Serbia, the state subsidizes 40 per cent of the insurance premium, but it has not stimulated peasants to insure their fields. The situation is even worse in livestock breeding, where only a negligible percentage of peasants insures their animals and barns, despite generous state subsidies.[7]

According to Danko, a local insurance agent, in 2013 in Gaj approximately 550 ha was insured in total, which covers less than 10 per cent of all fields of agricultural households in Gaj. In his opinion, even though peasants invest a lot in their production, very few realize the importance of insurance. Only a few insured wheat, because it ripens first, while they rarely insure corn or other crops (Figure 4.8). No one from the village in this period insured animals or barns.

> I don't understand what the problem is. Maybe it's a lack of money, but when you see how much they spend on agriculture, insurance is nothing compared to this. Maybe it is distrust of insurance companies. Maybe they are sceptical whether insurance companies will pay them for any damage. The awareness of the importance of insurance is slowly rising among agricultural producers. Today, the peasants are not illiterate. They know that with good machinery, fertilizers, good selection of seeds and protection they can achieve satisfactory yields. (Danko, July 2013, Gaj)

Figure 4.8 A corn cob ripening on the stalk, one of the crops commonly grown. Source: Author.

When I visited Gaj again in July 2017, I learned from another local insurance agent that the number of peasants who took agricultural insurance had continued to drop. Only 5 per cent of peasants took insurance against major risks such as hail and fire, while there was only one household which insured its purebred cattle, but the remaining animals were left uninsured. Jan, like his colleague, reckoned that the reasons behind this issue rest in cultural factors.

> They [the peasants] don't have a consciousness about this, and they don't have a culture of insuring their fields. All registered agricultural households that cultivate up to 20 ha can be reimbursed for agricultural insurance. Forty per cent is covered by the state, 30 per cent by the local municipality and the remaining 30 per cent peasants pay themselves. Yet, they do not take insurance. In one village close to the Romanian border, the situation is much better. Thirty per cent of them are insured, because they have a different culture. This is partly because they have a good cooperative which conditions them to be insured. This is not the case with Gaj. (Jan, July 2017, Gaj)

Both agents identified important aspects that discouraged peasants from making contracts with insurance companies. Peasants avoid dealing with the state bureaucracy and paperwork because of their distrust and scepticism – formative elements of the laissez-faire mentality, that affect the low level of cooperation with the state and insurance companies.

But apart from distrust and scepticism, the decision not to take insurance is grounded in peasants' own perceptions of risk, self-trusting risk management and years of experience with weather conditions that have rarely failed their assessments. Scattering of land plots, as already explained in Chapter 3 in 'Peasants' distrust of the state', represents one of the most practised and reliable ways of protection against risks. Relatively successful independent management of risks gives them fewer reasons to consider alternatives and risk mitigators. 'My land, my responsibility', an attitude often heard, captures the rationalization of peasants who are not used to sharing the responsibility and risks for their own land, even in cases which can benefit them.

Such attitudes have resulted in the poor market of agricultural insurance, which offers only basic premiums for which even the peasants themselves are not interested in great numbers. Yet in other cases, peasants who work in related occupations cannot insure their products even if they want to, because insurance does not cover risks that are common in their business. This was the case with Zoltan, who together with his Dutch partner invested in horticulture and plantations of peony in 2004. They planted 5 ha of peony using modern technology. They wanted to insure their investment of approximately 600,000 flowers. But the insurance companies could not offer Zoltan an insurance plan because the existing insurance packages were tailored only for farming, which do not match risks related to peony. Insurance companies tried to offer them a package that offered insurance against freezing, but the peony is strong and durable and not easily susceptible to frost. The second solution was a package that insured against damage from hail, but the plant blooms in May which is the month with the least percentage of hail in a year. Zoltan, however, could not insure his fields against aphid and plant lice, which are specific risks related to peony, because the insurance market had not developed programmes for horticultural and other diversified activities in agriculture.

Insurance also does not cover field thefts. Peasants' fields have always been subjected to the 'neighbourhood effect' (McCloskey 1991, 348). Trespassing and thefts that result in the destruction of crops and grass or quarrels between neighbours are persistent issues for peasants in Gaj. Sometimes they are of greater concern than the fluctuation of prices or weather hazards, which statistically occur less frequently in comparison to an immediate threat caused by the neighbours. Thefts and crop destruction, thus, present a significant risk. But agricultural insurance does not provide protection from field thefts and damage that occurs either because of theft or animal intrusion. The risks would be too high, local insurance agents agree, and people would have an incentive to steal or to let their animals intentionally graze the fields. Field protection, therefore, is one of the biggest concerns of peasants, and one that they have autonomously coped with for decades.

Protection against field theft

Until 2016, field thefts represented a serious problem in Gaj. Peasants' losses were measured sometimes in tonnes of corn, dozens of bales of hay, or hundreds of kilograms of cabbage. Peasants tried to draw attention to the problem at the local council and municipality meetings and find solutions for frequent field thefts. The police were not of much help given that they did not want to prosecute locally identified thieves because of their social situation. From 2013 to 2015 the village council hired two seasonal guards who underwent brief training and got the necessary equipment and a motorbike. Despite their busy working hours, they could not protect all fields in the vast village territory, and thefts continued.

Peasants wanted to stop the agony. They self-organized to find the solution. Some peasants surveilled their own fields, and others decided to jointly hire a professional security agency during the two most important months when threshing took place. The guards that were hired by the village council provided additional security. Upon my visit to the village in 2017, I learned that field thefts had almost vanished. The security agency, being better equipped with people and vehicles, was able to patrol through the night and surveil all the fields in the village territory. 'Fear protects the fields, not the guardian' one of the peasants noted with satisfaction, reacting to the change that came after the peasants' self-organization had put an end to the field thefts. But this self-organization was also crucial for restoring the status quo ante when the poor were allowed to glean again, after temporary suspension of the custom because of field thefts. By investing labour in collecting leftovers, gleaning enabled the poor to maintain dignity in the local moral universe and more importantly, escape the symbolic ghettoizing of the poor in the category of thieves.

Agricultural pensions

Peasants in Yugoslavia were only included in the existing compulsory pension insurance scheme quite late on, in the mid-1980s. The then

Yugoslav social politics often failed to attain its set goals and meet the needs of existing insurees due to frequent financial crises (Šućur 2003). The state was, on the one hand, faced with a massive increase in the number of pensioners from the industry sector, which postponed the inclusion of peasants in compulsory pension insurance. Social policy, on the other hand, had to resolve the pressing issue of growing unemployment that was galvanized by increasing rural-to-urban migration (Grandits 2012).

There were several attempts to include peasants in pension insurance schemes before it became compulsory. In the late seventies, pension insurance was voluntary, but peasants were not willing to insure as they relied on their property, kinship and family networks. In 1982 compulsory insurance was introduced only for peasants who were associated with cooperatives or in various arrangements worked with state farms. But these attempts were unsuccessful and did not result in an increased number of insured peasants. As of 1986, agricultural pension insurance was compulsory for all peasants. Since then, all peasants have been obliged since to pay pension contributions like any other insurees. The law anticipates penalties for those who do not comply with this obligation (Mijatović 2010, 13–15). But the overwhelming majority of peasants reject compulsory pensions, despite confronting the law and existing requirements.

The state in various ways tried to force peasants to enter the system of compulsory pension insurance or to pay their debts. One of the latest attempts was a ban on access to subsidies, which pertained to those peasants who did not pay their contributions and had debts to the pensions fund. By equalizing one economic stimulating measure such as subsidies with a constitutional right to having a pension, the state not only demonstrated arbitrariness in interpreting its own laws but also revealed the magnitude of its weakness regarding including peasants in the compulsory pension scheme. In response, many peasants from Gaj simply gave up their subsidies, while others used some of the already-described informal ways (see earlier in this chapter: 'Subsidies and spontaneous social order').

Another measure that the state imposed was pressing the banking sector to deny loans to peasants who had unpaid contributions and debts to the pension fund. Similarly, this did not particularly affect the peasants from my fieldwork, because even before the measure many had avoided dealing with the banks. Safety networks, at least in Gaj and neighbouring villages, appear to be the most important and reliable resource for borrowing and crediting agricultural and private investments, with the lowest overhead costs. The great majority of interviewed peasants agreed that safety networks can stand in for bank crediting in agriculture, being based on trust transfer and maintaining social credentials – both important local values that I discussed in Chapter 3.

Apart from its ineffectiveness, the current compulsory pension scheme is deeply problematic. It creates conflicts in rural areas and accelerates social stratification. For example, a peasant who cultivates 1 ha and another who cultivates over 100 ha pay the same contributions for pension insurance. Likewise, the number of years they have been paying for the pension insurance does not matter either, because they eventually receive an equal pension (c. 90 euros). Pensioners from Gaj commonly emphasize how unfair it is that a person who has been paying his/her pension contributions since 1986 and another who may have been paying contributions only for the last 15 years receive, in the end, the same pension. Such regulation had demotivated many of my informants when it came to changing their minds and contributing to the pension insurance.

The scale of the problem has been highlighted by former minister of agriculture Ivana Dulić-Marković who blames the slow reaction of the Ministry of Agriculture, which had remained silent when compulsory pensions insurance and later penalizations were imposed on peasants. The Ministry of Agriculture is trying to resolve this burning issue, because compulsory pension insurance is not sustainable for peasants. Agricultural pension insurances have dramatically decreased, and their number has shrunk from 222,986, in 2008, to 142,252, in 2022, with a continuing downward trend.[8] Peasants currently are among the biggest debtors to the state, owing approximately two billion euros for unpaid compulsory pension insurance contributions, which is only the numerical scale of the problem. The debts themselves are likely uncollectable, and the Ministry of Agriculture is developing a plan for writing-off interest and for debt rescheduling for peasants.[9]

The crucial reason which makes peasants from Gaj, Malo Bavanište and Beli Breg, such enemies of compulsory pension insurance rests in their well-considered decisions that involve reliance on their available material and social capital (family or kinship). In Gaj, for example, most peasants do not pay contributions to the pension fund, nor do they plan to. It is a common situation that in one household with several agriculturally active members, only one (or none) is regularly paying pension contributions. In some other households, members used to pay pension contributions in the past but not anymore, and lower income was just one among many reasons. Individually, most of the peasants I interviewed owed over a million Serbian dinars to the pension fund. In their calculations of costs and benefits, peasants consider pension contributions to be unnecessary.

Their logic can be generally boiled down as follows. A peasant pensioner who owns for example 5–6 ha of land – and a lot of people own between 5 and 10 ha – can rent out their land for 220 euros on average per 0.5 ha. Depending on the quality of land the price may go up to 250 euros. As I explained earlier in 'Subsidies and spontaneous social order', the landowner will also take subsidies for 5–6 ha which she or he rents out. In addition to subsidies, from the lease of land, a peasant can have at least 180 euros monthly. From the garden, livestock, and other additional resources such as sale of meat or milk products, or *zimnica*, peasants accrue not only additional income but significantly save on their expenditure for food. Overall, relying on their own resources provides them with more financial means than they would be able to get from a state pension (c. 90 euros per month). In the context of their calculation, investing in state pension insurance is seen as a pure loss.

In other households where one or more members are employed in public, state or private sector, they are the official providers of the social, health and pension insurance for other family members (underage children and spouse). From their point of view, paying pension contributions for other family member(s) who are involved in farming is pure loss. That money can be directed instead to buying land or investing in a private insurance plan.

The decision to reject paying pension contributions rests, for some of the interviewed peasants, in the social capital they possess; that is, in safety networks of family and kinship. It is largely expected that children should provide for parents in their old age, or that those who stay in the household should look after their parents, although this convention is now more flexible than in the past. It is still rare in Gaj to encounter family members who live in separate households. The family and kinship networks and their mutual expectations are the most important variable in delivering decisions vis-à-vis externally imposed demands. In contrast, those who cannot rely on such capital, opt for the pension insurance instead.

A local doctor pointed out to me one, pragmatic, reason that persuades peasants that their decision not to contribute to the compulsory pension and social insurance is the right one. According to the Serbian Constitution every citizen in Serbia after the age 62 automatically receives the right to health insurance. Since the age limit for pensions is 62 for women and 65 for men, this means that peasants get the right to free health insurance even without becoming pensioners, which strengthens their opinion that pensions are not necessary to enable their social and health coverage.

Peasants, as we see by now, reject compulsory pension insurance because they have material and social resources to rely on and, thus, autonomy in decision-making. Their attitudes are based on the belief that their own resources will provide them with better financial provisions and security in the long run than would be the case with a state pension. Apart from these essential reasons, institutional factors such as the unfair pension scheme, or bans on subsidies or bank investment loans only prolong the separation between peasants and the state in the long run. The outcome is that the state did not achieve inclusion of peasants in the compulsory pension insurance scheme, which had been promoted as one of the major conditions in enabling rural development after 2000.

Village associations

The local municipality's support of the village associations represents domestic implementation of CAP's policy that, apart from agricultural activities, finances initiatives that aim to enrich rural development and the local environment (Swain 2016). The village associations are perceived as means to mobilize the rural population and make them more engaged in local affairs. In South-eastern Europe the lack of social participation is generally interpreted as a socialist legacy where, because of the paternalistic role of the state, people became less motivated to involve themselves in common issues and civil initiatives (Swain 2016; Vuković 2013; Dargan and Shucksmith 2008). The CAP's policy, therefore, anticipates changing this and motivating people (particularly from post-socialist rural areas) to engage with and contribute to their social and economic wellbeing.

In Gaj, there are some 12 registered associations and sports clubs that Kovin municipality financially supports. Some of these associations and sports clubs were founded before 2000, such as the associations of pensioners, hunters, fishermen, firefighters, chess-players and the Češka beseda (Czech association). The association of firefighters is the oldest in the village, founded in 1920, and it has operated continuously since. As with associations that were founded before 2000, it did not have regular financing. Associations faced serious financial problems, lacked elementary means such as space and equipment or were dependent on the goodwill of local elites to support their functioning. Since 2000, all registered village associations have had regular, though modest, funds and enjoy – at least nominally – more support from the local municipality. Depending on the budget, the municipality usually distributes an equal amount to all registered associations.

Associations established after 2000 in Gaj were grouped around the same goals: to promote women and civic cooperation and activities. Upon my arrival in the village in 2013, I became acquainted with several associations that had similar names. Sometimes it was hard to distinguish between them and their goals because they all organized the same events, such as March 8, humanitarian action 'A cake for a patient', a sourdough-making competition or Christmas cake. Later I learned that the presidents of these similar associations were once in a single organization which then split. Some of these associations are run by one or two persons at most with only nominal members, while others resemble real associations with a president, secretary and regular members.

Leaders of these competing associations gossiped about each other on various occasions and accused the other side of abusing municipality funds, or of making profits through the associations or for keeping money from humanitarian events for themselves. Despite mutual accusations, the associations basically organize events for the same reasons. They collect money through charging for the events' dinners and tickets, organizing a tombola or occasional village parties. Some of these associations invest the collected money into future events or devote some part to humanitarian purposes. In one case, the association invested money in cutlery and dishes that they rent out to others who organize birthday parties, weddings and other big celebrations. The predominantly entrepreneurial character of these civil associations led many villagers to think that the core of their conflicts rests in the struggle for personal profits, rather than in differences in value orientations and agendas of the associations.

One of the leaders of the associations confirmed to me that it was an open secret that everyone who runs an association does it for personal benefit, which was the case for her, too. She said to me once: 'I put association's money in my pocket.' Because of such an attitude some villagers presumably do not have an exclusively positive opinion of the associations. In their view, some of the associations are meaningless because they do not fulfil the goals they are organized for and are mostly based on celebrations, music, drinking and eating. The president of the local council shared such an opinion and explained the situation with associations in the following way:

> Many associations do not organize events the municipality gives them money for. They spend the money, and later they justify it somehow, but almost no one has fulfilled the association's goals. Even if they have noble ideas, they quickly dissipate upon receiving the money. Some of them have never seen 400 or 800 euros in cash. That's why these associations are rapidly shutting down, and the new ones replace them. (Edvard, July 2017, Gaj)

It would be, however, mistaken to say that all associations in the village are motivated by financial gain. Some associations, for example, spend the funds they get from the municipality on the celebration of the association's *slava* (orthodox saint protector of the association), after which there remain few funds for conducting regular activities. They gather only once in a year to celebrate *slava*, and on that occasion they organize free dinners for their members and guests and take care of music and creating a good atmosphere. *Slava* or association's dinners are the most successful way of bonding their members, but after that event little enthusiasm and will is left to work jointly on any further association goals.

A deeper look at the phenomenon of civic associations in the village reveals a more interesting picture. Through the associations, the members meet different personal, entrepreneurial, or social needs, and the municipality, through securing funding, unknowingly supports their goals. In the case of 'entrepreneurial' associations, their members get the opportunity to earn money quickly and informally mimic private business. But the difference matters here. Through the associations they are shielded away from the negative aspects that private business brings, such as navigating through regulations and bureaucracy, high risks, uncertain revenues or rising costs and persisting despite failure. They get a better deal with associations and do not report their revenues to anyone. In other words, they earn money without taking risks as long as the association exists. In the case of associations that meet only for *slava*, their members see in associations' funds a resource through which they realize the need for social sharing, which the local culture of *slava* embodies. The funds are thus, an investment in hospitality and maintaining social networks of friendships and kinship by providing free dinners, setting up a pleasant and relaxed atmosphere filled with music, singing and dancing – which they otherwise would not be able to afford on their own. These examples of associations significantly depart from ideals captured in CAP. Yet, they reveal what the local population prioritizes, and what the translation of state rural development ideas looks like when applied in context.

Free riding

People from Gaj and neighbouring villages who are not involved in farming but in other occupations are critical of peasants' behaviour, especially of their informal ways of 'getting things done'. They perceive peasants, their co-villagers, as free riders. Their resentment toward peasants is mainly anchored in disproportionate contributions to the common good which others maintain through various taxes, and peasants don't. One of the common opinions is that peasants do not pay VAT and local taxes, compulsory pension and social contributions, nor land taxes; they do not report income; and they do not employ anyone, yet the state keeps subsidizing them and, unlike for others, treats them in a special, benevolent way. As an illustration, peasants in the municipality of Jagodina were exempted from paying land taxes for several consecutive years. The municipality justified such a measure as a support for rural and agricultural development.[10]

In Gaj, one case emblematically captured the tension between the villagers and peasants. It concerned the cancellation of the local taxes called *samodoprinosi*. In 1946, *samodoprinosi* were inaugurated and levied in all villages in Yugoslavia (Novaković and Radojević 2014). As of then, the municipality of Kovin collected the tax through automatically deducting 3 per cent from the salaries of all employed people. After 2000, all villages had the right to vote on local elections and decide whether they would like to continue with the socialist legacy of *samodoprinosi*. Gaj was the last village to keep *samodoprinosi*, until 2012, a fact of which local people were proud. People still refer to *samodoprinosi* in a very positive and nostalgic way. During that time, the infrastructure of the village, particularly agricultural roads, was well maintained: parks, sports areas, and children's playgrounds were in better condition, every street had its own lighting and sidewalks and the village was cleaner and greener. Some cultural associations from the village such as the Česká beseda (Czech association) were financed from the tax. But the tax was not voted for in 2012, and resentment was the main reason why villagers rejected it. A few villagers with whom I discussed these election results, explained to me that peasants, who use and depend on village infrastructure more than anyone else, should have contributed the same as other employees. But this was not the case. Villagers saw in such an attitude a paradigmatic peasant behaviour – a propensity to free ride collective benefits which others pay and maintain. Before 2012, people's salaries from Gaj were taxed, while the Kovin Municipality was supposed to tax peasants based on the land they cultivated. Miloš, a self-employed carpenter from Gaj, explained how *samodoprinosi* remained the exclusive burden of employed people.

> Because of political games by the state, and lazy administrative updates in the municipality of Kovin, peasants have not been taxed for many years and the municipality easily gave up collecting their taxes, while the burden remained on employees in other sectors. People had enough, and didn't want to contribute anymore. (February 2013, Gaj)

Peasants' free-riding makes villagers also critical of agricultural subsidies they receive, because they think peasants give much less in return and pay back almost nothing to the state. Perhaps this may be one of the reasons why some villagers are not sympathetic when peasants suffer losses or when they are cheated, as in the case of local cooperative I discussed in Chapter 3 'The collapse of a local private cooperative'. These factors add to the complex social relations and divisions in the village by aligning with the side of the local businessman, who, in their view creates jobs in the local setting, and 'thanks to whom', villagers often stress, 'dozens of families have a regular income'. Villagers cannot comprehend state benevolence toward peasants who owe billions of euros for compulsory pension contributions which will be, as it seems, written off by the state. If the situation had been reversed, villagers argue, they would have ended up in jail.

The resentments and existing tensions between villagers and peasants in Gaj, emerge because of the perception of unequal participation for the common good among them and the special treatment of the peasants by the state. The perceived special status of the peasants certainly does not stem from their weakness, as was often claimed in the scholarship that I critically engage with in Chapter 2. Peasants in Serbia have been strongly embedded both in national history and politics, through symbols and political campaigns, throughout the twentieth century (see Naumović 1995, 2009). Remaining in power depends a great deal on regions with rural populations. After all, in Serbia it has been always the case. Politicians, thus, must be careful in approaching voters and advocating politics that will be broad enough to catch-all, and at the same time narrow enough for peasants to be able to recognize their unspoken understanding with the state, as discussed earlier in 'Subsidies are flawed but they continue. Why?' and 'Direct trade and informal markets: what do they reveal about peasants and the state?'

Taking a different approach would mean losing the peasants' support and, ultimately, losing the election. But such political calculations are usually a double-edged sword. When the enforcement of state laws and regulations becomes dependent on the political estimation, free riding of peasants and strengthening of their autonomy comes as a natural consequence, but it returns later as a boomerang when the adoption of agricultural and rural policies gets hard or unenforceable. In the remainder of the book, we will discover whether free riding is an entirely negative feature of peasants' behaviour, or if it may also create positive externalities for the local community that official estimations of development cannot detect.

'Local as resource' in grasping what might go wrong with state policies

One of the aims of this book has been to discover in what manner state plans for rural development get adopted in the countryside, and how peasants relate to the existing state ideas of rural development. Subsidies, trading of products, livestock breeding, agricultural insurance, agricultural pensions and village associations have served as a terrain where I tried to find answers to my research questions. You may wonder why I focus only on these aspects and not on some other state programmes. Farming, trade, livestock breeding, risk mitigation, provisions for elderly and social activities represent the core of the village life, where the state plans tried to intervene and which the state tried to regulate through subsidies, trade chains and rules, agricultural insurance, agricultural pensions and village associations.

In the example of Gaj and neighbouring villages, I show why these policies are doomed to fail. The subsidies turned into ineffective agricultural policy. The local arrangements changed the flow of the subsidies and made the agriculturally inactive population its main beneficiaries. Likewise, the trading activities, despite state regulations and support for strengthening new trade chains and rules, did not change much from previous times and continue to be mostly or entirely informal. The state focuses attention and generous support on improving the devastated condition of the livestock sector, yet the rapid decrease in livestock households is currently more conditioned by fragile traditional livestock breeding arrangements in the village. The state is persistent in devoting generous support for agricultural insurance, yet the peasants are more confident in their own risk-managing strategies and thus reject insurance in great numbers. A similar situation exists with agricultural pensions that, although being compulsory, peasants reject in great numbers because their material (land and assets) and social (family and kinship networks) capital provide them with better and more comprehensive care. Through local municipalities, the state attempts to involve the local population in working together for the common good through village associations. Yet, in practice, these associations attain entrepreneurial and entertainment functions which radically depart from their projected goals.

These examples indicate, as the argument of the book goes, that individual and local values such as a sense of autonomy, land ownership, village ethics and the individualism – which shape various social and economic relations in the village – form the laissez-faire mentality and maintain peasants' resilience without, or in spite of, state policies for rural development. By now we can see that in encounters with the state policies, peasants' practices modified policies to the extent that they serve as means to attain individual and local ends, in which case agricultural and rural development policies became skewed, as happened with subsidies and village associations. Or, peasants' practices circumvent state policies, because they do not match individual or local visions of life, work and trade, as happened with agricultural insurance, agricultural pensions, livestock farming and trade regulations.

Any state rural policy that aims to succeed needs to understand first the local context in which the policy is planned to be implemented. Some inquiring wouldn't be a bad idea. But state policymakers rarely or never do that. Instead, they continue to impose rural development plans from the top. And if they fail, as is often the case, they invest additional effort in making new plans, increasing regulations and adding new bureaucrats, who are supposed to make things work. Endless expansion of state institutions on the local level is supposed to ensure the implementation of the policies. Instead of rural development, such state expansion generates the chronic problem of local clientelism, cronyism, corruption and rent-seeking, as the next chapter will reveal.

Notes

1 Development has been a highly charged concept for a long time. Scholarly criticism of development generally follows two themes: deconstruction of the concept as a post-war instrument of the West to continue its influence on the global politics and economy; inadequacies of the concept in the applied contexts when the development projects lead to failure and brings new or prolongs the existing inequalities (Rangan 2000, 136–53).

2 See https://n1info.rs/biznis/a131806-subvencije-poljoprivredi-smanjene-zbog-zloupotreba/.
3 See https://www.rts.rs/lat/vesti/Ekonomija/1493438/Manje+subvencije+za+ratare,+ko+pla%C4%87a+ceh.html.
4 There were several massive protests of peasants that were organized as electoral pressure before the parliamentary election in December 2023. One of several peasants' demands was higher subsidies. The other was liberalization of the export of agricultural goods which had been prevented since the outbreak of the Russian-Ukrainian war in 2022, when the government imposed a ban on exporting grains as a measure for protecting Serbian grain reserves. The government responded by accepting a delegation of agricultural producers and agreed with their demand for higher subsidies among others. It remains to be seen in the coming years whether the promised increase will contribute to the betterment of production, or it will just perpetuate the circle of existing practices.
5 Interview with Zaharije Trnavčević, Belgrade, 4 July 2014.
6 See https://www.ecinst.org.rs/sites/default/files/prezentacije/poljoprivredni/Drugi-poljoprivredni-forum-Prezentacija-govornika-Vladan-Manic.pdf, accessed 13 October 2017.
7 See https://blog.deltaagrar.rs/2014/osiguranje-u-poljoprivredi/, accessed 13 October 2017.
8 See the article 'Prepolovljen broj poljoprivrednih penzionera' [The number of agricultural pensioners has been halved] by Jasna Petrović-Stojanović, 21 March 2023, *Politika*, https://www.politika.rs/sr/clanak/543841/Prepolovljen-broj-poljoprivrednih-penzionera.
9 See https://novaekonomija.rs/vesti-iz-zemlje/resenje-za-poljoprivredne-penzije-do-kraja-godine.
10 See https://www.b92.net/biz/vesti/srbija/jagodina-paori-oslobodeni-poreza-781460, accessed 13 October 2014.

5
Local politics and rural development

One of the most salient characteristics of post-socialist transformations in Serbia has been an unprecedented expansion of political elites both on a national and local level. Such a trend initiated a rise of a new political culture that determined the mainstream understanding of politics, the role of elites and other political subjects after 2000. It has been translated into every field including rural development. Local political elites started to play an important role as intermediaries in state-sponsored development of infrastructure, agriculture, welfare or public provisions. They became enablers of the development rhetoric that is often fairly divorced from practically achievable goals, but it is strongly tied to political clientelism and rent-seeking (cf. Rangan 2000, 141–4).

The expansion of elites became part of the larger phenomenon in Eastern Europe after the fall of the Berlin Wall. The changes that affected the political systems of many Eastern European countries emerged during the democratization process that was supposed to result in the separation of the party and the state. But contrary to the expectations, the process of separation has scarcely been linear, stable or unchallenged on the path toward democratization, demonstrating the dual nature of the separation (Ganev 2001, 2007). In most Eastern European countries, 'the process of separation was marked by a struggle for control over resources, and the persistent efforts of incumbents to carve out domains of private power directly undermined the organizational integrity of public agencies' (Ganev 2007, 49; see Grzymala-Busse and Luong 2002, 537). Building new institutions dwelled on the existing structures, and on both formal and informal practices inherited from communist times 'because they have constituted the primary resources available to elites competing for authority' (Grzymala-Busse and Luong 2002, 535).

The proliferation of elites and their clientelist networks all the way down to the smallest local-level functionaries, thus, has subordinated institution building to chronic nepotism (Solnick 1998, Ganev 2013).

The emerging democratic voting system and state financing of political parties generated a new electoral market both on the national and the local level (Elster et al. 1998, Verdery 2002). Such developments created unruly coalitions and 'loose clusterings of elites […] who cooperate to pursue or control wealth and other resources' (Verdery 1996, 193). By broadening the state networks and involving local actors in official affairs the post-socialist states enabled enduring political systems in which local elites play a significant role (cf. Ferguson and Gupta 2002; Ganev 2013).

Since 2000, the ruling parties in Serbia have focused on enabling the local elites to secure the party votes and support on the local level, instead of encouraging them to work on institutional consolidation. The allotted responsibilities additionally empowered local elites in managing the lives of ordinary people (Verdery 2002). Through local elites in Gaj and the neighbouring villages we may understand better the character and values that determine the political system, both on national and local levels. In this chapter, I aim to enlighten their contribution to the state of politics after 2000, particularly in relation to rural development, elections and political participation. Local political arrangements are, however, not complete without peasants' understanding of politics and political participation, which is why peasants are apart from the elites crucial for their perpetuation.

Local elites

Swain sees rural transition, development and prosperity in post-socialist rural Central Europe and the Balkans as dependent mostly on 'the chance factor of the character and personality of the mayor, or other key individuals, rather than institutional support' (Swain 2000, 21). Two decades later, this still holds true, and is an important facet of rural development. Swain stresses also that national parties play an insignificant role at the local level. My evidence counters it and reveals that the ruling party(s) that shape national politics represent an important factor in local life. It can be seen through the professionalization of elites at the local level, who develop political careers and live exclusively from politics. Whether they take sides with the dominant, ruling party or act as an opposition, there is a strong belief that being close to politics, nurturing political connections and having skills in navigating different political demands is the only way to secure the personal gain but also the success and prosperity of the village.

In Gaj there are approximately 20–30 people who live exclusively from politics and rotate through various elected positions on the village and municipality councils. As a rule, they are also members of different committees at the municipality and village levels. Since 2000, bureaucratic expansion has slowly secured its path, resulting in the creation of various commissions, agencies and centres that are financed by the state, thanks to which local career politicians can make a living and become involved in different political activities. Kovin municipality, for example, has 36,800 inhabitants and 42 diverse commissions that during their mandate may engage 240–50 honorary members. The 'Council for interethnic relations', 'Council for youth', 'Commission for distribution of funds to associations', 'Commission for distribution of funds to churches and religious communities', 'Council for the employment', 'Commission for the regulations' and 'Commission for plans', to name a few, each meet a couple of times per year; their mandate is tied up with the mandate of the party and coalitions that govern the municipality, which are generally in force for between one and a half to two years.

For career politicians from Gaj, these municipality commissions and village councils represent a financial and political resource: financial, in the sense that individuals are paid for being members of these bodies; political, in the sense that incumbents maintain close connections to the centre of political power and information, which they can use for creating new career opportunities in politics, public services or alliances. Local political elites almost always align with the side of those who hold the power, either by membership in the party that runs the municipality (and the state) or with its coalition partners. Since the party that governs the municipality and their coalition partners nominates future members of the municipality's 42 commissions that, later, need to be approved by the municipality council, it rarely happens that someone who is in opposition gets nominated, let alone selected. The ruling party in such a way secures that the commissions deliberate decisions in its favour. Local politicians confirmed this practice, reckoning that the purpose of these commissions is impaired given that they exist only nominally to fulfil the requested form of democratic pluralism of the local government. Voting on certain issues is carried out according to a party directive. In practice, this means that the party nominates certain solutions, projects, plans and persons who should take over important public positions, while the people who sit in various commissions and councils are required only to approve what the party has nominated.

Svetlana's experience captures how strongly the logic behind the management of the village council and municipality commissions influences village life. Svetlana was a councillor in Gaj for a short period. She often had to vote and decide on things against her principles, because her colleagues asked her to vote in a way the ruling party requested for the local level. Hampering the work of opposition representatives is one of such requirements. On one occasion, the village councillors were deliberating whether they should allow the use of the public centre for culture for an event that was being planned by a political opponent from the village. They were instructed to vote against it, and they decided not to allow the use of the venue to this person. Even though Svetlana was privately against it, she did not have a choice, and so added her voice to the foregone decision. She told me, 'I made a decision against my principles and could not sleep for three days because of this. I couldn't wait for my mandate to end. After this experience, I have never run for councillor again' (Svetlana, April 2013, Gaj).

Svetlana's example in fact unmasks the institutional division of power on the local level. On the surface, the municipality seems like a democratized institution that shares power and authority with the associated commissions and village councils that manage life together at the local level. Yet in reality this is obviously not the case, since the ruling party influences decisions through its channels of loyal people, councils, commissions and boards, and in such a way decreases any opportunity to itself be controlled or hampered. The local politics reflect tendencies at the state level toward more centralization of power and decision-making that have started to develop over the past decade. When I started my fieldwork in early 2013 this trend was already somewhat apparent, but over time it has taken a more explicit form. In 2017, for example, of the village council's nine members, only one was not a member of the ruling party – but was a member of its coalition partner. Over the years, in Gaj it has become harder to run a campaign independently or as an opposition party member against the ruling machinery which controls everything from elections and employment, to membership in village and municipal councils and commissions. Nada, at the time the only village councillor who was not a member of the ruling party, summarized prevailing local predicaments in the following way.

> In Serbia and Kovin municipality respectively, we have currently almost a one-party system, and there is no employment bureau anymore, but only the Serbian Progressive Party (SPP).[1] They grew

into a machine which entices people whom they manipulate. (Nađa, July 2017, Gaj)

Even though it would be mistaken to say that all political elites from Gaj support the SPP, it can still be argued that there is a propensity to side with the party or leaders who are in power. Serbian politician Vuk Drašković precisely explained the phenomenon with an anecdote that captures well the logic of political reasoning, both on a local and national level. At one of the first mass meetings against president Slobodan Milošević's regime during the 1990s, Drašković, at the time one of the biggest enemies of the regime, approached a man who was very vocal in speaking out against Slobodan Milošević and the political situation in general. Drašković asked him: 'For whom are you going to vote in the next elections?', expecting that the man would say for him and his opposition partners, but the man answered, 'For Milošević, of course'.

In the perception of people and elites, the political mainstream embodied in the ruling party is a familiar option even if it may not be satisfactory. When people are about to experience a change, even if it is a change for the better, they might often be reluctant and unready, and feel the fear of change at the same time. On the other hand, life in a status quo that lasts for a long time is at least constant, whether under either bad or good conditions, and people become attached to and dependent on predictability. In the first case, the predictability is embodied in low expectations that something will change in a positive way, while in the latter, in low expectations that something will go wrong. The same perception also applies to regional and local political elites who maintain the existing political system. They hold onto those they know the best, and from whom they know what they can expect. Local elites know their place in the existing political hierarchy and, more importantly, what they can expect in return.

Who is the local elite?

Political elites in Gaj are of different social and educational backgrounds. Some have regular or semi-regular jobs, are unemployed or are on disability benefits; some hold public positions, or run private businesses or are workers with or without a high school diploma. Politics involves both women and men, although more men participate in daily politics and elections. Most of the elite do not work in agriculture and, presumably, have little land.

Locals regard politics as reserved for people with fewer obligations and set working hours that give them time to dedicate themselves to other activities and politics. Peasants by rule do not belong to the local elite, even though they are friends with some of the main political figures in the village. One of the former members in the council of the Orthodox church explained to me that the church council is composed of *paori* [peasants], ensuring that 'there is no politics in church'. He certainly did not mean that peasants are apolitical, but rather that they stay out of politics. Unlike peasants, the priest himself takes on both spiritual and political roles in the village; although he does not participate in the elections, he influences political events in the village in other subtle ways.

Through the organization of the church and church council the priest pays attention to maintaining a local political balance. The council consists of 12 members, who should be honourable and religious people. Each member of the council has a mandate of six years. The rule of the church orders that the council always has six new and six old, previously selected, members. When the priest came to the village in 2012 some of the old members of the council did not have a good relationship with the people who back then governed the village and were their public opponents. Soon after his arrival, the priest grasped the local relationships and wanted to impose himself as a loyal partner of the local leaders. The priest wished to 'neutralize the influence of a few problematic members of the church council, because they directly attacked the village council, and the church financially depends on it' (Priest, February 2013, Gaj). In an earlier interview with the president of the village council I learned that the church has its own resources and does not depend on the council. The priest, nevertheless, by influencing church members wanted to ensure the firm alliance between the church and the village leadership. When the selection of the president of the church council approached, the priest lobbied among other church members not to vote for 'problematic men and to choose a neutral president who will not provoke the village council' (Priest, February 2013, Gaj). The priest likewise used his authority and offered honourable seats to the president of the village and his close colleagues from the council. In return, the priest became a member of the board of the village football club that is financed through the village council. The pragmatic priest, upon his arrival to the village 'attempted to evict politics from the church council' (Priest, February 2013, Gaj) but, in effect, he was doing the opposite.

The example of the priest is symptomatic of the situation in the village because it depicts the dominant rationale of why people become involved in politics. A common expression 'Lakše vučem za selo' (getting things easier for the village) – which can be seen as a vernacular idiom of rural development – points to the shared understanding according to which people who have some political authority or function are closer to information and local decision-makers, and can persuade them to finance or do necessary things for the village. It emphasizes the importance of networks which reveal the ambivalent nature of relationships that at same time can be used in social and instrumental ways, particularly in informal exchanges, differently known as 'economies of favours' (Ledeneva 1998). They ensure among others vertical (patronage, protection, favouritism) and horizontal (reciprocity, mutual understanding, exchange of information) patterns of exchange which, when necessary, can swiftly be instrumentalized for various transactions, both material and in kind (Ledeneva 1998).

In Gaj, it is broadly accepted that those who run village associations should be involved in politics because in such a way they may get better connections that will enable benefits or better financing that otherwise they would not be able to access. For example, the president of the association of firefighters justified his decision to be politically active in one of the commissions on behalf of SPP in the following way: 'I accepted the role partly because of the citizens, but mainly to get things easier for the association. There appeared certain problems. The association's office is in a building that is under the restitution process, and we will be very likely evicted from there' (Kađa, July 2013, Gaj). Kađa believed that through his political engagement and connections he may influence a slowing down of the process of eviction, or even its prevention.

The connection between politics and the various associations is one of the most discussed issues in the village. It often happens that members of the same family are strategically located in local political structures, so that they can use wisely all available resources. It was not surprising when, for example, a son who used to be a president of the 'Commission for distribution of funds to associations' approved a three times bigger budget for the association which his mother ran, while other associations received significantly less money. Because of this and many similar examples, people rightly believe that budget allocation for associations depends mostly on political belonging, clientelism and connections.

Another important aspect of the motto 'to get things easier for the village' rests in the public perception of rights. Todor was employed in the municipality of Kovin and decided to participate in one of the elections for the village council because he thought he was able to strategically use both resources. As an employee of the municipality, he was in possession of knowledge and information, and knew bureaucratic procedures, while as a village councillor he was able to propose solutions and projects that had a high likelihood of being accepted by the municipality. He said, 'I always take care that people get what they can within the boundaries of the law' (Todor, August 2017, Gaj). Todor's explanation suggests two things. First, people are not always aware of their rights because there is a lack of transparency. Second, the lack of transparency enables resources which are nominally public to be used in practice only by those who are privileged either by their political belonging or by their strategic knowledge and ability. Therefore, people like Todor, who are closer to the resources and concealed knowledge, may act as brokers of information, bridging the communication gap, which may simultaneously serve both personal and community needs, or entrepreneurial, representative or some other ends (see Jancsics 2018).

The motto 'to get things easier for the village' often appears to be an empty ideal of the local elite since, even when they sit in municipality or village councils or on municipality commissions, they are rarely in the position to make substantial changes in the village. Their roles are mainly constrained by managing daily infrastructure and communal tasks of repairing public surfaces and buildings, cleaning the parks and playgrounds. One reason for this is that the local municipality budget is relatively low, and another is that incoming investments are mainly diverted to reviving the urban centre rather than to the villages. A careful analysis of the number of meetings of municipality commissions clearly shows that the commissions for local economics, employment, urban planning, municipality budgets, health issues, and the funding of associations and churches have been the most active, while commissions for rural development and ecology have been the least active in the past.

The local elite have also contributed to the motto 'getting things easier for the village' becoming meaningless. Local elite are professionalized in using the rhetoric of development without clear ideas and means for the practical implementation of their goals. In interviews with two former presidents of the village council in the period from 2013 to 2017, I asked both to answer the same questions: why did they run for the presidency?; how they are going to improve the situation in the village?; and how they see the village at the end of their mandate? They answered the first question routinely as if they were in the middle of the election campaign, stressing that they wanted to help the village to prosper, as energetic individuals dedicated to bringing change. The answers related to the second question became loose and unconvincing; further probing revealed that they did not know how to access national or EU funds for rural development, and were unskilled and uninformed. When it came to the third question, they both honestly answered that they did not go far in their thinking about the future vision of Gaj. The longstanding issues of inexistent village canalization and a chapel, and informal landfill that needs to be removed from the village outskirts, for example, regularly serve as electoral promises that have helped many previous village presidents to win elections. But the enthusiasm for resolving these issues wanes as soon as the presidents realize that they do not know how to approach a solution, either bureaucratically or financially.

There is, nevertheless, an institutional explanation as to why the two presidents, and very likely those to come, do not have means to change much in the village nor to foster investments. The power of village presidents is symbolic, given that the authority of the village council has been significantly limited since 2013. The Law on Local Community abolished the authorities of *mesna zajednica* (local council) and transferred property and authorities that once belonged to the local (village) council to the municipality. The president of the village explained what their authority looks like in practice after the implementation of the new law.

> We literally cannot repair the streetlights in the village without asking the municipality. Everything has become so bureaucratized and slow. Everything has been reduced to writing letters and making requests to the municipality and waiting for their reply. And we depend on some bureaucrat who may agree or disagree with our requests. (President, village of Gaj, July 2017)

Yet, despite the lack of authority, candidates continue to run for the presidency of the village council. Becoming a village councillor, along with the growing influence of the SPP, proved to be a strategically important step in career development within the party hierarchy and division of functions. The village council became an important playground for electoral training and increasing awareness of the party presence in the village. Candidates who best perform the allocated tasks get later promoted to a better position within the municipality and the regional party board.

Although the SPP has accelerated the development of the political culture and local elite in Gaj, it is, however not its creator. The introduction of a multiparty system in the 1990s has created an influential figure in the village, someone who is seen as the most successful leader in the local recent past and whom the current elite consider to be their political father.

The political father

The patron, the political father in the case of our village, is incorporated in a broader set of relationships that form patron-client blocks that should ensure their solid operations, and preferably long-lasting mutually beneficial transactions (Lemarchand and Legg 1972).[2] The function of the political father may be that of a provider, protector or enabler, yet one of the most salient functions is political. The political father, his fathers and those to come, all reveal how patronage coalitions have permeated the political systems in the past and present, to the extent that their roles are often indistinguishable from those of political parties. In Serbia, but also in much of Eastern Europe and the Mediterranean, patronage coalitions may or may not be formalized through official political membership to enable them to conduct what is one of their main roles: taking on control of an entire block of votes and tendering the electoral potential in the village and the municipality at their disposal (Giordano 2012, 22).

The father in our village was close friends with directors of state companies in Kovin municipality who were also members of Slobodan Milošević's Socialist Party of Serbia and MPs in the parliament of the republic in the 1990s. The father became one of the most influential people in the municipality thanks to having a directorial position in one of the few remaining successful companies. His political rise started in 2000, and he has been continuously in power ever since, either as mayor of the municipality, president of the village council or a councillor in the municipality, remaining as director of the company the whole time. He maintains power through various coalitions, because of which he has changed between more than four political parties, including the last transition to SPP. The father was also the president of the village football club, and an honourable member of several organizations in the village and in the city of Kovin. Local rumours speculate that his influence spreads to almost all public institutions in Kovin and neighbouring villages.

He has accumulated power, wealth and influence, but is still politically active. It intrigues many why he continues to engage in local politics to such a degree, given that after the elections in 2013 he was only a village councillor. Different voices speculate that he is addicted to power. Some think that he cannot withdraw from politics as he may end up in prison for various alleged malfeasances. Whatever the reason, still the father 'is alpha and omega in the village, in the football club, he is asked about everything, he is in all structures' (Branko, August 2013, Gaj).

Recent studies in anthropology have dealt with powerful individuals in rural areas who have risen after the collapse of socialism and built their influence and networks partly by relying on the former structures and acquaintances, and partly on new clients (Giordano 2010, Verdery 2002). In establishing their networks, they follow the model of the behaviour of socialist bureaucrats who created their power base 'by accumulating clients and dependents and by cultivating far-flung networks through reciprocity' (Verdery 2002, 18). Careful maintaining of networks is of vital importance both for powerful individuals on one side and for the prosperity of the members of their networks on the other. The clients may help their powerful friends or patrons to be re-elected and to keep their control over resources and infrastructure and, in return, may hope for employment, personal gain or to climb up the political and social ladder. The network of the political father functions in the same way; his followers and supporters create a relatively closed system where only those within it may get employed in the existing (poor) job market and attain some of the available political roles. As in every network, those who are distant from the network's core face a decreasing level of intimacy with it, and vice versa (Giordano 2010, 19; Granovetter 1973; 2005; Burt 1992). The proper functioning of the network, thus, demands permanent activities around the core, like proving loyalty and friendship, doing various things for the core such as making services and favours and finally, availability and readiness to support the network, even in a situation where it is not possible to get what is expected right away, or when it is against one's personal principles. By rule, those who drop out from the inner circles are the first to turn their back and work against the father and the core.

I often heard during my fieldwork that the father did many positive things for the village and villagers, particularly when he was mayor of Kovin municipality. He enabled the building of a gas line in the village, road infrastructure was improved significantly, the village got a new football ground and kindergarten, the elementary school was renovated, as was the centre for culture and the church got a new roof. Others praised his charitable character. He paid the rent for the premises of the association of pensioners when they faced financial difficulties, sponsored graduate students from the village, donated money for humanitarian aid and supported families with a sick child – and there were many more examples of his generosity. Despite what people may think personally about the father, almost all emphasized to me that he was working committedly in the service of the village, which is why he enjoys great local devotion. Another reason why people respect the father is that he employed people from Gaj in the company where he works as a director, proving in this way his loyalty to the village. It is particularly interesting that almost all football players from the village club are employed in the company, or in the mine near Gaj. According to football players I talked to, it was compensation (or the players' condition) since players do not get paid by the club. Other people whom he employed are not necessarily his relatives, but may be friends, neighbours, or political allies.

People in Gaj regard the father as an employment bureau, to whom they come directly to ask for work. When he did not have a job to give, the father would offer what he had at his disposal at that time, until some job appeared: small political functions such as positions in the municipality commissions, or in one case safeguarding of electoral boxes for the presidential election in 2017. In return, the expanded network of his employees, political comrades and their families, as rumours spread, served as his electoral core, supporting him to remain in power in the village and at municipality level. One informant admitted that 'when he [the father] employed me in the mine where I still work, in return I became a member of his party. I was hanging posters for some time in the village, and had to spread propaganda' (Edvin, July 2013, Gaj). Some employees did not specify whether they were asked to vote for the father, while others admitted that they usually voted for him because they admire him as a person, particularly his energy and enthusiasm.

But a close analysis of the social relations reveals that the father's network is likely unstable, as probably most similar networks are. It functions only as long as the father controls and distributes resources to people, and wanes when people turn their backs, seeing he has become politically and economically weakened. His political influence is measured by the stability of the social network he has at his disposal. In Gaj, recent developments point to the somewhat increased weakness of the father's network, perhaps because the number of people he must satisfy now overwhelms the available economic and political resources at his control. His vulnerability showed in the local elections in 2013, when his party representatives got significantly fewer votes. One of his close partners commented on the voting results in the following way:

> We had a bad performance in this election because the company [that the father runs] didn't work successfully during this and last year, and many contractual workers were sent home. Their contracts were not prolonged, and many parents were angry with him [the father] because he did not keep their children in the company. (Nemanja, August 2013, Gaj)

Somewhat different accounts show that very loyal partners may turn their back on the father because of his false promises and their unfulfilled expectations. A very close friend and comrade of the father decided to terminate communication with him, because he could not find a job for her daughter, which she had taken personally and understood as a betrayal of their friendship. In the second case, the family which has been by the father's side since his political rise thought that their efforts were not properly compensated and decided to change party and align with another political front. A similar political shift, one with more extreme consequences, happened when one of the father's longstanding party members was removed from a political function because she did not do the job properly. In revenge she gave up her party membership the same day and joined another party. In return, the father, ordered the firing of her husband from the local company, and, so the rumour goes, this led ultimately to the couple's divorce.

In every set of relationships, as Frederik Barth (1966) observed in *Models of Social Organization*, people keep evaluating values that they have gained and lost in exchanges with other people. These evaluations are dynamic. They change after every action and influence decisions about future exchanges. Consequently, the less asymmetrical the relationships, the more likely that obligations in existing relationships will continue. Barth's observation is extraordinarily valid in the case of the fragility of clientelist networks in Gaj that are becoming weaker with increasing asymmetries. Likewise, Barth's observation is also insightful for understanding how local people perceive the value of politics and clientelist networks, as well as their obligations in such relationships. Clientelist networks are extremely competitive, and thus only those who succeed in keeping themselves near the very core may prosper, while others drop out and turn to other suitable arrangements. To attain what the people in these clientelist networks expect in return, they need to demonstrate effort and commitment. The successful functioning of the clientelist network is tested during and after elections, which reveals why the most competitive local elites are so dedicated to the process.

Elections and maintaining power

The generally peaceful life in Gaj becomes hectic during elections. The SPP became a pioneer in careful and diligent preparation of the elections over the course of the whole year, which other political parties had not practised before. Local elections today represent the culmination of dedicated work of local elite who are engaged in different activities throughout the year. The main motivation for their engagement is climbing up the hierarchy in the party and obtaining better political posts within the municipality.

The chief political actor in the village before the rise of the SPP was the party of the father. When the SPP started to dominate the political scene on the local and republic level, those who were independent first joined the SPP, while the party of the father was its main opponent on a local level. The SPP's campaign against the father, accompanied by accusations and defamations, resulted in the defeat of his party at the local elections in 2013.[3] Yet, despite fierce political struggles before elections, the party of the father turned out to be influential enough, which led to a coalition with the SPP in the local municipality. Soon thereafter, the father joined the SPP with a full membership, without any previous consultation with the members of his party. They simply followed the father and relied on his political assessment. A sympathizer justified his action in the following way: 'He [the father] assessed that they can survive with the SPP, and thus work better for Gaj and the youth' (Milica, July 2017, Gaj).

As of 2017, many who were previously the SPP's opponents were now in the party; only a few have left the party since, most likely because their political ambitions could not be satisfied. Overall, the political landscape in the village became more homogenized than it was the case in the beginning of 2013 when I started my fieldwork. Likewise, the local elite has been more practically involved in politics with the attention on the local voters. Their aim has been to keep voters alerted and remind them of the party's presence in the village. Activities that take place before, during and after elections create 'professional party warriors' from the local elite.

In one of my subsequent visits to the village in 2017, I collected examples indicative of the professionalization of the local elite. The SPP trains their party members by sending them to special briefings and to a school for politicians. The aim of the briefings is to train local politicians for public appearances – teaching them appropriate gestures and body movements and to helping them prepare political speeches and arguments. Some of the interlocutors had found these trainings unpleasant. Each participant in the school for politicians, for example, must stand in front of an instructor and speak a text for a given time, which many participants considered embarrassing and exposing. Those whose performances were not satisfactory were sent home to practise in front of the mirror.

Apart from moulding their public appearances, the SPP expects the local elite to keep villagers informed about the party activities, plans and events, and to increase the number of their followers. Their political meetings thus became regular and are even open to the public. Yet although it may seem on the surface that SPP members have gathered voluntarily, a great deal of subtle and open force is involved. The following extract reflects this aspect.

> At the party meetings that the president [of the village] holds there is one recurring issue which annoys everyone, and that is the fulfilment of so-called quotas and party discipline. He says this is what the top of the party demands, and it must be respected. Quotas mean that every village, city, and local community has its own quota how many people must be sent to mass meetings or events that the SPP organizes. Everyone is annoyed by this, but people respect it, nonetheless. He explained the system of quotas in the following way. When, for instance, a new fish shop or something else is opened in Kovin, the party can employ, say, 17 people in total. If we do not fulfil quotas that regional party board set for us, the party gives these places to those villages who had the best performance. For example, ten positions go to Deliblato, five to Mramorak, one to Dubovac, and only one or none to Gaj. If it happens that Gaj is ranked as the best among the villages, then the biggest share goes to Gaj and vice versa. This is the motive for all of us to work hard for Gaj, to fulfil quotas and get many new jobs which enables our party to stay in power, and our children to get employed. Then one woman asked whether this means that if she doesn't show up on a mass meeting, she will lose her job. Then president assured her it won't be the case and that someone will replace her, but next time she will have to return the favour. (Ilonka, July 2017, Gaj)

The party's discipline also assumed that president of the Gaj village council and his comrades should set an example and that after the election they should, among other things, engage in improving the village park. This particular action caused a lot of criticism and mockery among villagers, because the SPP members cleared some established and healthy bushes and pine trees from the park in order to plant new ones, 80 per cent of which dried up and died shortly after planting. In another similar action the SPP members cleared political posters from the trees and public walls, so showcasing to their voters and villagers that they were fulfilling their electoral promises – one of which was the care for the village environment.

The fierce struggle to gain the attention and support of voters is best shown through the electoral process, which is supposed to be a crown of successful functioning of the clientelist network. Local elite work hard to ensure victory, and in doing so they often use undemocratic methods. It is partly enabled by the marginal position of the village in relation to the cities, and the shared belief that the conduct of the electoral process there is more flexible in comparison to urban centres.

Elections to the village council

Candidates for the village council should ideally nominate themselves independently and invest their name and reputation in the election process. But, since everyone in the village knows who is supporting which party, in effect it turns out to be a local competition of parties. Given that having a seat on the village council may enable career advancement in the municipality and regional party board, or assist in obtaining public jobs, the local elite strive to ensure their safe passage in the village council in various ways. The SPP members in Gaj, for example, make a list of candidates who should sit in the council and make propagandist efforts to ensure that people are aware of these candidates. They even visit people in their homes, bringing small presents, or make phone calls to enquire informally as to who the family is going to support. Some employ more violent mafia-like methods and warn independent or opposition candidates that they should withdraw from the electoral competition. One of the very few opposition candidates in Gaj in 2017 had experienced similar threats during her campaign. SPP members demanded that she stop publicly attacking the party, threatening that if she did not, her small business might be closed. Ultimately, the elections were successful for the SPP, with eight out of nine members elected to the village council.

Ideally, the candidate who receives the most votes should secure the majority in the council and become selected as its president, as this person enjoys most trust and a good reputation in the village. But since the rise of the SPP, a tactic has been used to changing the process. These popular, well trusted individuals are only 'borrowed' for the election process, and, while elected as president may not, eventually, serve as such in the long term. Such candidates often accept the presidency only nominally, but after some time they are instructed to resign because of alleged personal and professional reasons. Then the council members vote for another candidate from among them (who is usually suggested by the father), regardless of how many votes the person had won at the original election. In such a way, the president of the council as initially elected by the people becomes a powerless figure whose potential aspirations to grow politically are removed right from the start. The real power is held in the hands of the party that controls the majority on the village council.

The role of village council president is also important because it serves to consolidate political animosities and enable political homogenization, which was the main SPP agenda at both local and national levels. In one of the earlier elections for the village council, a candidate who presented himself as an independent got the most votes but did not secure the majority among the council members (who were supporters of SPP). At the time, the father's party and the SPP were severe political enemies. The father and his group of politicians who entered the council had secured a majority in the council, and enabled that person to become the president. It was revealed later that the president was installed to bridge the father's party and the SPP, which soon after united into one party. More importantly, the new alliance enabled the father's political survival. The function of the village council, hence, serves as an important indicator of the real power and influence of political actors, but also as a forum for making alliances that can be translated to the municipality level.

Municipality and republic elections

Municipality and republic (parliamentary and presidential) elections should realize accumulated political capacity and alliances that have been created at the village level. For municipality-level elections the party nominates prospective candidates for the council, while for republic elections the local elite, locally selected and integrated into the municipality and village structures, is in charge of securing the victory of the party. The greater the importance of the elections, the more complex the methods used to persuade voters.

When municipality or republic elections approach, the local elite apply a variety of strategies to ensure a so-called safe vote. In Gaj, it seems that peasants, Roma and pensioners are targeted as three major categories of voters to whom the local elite devotes special attention. In the case of peasants, pre-electoral persuasion is rather subtle, but for Roma and pensioners it is open and direct, presumably related to their unfavourable social position. The voting capacity of peasants, Roma and pensioners is very important, if not decisive, at the local level; by securing their votes, the elite enable the perpetuation of the established political system.

In Gaj, voter-persuasion techniques practised by the local SPP members for municipality elections in 2013, and for national parliamentary elections in 2014 became increasingly straightforward. SPP members, for example, distributed packages with meat, sugar and oil to Roma and pensioners. Some leading entrepreneurs from the village joined the SPP campaign and distributed juice, milk, beer and other groceries in Roma quarters. Likewise, those in the Roma quarter whose electricity was shut off because of unpaid bills got their electricity reconnected temporarily, prior to the elections. Some people received money for voting for the SPP candidates. SPP representatives from Gaj and their friends drove people to polling stations to vote for the SPP, and gave them sandwiches and beverages as refreshment. The SPP also organized free ophthalmological and cardio check-ups in the village for the older population. On that occasion, older visitors received free reading glasses, some medicine and vitamins. When it came to the peasants, voter-persuasion was, however, more subtle. Peasants were given gifts – small bags containing a cup with the candidate's face on it, his manifesto and a pencil. Local elite and activists left these bags outside peasants' doors or on their gates. Some peasants were phoned on the day of the elections and were 'kindly reminded' to vote with their family members.

The political monopoly that the SPP has imposed on the public sphere was evident again in Gaj in 2016, shortly before a parliamentary election. A side episode captures well the level of control that the SPP now had over the village and the municipality. One family wanted to assist the Adventist church to organize a public lecture in Gaj devoted to 500 years of the Reformation. For this purpose, they needed a public building in Gaj. Apart from the historical development of the church, they wanted to enlighten people about the healthy lifestyle that the Adventists practise, and promote their health magazine. But the village council did not allow them to use the public building, with the following explanation:

> They said to us that SPP is taking care of the health of the population, and they already organize something similar, so they don't need one more lecture on a health topic. In fact, they told us that they plan to bring cardiovascular and ophthalmological practitioners to the village, to check blood pressure and give advice for free. Elections were approaching and they didn't want to lose primacy and control over the village, which is why they declined our request. (Petra, July 2017, Gaj)

The control of the public sphere by the SPP, apart from manipulating public opinion, should ensure that the party and its membership by remaining in power get the biggest share of the public finance, jobs in the public sector and other lucrative opportunities. In the 1990s, when the multiparty system was introduced in Serbia, the political offer expanded considerably. At the same time, the state started to finance parliamentary parties, which incentivized an expanding market for well-paid political careers (see Elster et al. 1998, 132–40). Since then, the post-election period has been, thus, the time when the share of public functions and jobs among the parliamentary parties and their membership is carefully planned and distributed.

In the local example, we can see to what extent the expectation and prospective rewards incentivize local elites to invest efforts and engage in political campaigning for the SPP. A local restaurant owner, known for often changing parties, joined the SPP as soon as it started to grow. During one municipality elections he hosted SPP members from the regional board, financed their stay and supported their campaign, hoping he would be properly compensated for his services after the elections. One of his party members assessed that he had invested between 4,000 and 5,000 euros in the campaign. When the SPP won the election, it started to shortlist party members for the available public jobs. The restaurant owner asked to become director of the library in a nearby city. The party accepted his request and placed him in the position. But a problem occurred when the party found out that he had submitted a false diploma, and in fact he had never graduated from university. The situation with the restaurant owner soon became overwhelmingly compromising for SPP, and they replaced him. The restaurant owner stayed 'empty-handed', as one of his party colleagues observed: 'He invested so much money and didn't get anything in return'. When I asked what he was supposed to get in return, she replied: 'Well, the position of the director of the library, where monthly salary goes up to 1,000 euros' (Tijana, August 2014, Gaj). From the later rumours, I learned that the false university diploma was only an excuse for the SPP to disqualify the restaurant owner from the competition, because several equally useful people from the SPP were competing for the same post.

This and similar local examples demonstrate that political positions annihilate the idea of gradual professional progress. Progress, unless political and utilitarian, is essentially irrelevant and futile. Instant, short-term political positions should enable the local elite to accumulate benefits from powerful networks, and prepare the grounds to easily amortize the loss of the position or power through another favourable arrangement. Ultimately, the bonds between the party comrades are not ideological but instrumental, with a high degree of competition, which often leads to intra-party conflicts. Among the local elite, politics is seen as transactional, functional as long as reciprocity exists and without much space for political idealists.

The peasants and politics

Peasants' understanding of the politics and clientelist networks does not differ much from the dominant one in Gaj. Peasants generally see politics as a shortcut to access either services or resources that the majority is not able to use or the things that, in normal circumstances, imply time-consuming bureaucratic and expensive procedures. Yet peasants are not creators of politics in the way in which the local elite are, because they do not practise politics professionally and, unlike the local elite, are not a homogeneous group with clear political ideas related to the peasantry, rural development and the peasant's status in society.

Peasants in Gaj and neighbouring villages simultaneously navigate between their strengths and weaknesses in the political context. Their political strength stems from their land ownership and autonomy that provides them with the awareness that they represent an important political and voting potential. Peasants from my research area generally do not depend on politics or clientelist networks; they are not interested in climbing the political hierarchy, and most of them have their own resources to rely on without looking for external support. Many of them support a party, but they rarely back it openly through having a party membership. For example, on the eve of local elections in 2013, the leader of the former association of peasants from Gaj proposed to other members that they should run for the municipality elections together with the SPP. He believed that developing a common agenda with the SPP might increase their chances of winning seats in the municipality council. Joining forces with the SPP was also meant to help the members to attain their goals: getting more state land on lease for members of the association – as I explained in 'Interpersonal distrust' in Chapter 3. But the idea was not acceptable to many members of the association, and they rejected the proposal. They believed if they joined the SPP their association would lose its identity and dissolve in internal political calculations. Members of the associations did not want to risk losing the trust of other peasants, on whose support they counted, and so decided to remain independent.

The SPP, on the other hand, was interested in peasants' association from Gaj because it already had a significant influence among peasants even without having political power. The party wanted the association as an ally because, on the republic level, peasants represent a significant part of the population. A common wisdom of political analysts suggests that the party that first wins elections in the villages will likely win elections across the whole of Serbia; and vice versa, the party that first loses the election in the villages will likely lose its power on a republic level. Investing in electoral campaigns in villages, persuasion of peasants, as well as continuously reminding peasants of the party presence, as we saw on the example of Gaj, are thus the necessary steps in securing political support from the peasants' constituency.

Peasants' weakness, on the other hand, stems from their feeling of vulnerability and marginality, which is described as a chronic problem in rural areas across South-eastern Europe (Giordano and Kostova, 2002). Peasants sense their weakness through the lack of representatives in the parliament, staged dialogues with the Ministry of Agriculture and the biggest agricultural associations and poor rule of law. Yet some peasants from Gaj had learned how to live with their own marginality. Sometimes it included disregarding the state rules, because they believed that the state did not care much about them anyway. In other cases, some opportunistic peasants believed that structural loopholes could only be overcome by supporting the ruling party. That was the obvious premise of the leader of the former association of the peasants from Gaj, who believed that making close ties with the local elites from the SPP, would enable 'getting things easier for their association'.

In rare situations, peasants from Gaj join political parties by following pure political inertia and such decisions are often not the result of thorough calculation of personal or political gains. They simply align with the stronger. The following anecdote is particularly illustrative. One day I met in a bakery a neighbour who was excited to show me photos from an excursion to one Serbian city she had visited on the previous day. In one of the photos, she was with the mayor of the city Dragan Marković Palma, who is also an MP in the republic parliament, and the leader of the party United Serbia, which is in coalition with the SPP. When I saw him in the photo, I asked her jovially 'You are with Palma?', referring to her political alliance, and she readily replied: 'Oh no, I was but now I am with the SPP'.

This example and my past extensive fieldwork experience in the Serbian villages, led me to conclude that peasants are prone to opt for populist parties such as the SPP or United Serbia. Even though peasants represent the core of their votes, these parties paradoxically do not have in their party programmes elaborate plans for the improvement of peasants' condition or rural development. The SPP's and United Serbia's programmes are focused instead on the protection of national territorial interests, rejecting Kosovo's independence, plans for economic growth and plans to solve unemployment. These parties do not have representatives of the peasantry in parliament, except for one MP, whom many consider not to be a real peasant. Yet peasants continue to support the SPP and United Serbia. By supporting the political mainstream, peasants in fact maintain the status quo that, although it might not actually bring direct and visible betterment of peasant conditions, attains long-term goals. It enables the ruling party to maintain power and to continue to nurture the benevolent treatment of the peasants in return. The benevolent approach to peasants in cases when their offences are tolerated, on the one hand aggravates tensions and feelings of injustices in the broader society and, on the other, points to the power games between peasants and the state embodied in the ruling party. The examples of subsidies, evasion of VAT or rejecting compulsory agricultural pensions that I discussed in Chapter 4 unmask the trade-offs of such relationships. The peasants return the favour by remaining the main supporters of the mainstream politics in Serbia (Isić 1995). In other words, 'the economic and social benefits received in the rural environment are usually repaid by voting support in the political environment' (Lemarchand and Legg 1972, 156). Other competing parties may not be for sustaining such preferential treatment of peasants and thus are not worth the risk.

Expansion of the local elites does not secure rural development

As of 2000, it was believed that the democratic transition would result in the supposed separation of the party and the state in Serbia. In effect, the proliferation of new authorities and institutions, instead of institutional democratization and division of power, favoured the existing (political) and newly created patron–client networks that run through the entire hierarchy of patronage, geographical regions and government. As elsewhere, clientelist networks revealed that their expansion had been motivated by highly rational strategy 'employed to remedy the state's failure or shortcoming' (Giordano 2012, 23). In distrustful societies like Serbia, where transition brought express social stratification of the population, insecure job market, institutional injustices and many other hardships, clientelist networks function to supplement the weak state, rule of law and the poor job market.

In such a context, believing that the state institutions will perform their function, or enable any reforms, without submission to the clientelist networks was at least naive. This chapter indicated that there is a high likelihood that the dynamic between the micro- and macro-level clientelist networks will pervert rural development plans and that the expansion of the state institutions and authorities on the local level inevitably leads to more clientelism, but not to rural development, as the second argument of the book suggests. In the case of clientelist networks, Lemarchand and Legg (1972, 176) came up with the evidence that when their 'transactions come to involve policy as well as more individualized forms of payoffs in exchange for political support, the long-term growth of the system, including its economic and political capacities, may be seriously impaired'. In such a context, the reforms and policies, instead of helping the system to integrate, become too fragmented and too personalized, and along the way intensify fractures in society.

Judging from the case of Gaj and neighbouring villages, the outcomes of the institutional expansion and increase of the local elite after 2000, supposed to enable rural development, were not spectacular. Politicization of local clientelist networks turned rural development into plain rhetoric, political mantra and opportunity. In such a political environment, peasants do not seem to care about rural development rhetoric, but instead focus on preserving the political status quo that would least endanger their plans and their status in society.

Notes

1 The SPP has been the ruling party on the local and national level since 2012.
2 There are several synonyms that are often used interchangeably such as simply 'patronage', 'machine politics' or 'political clientelism' that essentially refer to the same phenomenon: a personalized and reciprocal relationship between inferior and superior actors or groups who are commanding unequal resources and involving mutually beneficial transactions that may have political ramifications (Lemarchand and Legg 1972, 151–2). Patronage exists across different geographical regions regardless of their type of political organization and specialization.
3 The political father was accused of abusing the position of mayor by taking 14 ha of municipality land on lease on behalf of the company he runs. The leaflets with this content were distributed in the village on the eve of the local elections in 2013.

6
Whose rural development?

The state plans for rural development in Serbia, as we see by now, either turn into wasted attempts or plain rhetoric. In politicians' and policymakers' rhetoric, rural development miraculously happens while, instead of the rural population, they become its main promoters. Rural development is promoted usually as a top-down complex organization of plans, goals and ideology that should bring economic, social and environmental improvements to all categories of people in rural areas (Scoones 2009, Sachs 2005). Yet, such a political top-down approach is rarely questioned in public, despite state- and donor-led rural development projects that often fail to achieve their encompassing goals (see Blackburn and Holland, 1998; Holland and Blackburn 1998; Mosse 2001; Cooke and Kothari 2001; Hobart 1993; Chambers 1983; Higgott 1983). Moreover, plans that aim to improve rural conditions are based on mistaken premises as to how change occurs. Policymakers' ideas about change in rural areas are first formalized through project plans, laws and financial institutions (Apthorpe 1997, Von Benda-Beckmann 1993). They advocate an institutionalist approach, because 'institutions (most commonly conceptualised as organisations) are highly attractive to theorists, development policymakers and practitioners as they help to render legible "community" and codify the translation of individual into collective endeavours in a form that is visible, analysable and amenable to intervention and influence' (Cleaver 2001, 40). Yet further planning, bureaucratic adjustments and new regulations seldom enable targeted areas to better thrive. An emphasis on planning does not tell us *how* rural development in fact occurs on the ground.

Neglecting endogenous development and emic ideas on how communities define wellbeing, and how local forms of thriving may be achieved, left many policymakers, but also some scholars, ignorant about the ethical importance of endogenous development, spontaneous change and the role models in a community. These factors are rarely taken seriously in systematic observations of local development, perhaps because it is believed that they do not have a strong explanatory capacity and that they cannot comprehensively account for the change.

Gaj and neighbouring villages, nevertheless, offer evidence that endogenous rural development compared to state-led plans for rural development achieves wider effects. There are at least two reasons for this. First, there is a structural difference between state-led and endogenous rural development. Agricultural policies conducted by the Serbian Ministry of Agriculture since 2000 to the present are rudimentary and predominantly focused on the intensification of agricultural production. They are also exclusive, targeting only registered agricultural producers who actively practise agriculture. Ideas of development promoted by the Ministry are based on the selective bureaucratic implementation of agricultural schemas that predominantly exclude those who do not cultivate or possess land. Endogenous development, on the other hand, spreads horizontally and is more inclusive toward diverse categories of people and individual approaches to agriculture. It is based on the principal application of norms that hold local society together. Likewise, thriving from scratch in the local context is possible and common, unlike the existing Serbian state agricultural schemes that are aimed at supporting those producers who are already established. Second, the ideology of agricultural policymakers often does not comply with the ideology of producers, as evidenced in numerous agri-environmental and conservation schemes carried out across Europe (Burton et al. 2008, Medina and Potter 2017). Within endogenous development, sharing local values and worldviews is a necessary precondition for an internal realization of functional household and village organization. But if the local ideas and drivers of development that underpin certain society remain unknown, life beyond state planning and bureaucratic regulations will remain neglected, and we will never understand the power of individual and local ethics (Pandian 2009).

Deeper insights into endogenous development in Gaj, Beli Breg and Malo Bavanište reveal that local perceptions of autonomy, land ownership, dignity and hard work are identified by the people as the main drivers of rural development. This chapter discusses how local and individual visions of development are constituted, through several stories. Even though the practical influence of the selected cases is difficult to estimate, they nevertheless mirror a local trend and worldview of villagers for whom farming is either an additional or a prime source of income. They reveal paradigmatic local wisdom: development is an individual and rarely systematic achievement; wellbeing and success come as mixed outcomes of individual endeavours and virtues, village ethics and forward-looking; such aspects have always been agents of development in these villages. These and similar individual examples of thriving and achievements impact the broader community and bring structural shifts that are not planned, intentional or instructed from above.

Stories of development

Stories of development vary greatly in motivation and in the origin of the main characters, but also in the neighbourhoods that in different ways have significantly influenced, or were decisive for, the desire for change and success. Motivations and goals differ in the lower, the central and the upper village as well as in Beli Breg, a neighbouring village that territorially and administratively belongs to Gaj. These neighbourhoods display how ideas of development emerged and how they were realized, but also what triggered the desire for change.

Case studies from the lower village

The lower part of Gaj, Trnovača, spreads along the very long Dunavska street, that connects Gaj with Beli Breg, Malo Bavanište and the River Danube and the public beach. Nearby the beach is an operating coal mine, which makes this road very busy with transportation trucks, cars and agricultural machinery. From the end of the residential area along the way to the Danube spread spacious fields and orchards. But there is also an illegal dump just around the corner on the main exit from the village. The dump has been an issue for decades but has never been removed, even though its removal represents a long-standing political promise in every local election. Another infrastructural problem is the lack of a proper sewage system in the whole village, that affects Trnovača the most. During the summer months, due to its lower position and low water level, wastewater stays in the drainage channels, spreading unpleasant smells. This problem has been long ignored by the local politicians because fixing it requires an expensive and long-term investment, and one that is not visible and does not bring immediate political benefits. They instead focus on accomplishing short-term and visible goals.

Trnovača is a relatively recent addition to Gaj that grew during the 1950s and 1960s, thanks to newcomers who came from Southern and Eastern Serbia and Roma, and also several Hungarian families. There are many obvious signs that indicate the relative modesty of this quarter. Houses are small, simply constructed, less decorated, unfinished or unpainted. Front yards are significantly less clean and tidy in comparison to the central village, while streets are narrower but livelier and more crowded with children and a younger population in general. The whole atmosphere of this quarter feels more relaxed and carefree, particularly during summer when the air is filled with loud music that comes from open windows and cell phones. People buzz around, call and tease each other, children freely ride their bicycles on the streets, some play football or run around. The gates to the properties are mostly wide open, which is not typical for Gaj. Traditionally gates are opened only when people drive their car or machines out to the fields and are then immediately closed again for practical and safety reasons, since all gardens, stalls with animals, orchards and small plots are in the backyard, away from the street. People who are busy in their backyard may not want to be interrupted or may not hear who is coming. But in Trnovača, most households do not have land, animals, gardens or agricultural machines. There is nothing to protect except life and health. The occupations of people in Trnovača are mixed, ranging from small-scale peasants, day labourers and workers to professionals. Part of the population is unemployed, and these are mainly Roma. In its general appearance, Trnovača leaves the impression of a poor and neglected quarter.

Maruška's story

It was an early summer afternoon when Maruška unlocked the newly painted green gate and let me in, then locked the gate again. She cordially greeted a few people who hung out on the street but while she was shutting the gate she shook her head in a disapproving manner. I could see that she did not think highly of them. While we chatted briefly in the front yard, I could observe that her relatively small house and yard were spotlessly clean and neat. We moved into the house to hide from Banat's heat. Maruška immediately left the impression of being an agile and hardworking woman. Her movements were deft. Her words were clear and straightforward in a way that did not leave anything unexplained or misunderstood. She immediately initiated a discussion about her family living among Roma. She wanted to make sure that I understood that she and her family did not belong there, and their being so was a result of certain circumstances.

Maruška (age 54) was born into a poor Hungarian family in a neighbouring village and moved to Gaj when she was six. She married when she was 15 years old, to a Hungarian husband. When they married, they did not have anything. They lived in one improvised room under the barn, together with their two small sons. They did not have a bathroom, and the toilet was improvised and made out of wooden boards behind the barn. At that time, both had worked as day labourers, mostly in private households and a state agricultural farm in the village. From the money they saved, they bought a small plot of land and built a house. Then, they started a farm with 15 pigs. The farm was speedily growing and by the end of the year they had 60 pigs. Since the farm was expanding, they moved it to the summer ranch near the village and lived there for five years, together with their sons. Their sons, however, could not accept their family business, which they found embarrassing and stigmatizing. They asked their parents to shut down the farm because other people in the village looked down on them and called them 'piggers' (*svinjari*). Maruška believed that this stigma was the reason why her sons did not finish primary school, because of the teasing and provocation from other children.

Maruška and her husband eventually sold off the pigs and shut down the farm, but she swore she would one day show all these people who had mocked them. From the money from the pigs, they bought nearly 3 ha of land, two tractors and have now committed exclusively to agriculture. During the last 30 years, they have acquired all the necessary mechanization, a total 10 ha of their own land, and, moreover, have taken a further 7 ha on lease. In the meantime, they have expanded their household activities with cows, sheep and pigs. Maruška and her husband also built two houses for the two sons and organized two generous send-off parties for them when they joined the army. Likewise, when both sons got married, they organized big wedding ceremonies for them. Maruška reckons that all of this would not have been possible without the pig business: 'We thrived thanks to pigs, hard work and our own sweat'.

Although Maruška, her husband, their sons and their families live in two separate houses, they work the land and run the household together, and share all income equally. She is very proud of what they have achieved in the last 30 years and compared their success to the old well-known householders (*gazde*) from the village who failed.

> *Gazde* for whom we had previously worked for wages have ruined themselves, while we have thrived. This is because they strictly stick to the old, traditional, way of doing things, and the mothers-in-law have the last word. In our household we do it differently, we have a democratic approach, and we agree upon who is doing what. For the time being it functions. (Maruška, July 2013, Gaj)

Maruška is an example of a person whose success and wellbeing came as result of hard work and her desire for a better life and social recognition. Maruška stressed that one of the motivations for the thriving of her family was their social recognition. Through organization of big celebrations and enormous spending for her two sons – which is a local symbolic indicator of success and social stratification in the village – they have satisfied both the desire for showing off, and gaining public confirmation of their success.

Vasa's story

Vasa (age 74) has lived in Trnovača since he moved to Gaj when he was 14 years old from a poor mountain village from one of the former Yugoslav countries. His house, though slightly bigger and painted, does not stand out in its appearance from the rest of the neighbourhood, even though he is known as one of the better-off cattle breeders in the village. I learned later that this was partly a deliberate decision on his part, affected by his neighbourhood and the people with whom he has lived and cooperated for many years, most of whom are Roma.

When Vasa came to Gaj he worked as a day labourer and a shepherd. His wife (age 55) was born in Gaj, where they met and later married. Vasa's wife inherited some 2–3 ha of land, which became their basis for the enlargement of their household (land and property). They built a small house and soon started livestock breeding. From the first days until the present, they have been breeding cows. Their son, with whom they share a household, after elementary school dedicated himself to cattle breeding. In the beginning, they owned only two or three cattle but soon the herd started to grow and over the years they expanded it to 100 cattle. Along the way, they have been gradually buying land and today they possess some 40 ha. The wife is responsible for taking care of calves and dairy cows, the house and the garden, while Vasa and the son have been responsible for the cattle they have on the summer ranch near Gaj. Because of the size of the herd, it is cheaper and more convenient for them to keep them at the summer ranch throughout the year and to bring supplies from the village. Vasa and his son regularly commute several times a day between the ranch and the house. But during summer their working schedule gets more intense because they need to cultivate the fields, bale the hay, transport the crops to middlemen and maintain the summer ranch. Most of the work they do alone, in part thanks to owning the agricultural machinery necessary but also because they struggle to find reliable shepherds and day labourers, even among their neighbours. Their hard work has paid off in terms of self-sustainability and the capital they possess. More importantly, they have achieved a sustainable system, and make significant savings through the use of animal-based fertilizers which they produce within the household. This also gives positive results in terms of yields from their crops.

Both Vasa and his son think that a family may have a decent life with 30 ha of private land. Today they cultivate approximately 70 ha out of which 30 ha is leased state land that they took in 2013 as livestock breeders. Renting out the state land was an initiative from the local state of Kovin municipality and a supportive measure for livestock breeders that were facing a serious decline in animal husbandry. Yet, the family's current capital cannot be attributed to these state incentives, because they already possessed cattle and 40 ha of land before the measure came into effect. Vasa and his son think that their wellbeing was a product of their hard work, thriftiness and desire for a better life, and from the satisfaction they gained from managing to thrive out of poverty. Vasa explained his thriving and that of other peasants through the shift of the general mentality after 2000.

> When Tito was alive, there was something in people that they didn't want more, but after 2000 people wanted more and went for more. Suddenly everything became available to them. The products gained good price and they started to make a profit. In people is the desire for more. It's the game now. The land is cultivated better, otherwise it'd be neglected. (Vasa, August 2013, Gaj)

This extract reveals the importance of having an enthusiasm for production, at the local level, which when transferred to the macro level integrates within its reach a rising number of people who want to satisfy their needs for competition and self-realization. An enthusiasm for production likewise affects market prices and the supply and demand chain. Enthusiasm for production is gradually accompanied by social mobility that enables a transition from the status of poor to the status of being better off. If it occurs according to local norms of hard work, it is rewarded with dignity, respect and acknowledgment, as in Vasa's case.

Case studies from the central village

Most people's impression of the village is based on its centre. The church, school, park, shops, centre of culture and the few cafes along the regional road to the town of Bela Crkva, as well as several side streets on either side represent the heart of Gaj (Figure 6.1). This part of the village is inhabited mostly by people who are considered *Banaćani*, that is, families who have been living in Gaj for several generations and who have been working in agriculture ever since. In the central village, both modern dwellings as well as houses that date back to the first quarter of the twentieth century preserve the architectural style of Banat region. This architecture entails spacious and nicely decorated houses, with big wooden or metal gates that connect the two separate parts of the properties. Every house has a small green area in front of the house facing the street, which is maintained and decorated by householders themselves. The main yard, usually very large, is hidden from the street.

Figure 6.1 The street through central Gaj, showing typical houses of the area.
Source: Author.

Streets are spacious, with decent lighting, sidewalks and plenty of trees. The whole impression of the central village is a feeling of safety and serenity. People in the central village usually keep the gates of their properties shut, which represents the idiosyncratic living style of Banat's inhabitants. A great deal of family life takes place in the yard within the gates. This changes to some extent during the summer months when people gather on the streets for chat. The atmosphere of the central village differentiates it visibly from the quarter where Maruška and Vasa live, mostly in quiet and introvert – 'minding my own business' – way of life which is practised in the central village.

Goran's story

Goran (age 43) was born in Gaj. His father is also from Gaj, while his mother moved with her family to the village from East Serbia during the 1960s, and later married Goran's father. Goran finished primary school and three grades of the vocational school where he specialized to become an agricultural technician. Since the age of 10 he has worked in agriculture, and he has always seen himself doing so. Goran had tried a small private business during the 1990s to diversify his income and support the household. He bought a truck and did unreported transport services for 10 years, but even when running the business, he never ceased to work the land.

By the 1990s, Goran and his father had only 2 ha of land and took an additional 15–20 ha on lease. Before the 1990s, land could be taken on lease easily, but a lease itself was very expensive. From the 1990s to 2000, due to the political situation in the country, leasing became cheaper, but the land was poorly maintained given the fact that people did not have the means to invest in production, nor did they have the necessary machinery. 'Back then the land was cultivated very primitively', Goran asserted. During this same period, because of poor productivity, low prices of agricultural products and economic sanctions, land was cheap. Goran and his father seized this as an opportunity and started to buy from 2.5 to 3 ha annually.

Goran significantly advanced the household when in 1995 he started an informal cooperation with his neighbour. Their cooperation worked productively for 10 years. They helped each other out in different agricultural work, in combining machines, and even some land. The cooperative, as a product of trust and good organization, brought mutual benefit and prosperity to Goran and his partner. It even accelerated their private investments. During this time, for example, Goran invested in expanding agricultural buildings and a separate barn for machines and storing crops. In 2005, Goran and his partner realized that they had each become big enough and capable of running independent businesses and decided to end their cooperation in a friendly and understanding atmosphere.

Goran's entrepreneurial initiatives, economic intuition and the cooperation with his neighbour, as well as the small business that he practised for 10 years, helped him to invest in his production and accumulate land when it was cheap and when farming was unpopular. He grew into one of the most successful producers in the village and today he has 60 ha of his own land and takes an additional 60 ha on lease. In 2013 the Kovin municipality rewarded him for being one of the most successful agricultural producers in the area. People like him who seized the opportunity and invested in their work, already stood out before the implementation of the agricultural subsidies in 2006. These indeed speeded up the development of peasants like Goran, but they couldn't solely account for their economic growth, in Goran's opinion. The readiness to invest in production and to expand one's property are according to Goran the most important factors for development.

> Today the land is in the hands of those who want to work it properly, and many have thrived as *gazde*. Nowadays all producers compete to work better; much attention is given to proper care and treatment of the land. Some 20 people from the village have thrived and cultivated from 20 to 90 ha of their own land. Before 2000, the most successful guy had approximately 25 ha. Today those with 30 ha have a decent life but with this money they cannot invest in land, nor in machines. They can only maintain their existing household. People here aren't aware they're decaying when they keep the same amount of land and don't expand their property. Those who keep working just 10 ha are first to collapse because they think they can live like in the 1980s when 10 ha was satisfactory. (Goran, August 2013, Gaj)

Goran's example reveals that development may be incentivized by a forward-looking approach, rather than by the current political and economic conditions. Setting an example through the diligent and careful treatment of the land and crops, gradually becomes a local pattern of work, as Burton rightly wrote: 'The symbolic value of the crop is thus in that it displays the farmer's commitment to agriculture as a way of life, to the soil and to the crop, and not in its display of the profitability of the farm' (Burton 2004, 209). Only later do these values translate into competition which manifests both as social pressure and enthusiasm for production. Eventually, the synergy of these elements influences new local attitudes toward land, farming, success and understanding of development, which is, among middle-level and bigger peasants, perceived as both an entrepreneurial endeavour and an act of virtue.

Dragan's story

Dragan (age 50) was born and raised in Gaj in an old and respected Banat family. The family's house, one of the oldest in the village centre, retains a Banat's charm despite being recently renovated. In the nineteenth century and interwar period, mostly better off Serbian families had settled and built their houses in the core of the village, while its periphery was populated by poorer dwellers and newcomers. Living in the centre of the village now, like then, reflects the higher social status and influence of families. Some have failed in preserving their old reputations, but Dragan and his parents have succeeded in doing so and are still considered as one of the better-off and most respected households.

Dragan's family has been working in agriculture for generations. Dragan, though, did not always plan to stay in the village and work on the land. After high school he started studies and lived in Belgrade for three years. But he quit his studies because his parents could not finance him in the 1990s, during the harshest economic and political circumstances. He returned to Gaj and started to work as a technician in a state company in Kovin, but the salary was small and irregular. When the company was privatized in 2003, he decided to quit his job and since then he has been dedicated to agriculture only.

By the late 1980s, his parents possessed and cultivated some 20 ha of land, which at that time represented real wealth. When Dragan took over the household, it grew steadily. Since 2006/7 the price of land has risen by 100 per cent while the rise of crop prices was getting lower due to agricultural subsidies. Despite low prices of agricultural products, Dragan wanted to expand his household and work without getting into debt with private cooperatives or banks. He knew that with the implementation of improved agrotechnological measures he could attain higher yields. He wanted to learn more about farming and went to the United States for a month. During this time Dragan visited several farms and educated himself about the ways in which American farmers improve their production. His newly gained knowledge gradually yielded results.

Today Dragan owns 30 ha of land and has an additional 40 ha on lease. Most of the agricultural jobs he does alone because he is equipped with all the necessary mechanization. Dragan believes that the milestone in his production was when he adopted new agri-methods. He considers that, unlike him, the 'majority of people in Gaj' are 'too conservative and sceptical of new things, and have doubts about anything that is considered either foreign or new' (Dragan, July 2017, Gaj).

Dragan's knowledge, skills and personal qualities enabled him to build a reputation as one of the most respected peasants and *gazde* in the broader village community. His work, dedication to farming and the village synthesized both personal and family reputation in the overarching task of maintaining and enlarging the family household. Dragan admitted that being raised in a patriarchal family, he did not have a choice but to adopt hard work habits and awareness of his family's reputation. In these factors, Dragan sees the main motivator of his later success.

Bogdan's story

Bogdan (age 47) was born in Gaj to a family of newcomers. His father moved to Gaj in 1966 from a poor village in eastern Serbia, while his mother came from the Dalmatia region in Croatia, famous for its poor soil and craggy landscapes. His parents met in Gaj and later got married. Bogdan's father was only 12 years old when he came to Gaj and was so poor that he did not have enough money for a bus ticket, and hiked to the village for more than 100 kilometres. In the beginning he lived in an improvised hut in a field and worked as a day labourer and a construction worker. When he became an adult, Bogdan's father was employed in a construction company. In the 1990s the company where he worked was shut down and he decided to start his own private business that involved Bogdan's mother, Bogdan and his brother. Bogdan describes this period as the beginning of their prosperity.

When Bogdan graduated from high school, he moved to Belgrade for studies, but he never finished them. After a couple of years, he returned to Gaj and started to work with his father. Bogdan worked just as hard as his father, mostly in construction. In 2005, Bogdan opened the currency exchange in the village which turned out to be a successful business move, because nothing similar existed in Gaj or nearby villages. Then, he opened the first large store in Gaj, and soon expanded the concept of stores to seven nearby villages. In summer 2017, when I visited his household again, I learned that he had opened a bakehouse

Figure 6.2 The baker at work. Source: Author.

that supplies his stores with bread and pastries (see Figures 6.2 and 6.3). Bogdan plans to further expand the business by opening a mill for the production and packing of flour. Apart from his regular business activities, Bogdan and his father jointly own and cultivate 5 ha of land which they work alone with their own mechanization.

Bogdan and his father represent one of the few pure entrepreneurial families in the village. For most people who combine farming with an additional occupation, it is a way to diversify income. For Bogdan and his father, farming is not a necessity. It represents rather the way to bond with the village more strongly. In a similar way, they understand their mission as entrepreneurs: half of their employees are from Gaj; they tend to support every initiative that comes from the villagers; they are committed to preserving local businesses in various ways.

> I always buy gas at the village gas station even though it is more expensive than in Kovin. Stuff for the house reparation I buy in Janko's shop even though it is more expensive than elsewhere. I want to leave my money in the village. I always try to help and support various cultural and social events because I want people to stay in here. If all would think like this then Gaj would be a much better place. Yet, despite political differences, I think we are united, and we find a compromise unlike other neighbouring villages.
> (Bogdan, August 2013, Gaj)

Figure 6.3 Heating the wood-fired bread oven in the bakery. Source: Author.

Bogdan's commitment to the village is widely acknowledged. On different occasions I witnessed people express very high opinions about Bogdan and his family. He is a titular president of the association of chess players, and he was a member of the village council. Although Bogdan admits that he does not have political ambitions, local SPP party members invite him to support their political campaigns and various events. Such situations are, nevertheless, inevitable in small communities particularly because people gravitate toward those who are considered better off and successful and who may be either a resource for, or leaders in, change.

Bogdan represents an economically influential man who to some extent has changed the landscape of the village. His businesses have not only improved the wellbeing of other villagers but have also contributed to the diversification of economic activities away from farming. His success also has a symbolic significance. Bogdan's wealth is socially accepted and acknowledged even though it does not spring from a 'true' Banat occupation – farming. Moreover, his family does not have Banat roots, but their proven loyalty to the village makes other people consider them 'real' *Banaćani* who adhere to the village values.

Case studies from the upper village

As we move away from the central village, the landscape changes too. The street that transects the upper village leads toward the fields and another village, 6 km from Gaj. The street that at one point turns into a gravel road has been the subject of one of the longstanding promises of local politicians, who as a rule use this road in campaigns to attract voters with promises about its final asphalting. On the eve of every election, the authorities add fresh gravel and roll it evenly, rather than asphalting it. With the first heavy rain, the road gets and remains destroyed until the next elections. During summer, people who live in this neighbourhood keep their windows shut due to huge amount of dust that spreads in the air, which is lifted by tractors, cars and trucks on such a busy road.

The second, long, street that crosses the upper village leads toward the cemetery and football playground. The streets in this neighbourhood are filled with houses that are smaller and modest in comparison to the central village. This quarter started to grow in the 1960s with newcomers predominantly from Eastern Serbia and Dalmatia in Croatia. Back then, it was one of the rare undeveloped areas in Gaj where building plots could be purchased. In this quarter live the least numbers of peasants, although almost all households possess some land. Since most of these families have newcomer origin, they have never been occupied with agriculture exclusively. They are mostly craftsmen (Figure 6.4), or workers in factories, public services or administration. Yet the gates on most of the households are kept shut and yards are neat and well maintained, which is a symbolical indicator that they have adopted the village values.

Ana and Damjan's story

Ana (age 42) and Damjan (age 40) are a couple, and both were born in Gaj. Ana's grandfather came from a very poor village in Southeastern Serbia, while Damjan's father came from South Serbia. Ana is a nurse in a city hospital, and Damjan is a policeman. Their parents were workers who possessed little land. During socialism this group of people was locally known as *polutani* (semi-workers, semi-peasants), because they cultivated the land in addition to their main occupation. Ana had some sporadic experience in agriculture when she went picking at state farms for pocket money during the summer while she was in high school. Damjan admits he was very poorly educated in agriculture, hardly knowing the difference between a cucumber and a courgette. Since their professions were poorly paid, and yet relatively

Figure 6.4 The tailor's work in progress. Source: Author.

stressful, they contemplated starting small farming production to secure additional income.

In 2004, Damjan built his first greenhouse without even elementary knowledge of farming. Apart from additional income, he saw in greenhouse production a way to secure personal independence. Ana was against his project at first, but she changed her mind when their child was on the way. They started with strawberries, but that greenhouse was destroyed one day in a heavy storm. The strawberries were almost ready for picking, and in five minutes they lost everything. Ana and Damjan were devastated. Soon after this event, they built a second greenhouse but with vegetables. They were gradually gaining knowledge and followed professional advice. In a relatively short period, their business expanded. They built two greenhouses that spread over 7 acres, and an additional three greenhouses for seedlings.

Damjan's ambition went further, and he founded an association of vegetable producers from Gaj, in 2011, with an idea to find a new market that the association could supply. The Kovin municipality gave them a free stall in the town's marketplace, as a gesture of support for the small agri-business and associations. The stall, however, was on the fringe of the marketplace, away from its core commercial area. Even their attempts to draw new customers with an attractive look to the stall, recognizable uniforms and logo, leaflets and promotions could not secure their business success. The members of the association lost enthusiasm after a series of failures. The association eventually fell apart. Yet this did not discourage Damjan and Ana, and they decided to independently lease a stall in the centre of Kovin marketplace instead. Such a business move turned out to be very successful and important for the expansion of the business. Because of their additional jobs in public sectors, they used the marketplace to promote their products at weekends, while selling bigger amounts direct from home.

Damjan and Ana represent a growing population in Gaj that is slowly turning toward professional agriculture. Although they still do not plan to quit their primary jobs due to the unstable political and economic situation, they are thinking of expanding the business and adding more greenhouses. Securing an additional income in their case was one of the main reasons for building the greenhouse. But through the farming, they gradually discovered the value in the autonomy of those working the land and producing vegetables. They realized that the greenhouse business made their family closer, and enabled them to have better family time, which they did not have before. The combination of autonomy and gradual economic prosperity has made their entrepreneurial endeavour survive two big setbacks – the damaged greenhouse and the failure of the association's stall at the Kovin marketplace. Like many people from the village, in pursuing a better life and change, Ana and Damjan were driven by a belief in the quality of their products and work commitment, autonomy, dignity and social recognition. Yet such common sense motivations are not considered scientific enough to explain local development, because they are not planned or directed from the top.

Ivica's story

Ivica (age 45) was born in Gaj to a family not originally from the village and came to Gaj in the 1960s. The family lived for a long time as tenants in the village in relative poverty. Ivica's father was a worker employed in a construction company, while his mother was a housewife. His father was an alcoholic, which is why he does not have many pleasant memories of his childhood nor of his parents' marriage. Their family reputation is associated with his father, who was known for violent behaviour and lack of respect.

Ivica was an excellent student in primary and high school, but his father was against his studies because they had neither land nor money to support his ambitions. After high school, he joined the army, where he was among the best and toughest soldiers in the group, despite his seemingly weak physical constitution. His accomplishments at military training were recognized with awards, several times. When Ivica returned home after the army, he did various jobs. He worked as a day labourer, then in private manufacture of fruit juices, he drove a taxi, sold smuggled cigarettes and was a bingo caller. He sometimes worked 12 hours a day. Despite his sometimes harsh life, Ivica never despaired. 'My optimism and vision kept me strong and persistent' (Ivica, February 2013, Gaj).

For the past decade, Ivica has worked in a successful company in a nearby town. His hard work and commitment have promoted him to chief of department with a high salary. But the general situation in the company as well as personal relationships among employees make Ivica very dissatisfied and unhappy. Even though his job has enabled him to travel the world and see the sea for the first time in his life, to renovate his household and buy some land, nonetheless, he considers leaving the company. Ivica was preparing to resign and to commit completely to agriculture. Since he was planning his resignation in advance, he started to buy the land and agricultural machinery. He bought 5 ha of land, expanded the garden, and invested in poultry. He found his motivation in acquiring land and building his own status of a respected householder. 'Every time I bought a piece of land, I had to fast for a whole year to pay off the debt, but one motive has always kept me going – that a poor man should earn capital – because my parents did not have a gram of land' (Ivica, February 2013, Gaj).

Ivica's dedication to farming and his hard work have enabled him to build a respected name – where his father failed – and to replace the bad image the village associates with his family. His religiosity additionally strengthens his social reputation, as was symbolically acknowledged when he was offered a place in the church council. According to people who know him, Ivica is a true and dedicated believer, who actively helps in maintaining a monastery near Gaj, and who also supports several Roma children with food and clothes. He explained his religiosity as the only choice he had in a world of constant poverty and unhappiness. He reckons that his hard life and many unfortunate events have contributed to the strengthening of his faith. 'I have always believed in God, but the hardness of life made me believe in God more than others' (Ivica, February 2013, Gaj). His religiosity and good reputation turned out to be crucial factors when he purchased land from pensioners from Gaj who did not want to sell it to anyone but him. 'They even were happy to wait for me until I repaid the land because they trusted in me and wanted to help me in fulfilling my ambitions' (Ivica, February 2013, Gaj).

Ivica's story reveals the importance of hard work, dedication to farming and religiosity for success in the micro-community. Among those who want to fully adopt village life these values today play an equally important role in social and economic integration as they did in the past.

Case study from Beli Breg

Beli Breg territorially and administratively belongs to Gaj, and is only a couple of kilometres from its centre, halfway between Malo Bavanište and Dubovac. The village faces the River Danube, which flows along its fringes. Between the village and river lie spacious fields consisting of sandy soil. Although farming on such soil is challenging, it turned out to be ideal for watermelons, which has made the village well known in the region. Despite the quality of the soil, most of the population works on the land, while only a few households combine livestock breeding with agriculture.

Beli Breg is a relatively new village that is populated by so called *došljaci* (newcomers) from Eastern and South Serbia, who came there in the early 1950s and 1960s. According to many villagers, Banat was for the newcomers the same as Switzerland is for Serbia today – a rich and promising land. After setting up a base in Beli Breg, most newcomer families were temporary workers in foreign countries (Austria, Switzerland, Germany), with the aim of saving enough money to purchase land and agricultural machinery. This has continued until today. Beli Breg has the highest rate of migrant workers in the region. Half of the families from Beli Breg are still temporarily based in foreign countries (as is the case also in Malo Bavanište, which has a similar demographic).

The wellbeing, wealth and success of Beli Breg's inhabitants are visibly manifested in the architectural appearance of the village. Most of the houses are relatively new, big and modern, with spacious grounds decorated with gypsum statues, swimming pools or fountains. Yet the village does not have a school, nor an asphalted road to link it with Kovin, Gaj and other surrounding villages. In 2014 people still used an old gravel road, complaining about the politicians who, during elections, made false promises about getting it asphalted. People commute regularly to Kovin or Gaj for their daily needs, because the village lacks shops, a post office, a pharmacy, or a health centre, which makes the road busy. In the winter when it is snowing, the village is cut off for couple of days because machines are busy clearing the town of Kovin, the regional roads and central villages. During such events, the inhabitants of Beli Breg usually organize themselves and clear the path using their own tractors and machines. The problem with the road reveals old infrastructural challenges of Beli Breg. The village only got electricity in 1971, two years before the road was built. Since then, existing modest infrastructural improvements have come mainly as the result of political pressures on local elites, rather than through planned development of the village.

Rista's story

Rista (age 56) was born in a village in Eastern Serbia. In 1964 his parents moved to Beli Breg, together with their children, thanks to the persuasion of Rista's aunt, who was already married and living in the village. The family sold all they had, which was not much. In the beginning they lived as tenants. When Rista finished primary school in Gaj he started to work as a day labourer, alongside his parents. Through their joint efforts they bought 2–3 ha of land in Beli Breg on which to build a house and use the rest for subsistence agriculture. At the time, Beli Breg was completely vacant, without any infrastructure and organized village life.

Their 2–3 ha of land, however, could not satisfy their growing family. Rista did not have many options at his disposal. In 1986 he decided to go to Switzerland and look for a job. In the beginning, he worked illegally on construction sites thanks to his friends who offered him work. Because of his unreported status, he was going back and forth between Switzerland and Serbia, often residing illegally in Switzerland, from which he was twice deported and banned from working. He nevertheless ignored the ban and returned every time. When he eventually resolved his residential status by working officially for a Swiss company, Rista, his wife and their youngest son all lived in Switzerland until 2007, while their older children remained in Beli Breg with their grandparents. He decided to return to Serbia because he never planned to stay abroad longer than necessary and was afraid that the hard work and Swiss discipline would destroy his health and sense of purpose. 'I didn't want to break my back for somebody else and make him rich. I wanted to do something for myself' (Rista, July 2013, Beli Breg).

When Rista left his village in 1986, his family lived in a small house without a bathroom in two rooms that he shared with his parents, children and wife. Today he lives in a spacious house with several bathrooms and rooms. Rista also owns 46 ha of land as well as agricultural machinery including harvesters, seeders, crowner and tractors. He is confident that people can live nicely from agriculture if they cultivate between 30 and 40 ha and do not indebt themselves buying seeds and fertilizers from private agricultural cooperatives. He does not lease additional land because he is satisfied with the work, and some additional income he generates from renting out machinery. Rista's plan was to be self-sufficient, doing all the work himself, without hiring day labourers, and this saves him a lot of money and trouble.

Apart from the desire for dignity, a better life and autonomy, Rista's story reveals a core dimension that is important for the newcomer families from Beli Breg (and also from Malo Bavanište). It explains their mass migration to foreign countries, and their significant mobility and adaptability. Rista holds that people from central Gaj did not have a need to migrate because they already possessed 10–15 ha of land and had to maintain the property and the family name. They needed to invest only hard work to maintain their household and their reputation, while others – like his family – had to start from scratch. Yet, families like Rista's struggle, not only to attain a better life and capital but also to get rid of the stigma of being newcomers that accompanies them even 60 years after moving to Gaj. Some better-off 'newcomers' are never fully and symbolically integrated in Gaj – or at least this is how they feel about it. The newcomers struggle for status and social recognition in the village, and this struggle usually manifests in megalomaniac indicators of success through building big houses on two or three floors, and yards with fountains and swimming pools. The appearance of their houses does not resemble Banat style, nor it is meant to, because they are in many regards different from *Banaćani*. They want to preserve their identity traits. The aim of their 'megalomania' is to impress lethargic *Banaćani* and make them ashamed when they compare themselves with the newcomers. Newcomers want *Banaćani* to understand that they are at least equal, if not better than them.

A few better-off people in the village have newcomer roots. One of them explained their success in the village through the comparison with lethargic *Banaćani*, and readiness of the newcomers to move and innovate.

> I came to Gaj from Izvor when I was only seven years old and wasn't the only one. We used to struggle, fail, and work hard, left behind our homes, and start new ones, unlike *Banaćani* who have

been living for decades and centuries in the same village. They are dummies, they have been working the land for a hundred years, constantly seeding the same crops: corn, wheat, sunflowers. Then sunflower, wheat, and corn again next season. They work five days in a year and the remaining time sit in front of their houses. And then they complain about the state. Or, if the state owes something to them they block the roads, but they never ask what they owe to the state. They don't pay taxes, but yet they are subsidized unlike locksmiths, bakers, carpenters. They say 'we feed Serbia' but they don't contribute to anything. *Banaćani* don't want to bother with anything too much. Apart from corn and wheat they will not try to plant let's say a chain of potato, paprika, carrots and sell it later because this demands a lot of work. They are traditional about everything and so in agriculture. (Branko, August 2014, Gaj)

The mobility and lifestyles of newcomers account for changes in the village. The newcomers have diversified social and economic practices and influenced local habits. First, they contributed to the proliferation of dominant occupations in the village. When newcomers settled in Gaj, most of them opted for entrepreneurial jobs and crafts, because the village was already populated and there was a lack of people with such skills. They filled the void. Second, those newcomers who settled in Beli Breg and Malo Bavanište and who embraced farming had to migrate first to foreign countries in order to build a household base in the village. Third, perhaps their most important contribution is not only in the economic prosperity of Gaj and surrounding villages. It is, rather, in the mindset they brought along. Their attitude of 'thriving from scratch' has shifted the mainstream understanding of development in the village as something that happens through generational and hereditary enlargement of property. Both newcomers and others in the village have taken this on, and made success possible and less abstract, even in an economically homogeneous environment that traditionally relies on crop farming and small-scale trade as the most common occupations. Jobs other than farming, such as rural tourism, applied arts or entrepreneurial jobs have been for a long time scarce. Over the past few years, several people in Gaj and neighbouring villages have opened small and successful businesses such as pastry shops, beauty salons and an office for proof editing and press preparation, and similar. We cannot know for sure to what extent newcomers' stories about thriving from scratch have affected the recent development of entrepreneurship in the village, but they have certainly become embedded in its social fabric and affected the shaping of the attitudes too.

Individual and local values explain development

Common to all the stories of development presented here is that their growth dates from before subsidies and state measures for supporting agriculture. In some cases, subsidies did stimulate production (as in Vasa's, Goran's, Dragan's and Rista's case), but they did not trigger the desire for growth, nor the achievements of these individuals. Moreover, Ivica, Bogdan, and Ana and Damjan had never been entitled to state subsidies because they were permanently employed and did not have a registered agricultural household. The growth achieved by my interlocutors was, rather, spontaneous and self-initiated. It emerged from their own hard work, but it was also accompanied by market prices that boosted their professional satisfaction and motivation. Their growth came also as a desire for distinction, social recognition, autonomy and land ownership, competition and cooperation. More than two centuries ago, utilitarian philosopher Jeremy Bentham ([1781] 2000) identified these variables as the important motivators of social action and cooperation.

> The pleasures of a good name are the pleasures that accompany the persuasion of a man's being in the acquisition or the possession of the good-will of the world about him; that is, of such members of society as he is likely to have concerns with; and as a means of it, either their love or their esteem, or both: and as a fruit of it, of his being in the way to have the benefit of their spontaneous and gratuitous services. These may likewise be called the pleasure of good repute, the pleasure of honour, or the pleasures of the moral sanction. (VII, 36)

Although development cannot be explained solely in utilitarian terms, these social variables, nevertheless, are important because they reveal the role of the local community in assessing, acknowledging or disapproving of somebody's success. Successful individual endeavours represent the result of a complex interplay between individual values and uneasiness in Mises's sense, and the values that shape a local group and its expectations (Mises 2007, 11–30). Success may indeed be individual, but it is meaningful only in the community. Its maintenance implies certain liabilities on the part of those who are considered successful, such as spreading knowledge and information or providing support to peers. Collective representations of what is considered good and important in life equally matters, becoming values that are represented through the influence of exemplary persons (Robbins 2015, Robbins and Sommerschuh 2016, 7–8). These people in fact shape the community and impose new standards, unlike state strategies and plans that in the local context seem abstract and distant. An agricultural engineer from the Kovin municipality confirmed the importance of exemplary people in the local community, having observed through his work that better-off peasants spread information willingly, supported farming novices and served as role models for others in the village. Their success not only created positive externalities for other people but also for the gradual improvement of agriculture in the community.

Thriving that occurs as a combination of individual and collective virtues can, as in the example of Gaj, explain the paradox of why agriculture is slowly growing on the one hand, while state measures for agriculture and rural development are facing a continuous collapse on the other. Statistically, Serbian agriculture on average maintains the trend that was first identified back in 2010 (Volk et al. 2010). Serbia has a better export–import ratio in comparison to neighbouring Croatia, which is receiving higher agricultural subsidies. Serbia has a positive agri-food trade balance, while other Balkan countries are net importers. Each of these states except Serbia has 'run a trade deficit in agri-food goods with the EU 27 over recent years, and except for FYR Macedonia, this deficit shows an increasing tendency' (Volk et al. 2010, 22–5). This certainly could not be the result of subsidies that were introduced in 2006 in Serbia. On the other hand, when agricultural subsidies reached their financial peak in 2012, two years after Volk et al.'s (2010) report, they made only 8 per cent of the gross income of middle-sized peasants. In later years, the trend of further reductions in subsidies has continued, as I already discussed in Chapter 4 under 'Subsidies', and this measure clearly did not contribute to the increased productivity of agriculture.

If not state institutions and plans, what then motivates rural development? McCloskey unravels the ideology of development saying that 'it won't suffice, as the World Bank nowadays recommends, to add institutions and stir' (McCloskey 2016b, 10). The ideas of thriving first occurred in the mindsets of ordinary people (McCloskey 2006). They attributed value to farming and imposed ethics on working the land and maintaining the household. With hard work comes motivation.

Table 6.1 Land utilized by agricultural households in Vojvodina (hectares).

No land	6,054
<=2 ha	68,683
2.01–5 ha	28,269
5.01–10 ha	18,959
10.01–20 ha	11,553
20.01–50 ha	8,563
50.01–100 ha	3,912
>100 ha	1,631
TOTAL	147,624

Source: *Statistical Yearbook of the Republic of Serbia* (2016, 240). Copyright SORS. Reproduced by permission.

Village and individual ethics create the climate in the village for things to happen in a certain way. The climate in the community spurs the enthusiasm for production – not because of the subsidies or measures for the support of livestock for example, but because of the value added to this work. It is true that Goran, who cultivates 120 ha, and Ivica, who cultivates 5 ha, cannot be compared and will never be monetarily equal. But both are driven by the same ideals which they practise in their lives: becoming a good and dignified householder. It is the same motivation that accounts for prosperity in both cases.

Let me illustrate further the point of thriving in Serbia, and concretely in Gaj, Beli Breg and Malo Bavanište. Table 6.1 presents data on the scope of land that is utilized by agricultural households in Vojvodina. Data like this, as well as GDP, are usually taken as indicators of rural development and are reproduced in numerous national and international policy reports and academic publications. A superficial look at the data might see it as pessimistic, as the largest number of households either do not have land or have less than 2 ha. The real situation and dynamics of land utilization I captured in Gaj and neighbouring villages does not, however, match the data in the table.

People who either have no land or have less than 2 ha (and make up approximately 45 per cent of the landlords in Vojvodina) do not actually represent the active agricultural population in Gaj and neighbouring villages. First, because those who do not have land do not deal with agriculture. Second, those who have less than 2 ha rarely work the land, either because it is not profitable or because they are retired. As already explained in Chapter 4, in 'Subsidies', people who possess up to 2 ha represent the core of land suppliers in Gaj, Beli Breg and Malo Bavanište, and rent it out to some of the three categories of producers that I extracted from my informal survey:

1. Producers such as Damjan and Ana, Ivica and Bogdan, who own and cultivate 2–5 ha of land, and combine agriculture with some additional or primary occupation. They cultivate their own land, and sometimes take additional land on lease. These make up 15 per cent of the village population.
2. People who cultivate 5.01–20 ha. Many people from this category take additional land on lease and diversify agricultural activities with livestock breeding, greenhouses or orchards, as in Maruška's case. These make up 15 per cent of the village population.
3. Vasa, Goran, Dragan and Rista are representative of peasants who usually combine their own and leased land, cultivating middle- and bigger-sized holdings of 20 ha and above. These make up 30 per cent of the village population.

The village context reveals that indicators of development cannot only be tangible statistical data on land utilization. In this chapter, I attempted to show that an area of cultivated land indeed does not ultimately determine the level of personal satisfaction or growth. Those who own or cultivate less than 10 ha, do not consider themselves unsuccessful, less developed or poor. On the contrary. Ana and Damjan, Maruška and Ivica think they are slowly thriving and living a dignified life. Their sense of growth is more related to variables that cannot be measured or precisely captured in policy reports. By imposing only tangible indicators of peasants' development such as utilized land and income (that may not match the real situation in the field, as is the case in my research area) there is a threat of perpetuating the image of peasants as victims of the market economy instead of competent and resilient participants and creators of the society. What policy data on rural development also cannot capture is that endogenous development is egalitarian in its principles, that is laissez-faire and autonomous, that is virtuous and spreads horizontally by involving diverse people whose competencies and approaches to agriculture differ. In other words, it is more inclusive than most state-led plans for rural development.

Who is rural development aimed at?

The officials and the local population from Gaj, Beli Breg and Malo Bavanište believe that the main problems of rural development in their areas are grounded in poor infrastructure, the lack of rule of law and clientelism. Rural development projects did not deal systematically with the problem of rural infrastructure. Examples from the lower and upper parts of Gaj and from Beli Breg demonstrate that the lack of asphalted roads represents a longstanding issue. Regional connections through highways are poor. Rivers that may be used for transportation of agricultural products are almost non-existent, even though the Danube flows through a significant part of Banat region and is only seven kilometres away from Gaj. An illegal dump and the lack of a sewage system make the environment unhealthy for people, animals and agriculture. Gaj, like almost every village in the Vojvodina region has an insufficient irrigation system, while the existing irrigation canals are poorly maintained. The village pastures do not have electricity, water or asphalted roads, which hampers the production and trade of milk and livestock.

The rule of law, as discussed in Chapter 3 ('Distrust') and Chapter 4 ('Trading of products' and 'Livestock breeding') is seriously compromised. Some of the longstanding issues are debt collection for peasants who have been damaged financially, who cannot rely on legal institutions even in cases when they win the dispute. Such events prevent trust and discourage peasants from seeking and believing in legal justice. In addition, clientelism privatizes the state and this affects not only the selective application of law but also market relationships. Some peasants that I interviewed believe that monopolies in Serbian agriculture are generated by the government, which has granted monopolies to a few favoured export/import companies who are close to the Serbian Progressive Party (SPP) and are its main financiers. The laws and regulations, the peasants believe, are made to protect the interests of monopolists and are for others futile. Some peasants blamed the lack of cooperation between themselves for producing this situation. Even though they personally may not be interested in joining associations, they, nevertheless, are aware that the lack of peasants' associations weakens not only their negotiation power and legal position but also impairs their participation in the market, and gives the advantage to monopolists. For example, without associations peasants are not able to import cheaper inputs and fertilizers or export their products. In comparison to other neighbouring countries, ever since 2010 Serbia has adopted customs barriers and has higher customs duties of up to 40 per cent (Volk et al. 2010, 26). As a result of various bans, peasants seldom sell their products through the legal channels, to buyers from the nearby Balkan countries. Clientelism is also mirrored in access to commodity reserves, and peasants agree that they are available only for the minority, usually the biggest producers who are also supporters and financiers of the SPP.

But clientelism, lack of rule of law and poor infrastructure are in fact, symptoms of a larger problem: a systematic approach to agriculture does not exist. For former minister of agriculture Dragan Glamočić, it is the greatest obstacle for rural development in Serbia.

> Agriculture is not essentially important to politicians even though most voters live in villages. [...] They issued the strategy [for rural development] only because it was necessary for the accession to the EU and not because it represents a genuine political interest. The lack of professionals is also one of the main problems because people who create agrarian politics are not related to agriculture. They go with every shift of political structures. The new ones who come bring along their people who are not professionals either and it goes like this for decades. We have several renowned agricultural institutions that are not connected with the ministry and that are not used as a resource of knowledge. Only some politically suitable professionals happen to be in the ministry, but this is the problem. Masses of people, thousands of people, could have worked together, and the state and the ministry could have benefited from their knowledge, but they stayed on the margins of the system. We have a situation where the whole agriculture depends on a few people. There is no communication between professionals, ministry, and the peasants. They don't listen to peasants. As long as we have disconnected system, anyone can become a minister, but he will not be able to change the situation. (Dragan Glamočić, 25 July 2017, Ministry of Agriculture of Republic of Serbia, Belgrade)

The perspectives of peasants resonate well with the one presented by the former minister. The biggest fear among peasants is that the systemic problems will remain untackled for a long time, because rural development is trapped in the clientelist networks and political marketing. Under such conditions, peasants often feel that the existing system does not enable them to thrive more than they currently do and are able to.

Let me try to answer the question from the beginning of this section: Who is rural development aimed at? Hobart advises us that 'it is useful to remember that development is big business' (Hobart 1993, 2). As long as rural development as a lucrative business concerns mostly governing elites and their clientelist networks but not the majority of rural population, we cannot talk about systematic rural development. Likewise, as long as clientelist networks thrive, they cannot generate development but instead will generate more clientelism, favouritism and rent-seeking. What the state envisions as a path to rural development is potentially very corruptive, in essence favouring the clique that develops by using public resources and institutions, while the rural population develops thanks to itself, in spite of or contrary to political circumstances and set goals. The rural population, thus, relies on its own internal drivers, which are divorced from state plans for the betterment of rural life. For the time being, it seems as if state and endogenous development run two separate lives.

7
Roma and rural development

Rural development cannot be understood completely without considering Roma, the third-largest ethnic group in Serbia. Roma make up approximately 10–15 per cent of the entire population in Vojvodina villages, where their poverty and marginalization are more evident and severe than elsewhere. Betterment of the Roma position in Serbian society has been envisaged by different government[1] and non-governmental projects that have been conducted continuously since 2000. Because of the high unemployment rate and poor education among Roma, the chief goal has been inclusion of Roma through education, access to health services, access to the labour market, political representation, and reduction of poverty. There are several reasons for the poor status of Roma in Serbian society. As in other parts of Eastern Europe, even though many Roma have had sedentary, rather than nomadic, lifestyles for centuries they have been permanently exposed to social, political and ethnic marginalization (Barany 2002, Giordano and Kostova 2006; Ruegg et al. 2006; Stewart 2002; Kovacs 2015). Their deprivation becomes intergenerational and turns into a continuous poverty trap (Bodewig and Sethi 2005). Moreover, their poverty becomes ethnicized and perpetuates the image of Roma as professional aid-seekers, lazy and unreliable persons among whom petty crime and theft are endemic, as an intrinsic ethnic feature (Schwarcz 2012). Informality also becomes 'the part of their assigned and assumed identity' which 'contributes to forming the stereotype that has stuck for years – portrayed negatively in terms of vagrancy and laziness, or positively as the expression of their freedom and detachment from 'bourgeois' values' (Ruegg 2013, 300). For these reasons, state policies in Serbia aim to facilitate the transition of Roma from informal to the state, formal, realms that would include public education, reported jobs, termination of child labour and marriages and social rehabilitation after criminal offences.

In Gaj, Roma make up 15 per cent of the overall population. Only a small number are self-employed, or are communal or guest workers. The significant majority are unemployed or work occasionally as day labourers in agriculture. Most Roma do not possess land, and they almost never obtain leased land in order to start agricultural activities. One of the reasons is that they lack not only the necessary agricultural mechanization and premises but also the skills for farming. Perhaps this is why they do not consider themselves to be peasants. Roma, however, belong to the social and economic environment of the village and contribute to rural development in ways that are not anticipated by the state programmes for rural development. Rural development programmes do not explicitly exclude Roma, but implicitly they do, as they mainly focus on the agricultural population to which the Roma do not belong.

But Roma find their own mechanisms to improve their condition. This chapter reveals that unemployed and poor Roma are not passive recipients either of state aid or of their daily predicaments. Romas' aspirations for better living have been underpinned by similar motivations and values to those that push peasants forward. Peasants and Roma strive to similar ends – preserving or acquiring property and dignity. These are the values that are strongly entrenched in the village system and represent criteria for the evaluation of the level of integration in the village society. The realization of these values, thus, has been a long-standing imperative for Roma. Romas' attempts to improve their social standing in Gaj differ in ways and approaches which are mostly determined by their existing condition in the village.

Roma in Gaj: on essentialization and differentiation

In Gaj, the social status of Roma differs from case to case. Roma are not a homogeneous group. Scholars rightly emphasize that essentialization of Roma produced interpretations which lack insights about their social stratification, existing conflicts or inter-group animosities (Podolinska 2017, Stewart 2013, Barth 1975, Okely 1997). There are many layers of interpersonal differences and animosities among Roma that determine how Roma regard each other, on the one hand, and the external perception of them on the other.

Roma from Gaj differentiate between those who are so-called *Domaći Cigani* (Domestic Gypsies) and those who settled in the village relatively recently. *Domaći Cigani* have lived in the village for at least two centuries; they are assimilated into the dominant village culture; some of them have married ethnic Serbs, but rarely Hungarians or Czechs. It is often heard, both from Roma and non-Roma, that these long-settled Roma deny their Roma origin, and do not want to be associated with Roma culture whatsoever, which is why they declare themselves to be Serbs, Orthodox Christians and *Banaćani* (domestic people from Banat region). Political attempts during the late eighteenth century Austo-Hungarian empire to convert Roma from the region into new peasants (Neubaurer), and force them to cultivate the land, proved futile (Pavkovic 2009, 81). Rather than working in agriculture, *Domaći Cigani* used to work jobs that were considered marginal in the village, such as grave diggers, blacksmiths, broom makers or day labourers (see Pavkovic 2009, 69–121).

Over the years, their living conditions have improved significantly, and they mostly set up their households in the upper village (see Chapter 6). Some went to work abroad when Yugoslavia liberated the flow of the workforce and its migration to western Europe in the 1960s and 1970s (Banić-Grubišić 2011). They have since returned, either to spend their retirement years in Gaj or to start up small businesses. *Domaći Cigani* have little land and mostly do gardening, but not agriculture. Others work in the communal sector, run small businesses or still work abroad. *Domaći Cigani* are positively valued by other ethnicities in the village. They are sometimes also subject to envy, as one of my interlocutors, a retired Roma and former guest worker, emphasized:

> Today my friends can work as servants in my household, as I used to serve them when I was a little boy, and they envy me, but no one has asked me what I have been through and how much I struggled to earn the money. (Sima, May 2013, Gaj)

In Gaj in the lower village (see Chapter 6), the social and economic situation among Roma residents is more balanced. They built their modest houses only a couple of decades ago and mostly belong to the Orthodox denomination. They declare themselves to be Roma and Serbs interchangeably, sometimes even as *Cigani* (Gypsies). They maintain regular social ties with other Roma and ethnicities from the neighbourhood. Some of them do not speak the Romani language, but they mostly understand it. One small group of Roma are neo-Protestants and they exclusively identify as Roma and nurture their language. In the lower village, Roma are mostly social beneficiaries with a few exceptions. They diversify their income either by taking up seasonal work during the summer months, gleaning or collecting scrap metal, or are asylum seekers. However, even though they seemingly live similar lives and have similar incomes, according to my Roma interlocutor from the lower village, they are significantly different.

> Here live mostly Orthodox Christians. They celebrate *Gospojina*, *Aranđelovdan*, and *Sapasovdan* as village *slava*. There are no Roma Muslims in the village. We differentiate ourselves by our origin: there are Romanian Roma – *Banjaši*, *Cigani Čergari* [nomadic Gypsies] and so called *domaći* [domestic Gypsies]. Some of the Roma families who used to live as *Čergari* also live in the Roma quarter [in the lower village], near the Danube, and they still sell their daughters. (Đurđa, February 2013, Gaj)

This excerpt points to inter-Roma differences in their social and cultural adaptation to the sedentary life which presupposes relinquishing some of the features of Roma culture and adoption of the dominant Orthodox religion as well as new 'civilized' values such as schooling of children or ceasing the custom of teen marriage. Unlike Roma who have adopted 'civilization', *Čergari* who live in the same neighbourhood and have a sedentary lifestyle still preserve their tradition, which is why they are at the lowest hierarchy level and are considered inferior to the rest of the Roma from Gaj. But my extensive research in the village revealed that the diversity and social stratification of Roma matters only in the Roma quarter (lower village). Their mutual differences are irrelevant beyond the Roma communities in Gaj because they do not affect the dominant, outsiders', perception of Roma. Toša, a retired communal worker from Gaj, explained such paradox though the stigmatized perception of Roma in the village.

> Roma who live in this quarter are mostly from somewhere from Banat in Serbia or from Romania. They come, stay, and some of them work. Some of them have been here for two or three generations and they have almost or completely forgotten the Romani language. They mostly speak Serbian. […] But not all Roma are the same. I personally don't like when they are put in the same basket my daughter who finished school and some Roma who beg, who didn't spend a day at school. But, for the outside world we are all the same. Even if a Serbian is an alcoholic, a scam or lazy,

such a Serb is always better than the best *Ciganin* [a male Roma]. (Toša, July 2017, Gaj)

Such conditions inspire some of Roma to improve their status and attain social recognition from the broader society. Roma from the lower village represent the focus of my ethnography, which portrays practices related to the betterment of their livelihoods and attaining long-term goals: property, security and social recognition. The identity and social differences in their status, culture and living standards, thus, trigger different solutions for attaining the desired values. In improving their own living conditions, Roma often apply solutions that run contrary to government plans that are supposed to better integrate Roma in the system. *Asylum-seeking, religious conversion* and *gleaning* are not, of course, the only means of bettering their individual living conditions but are the most salient among those observed. These practices reveal how they affect inter-Roma relationships in the lower village, and the perception of Roma and their achievements by non-Roma residents.

Asylum-seeking

The first wave of Roma from Gaj who went to the European Union (EU) in order to seek asylum took place in 1999 and 2000, and until today this practice has remained a regular solution for many Roma who want to improve their living conditions. After the civil war in the territory of former Yugoslavia (1995) and the conflict in Kosovo (1999), Serbia is considered a relatively stable democratic and peaceful country whose citizens should not seek asylum. By signing the readmission agreement with the European Union in 2007, Serbia became obliged to take care of those Serbian citizens who enter the EU illegally. The asylum seekers from Serbia, among them Roma, go to some of the EU countries and seek asylum there based on ethnic discrimination. Yet, these countries often consider such requests ungrounded because it is believed that the discrimination of Roma in Serbia is less institutional than interpersonal and cultural. Without officially granted rights to stay in the EU, Roma become identified as illegal immigrants and are obliged to leave the EU. They consequently get banned from entering the EU for several years. But, after the expiration of the ban, a significant number of Roma, as indicated by my research fieldwork, had, as a rule, tried to repeat the same procedure.

Despite awareness about the strict asylum rules and hard access to the EU, my Roma interlocutors sought asylum not because they believed they would eventually get accepted by a foreign country, but rather because it has become a proven short-term strategy for the improvement of living conditions. There are three common rationales that play an important role in the decision of when and how to undertake asylum seeking.

Some Roma decide to seek asylum and to stay abroad from 3 to 6 months maximum, which is the necessary duration for the processing of their asylum applications until the point they are turned down. During this time, they mostly work illegally and in addition save up some money that foreign authorities provide them for food and housing. Before coming to the EU, they plan the route thoroughly, including the means of transportation and organization of the whole endeavour. Some Roma pay informal organizations to take them across the border, but it remains unclear whether this method also implies illegal crossing of borders.[2] Once they arrive at a destination, they either have an appointed person (a friend or relative) who guides them to the right institutions, or they have already been instructed at home as to where to go and how to present their case. Roma openly share their experiences, information and suggestions on social networks, where they post their videos, comments and the latest news related to asylum in the EU. Ivan, who attempted asylum-seeking, explained that shared personal experiences are a key factor when people decide in which country they will seek asylum.

> We mostly get in touch with our friends, neighbours, or cousins who are in Europe. This is much easier today because of the internet, Facebook, Viber and emails. I write to some people on Facebook who are in asylum to find out how it is there and how much they get paid. Then someone says that Norwegians turn asylum-seekers down, that Switzerland is hard to enter because of the borders, that asylum is best paid in Belgium, but the accommodation is bad, that France has the best conditions, but it is hard to get there. All in all, after we get information about which country is good, we organize ourselves and go. (Ivan, July 2014, Gaj)

In some other cases, when Roma from Gaj arrived in one of the EU countries they attempted to stay there for a longer period. Those are usually more experienced people who already know the law procedures and their rights. When they get denied the right to stay legally, they filed an appeal against the decision, and when they got denied again, they had the right to another appeal which when turned down meant they had to leave the country. The whole procedure, however, as my informants say may take longer than a year, which gave them time to work sporadically and save up more money.

Only for a tiny minority the asylum was not about the short-term strategy for obtaining cash, but about getting work permits and foreign citizenship. My interlocutors told me about their neighbours who in their attempt to achieve this goal were marrying EU citizens 'for the papers', but almost all transactions ended unsuccessfully because their alleged partners cheated them for money and reported them to the police or asylum authorities. As in other cases, they were sent home and got banned from entering the EU countries for several years.

Roma from Gaj who have experience with asylum consider it the most reliable way to achieve financial means and to support family members in their home country. Asylum provides an opportunity for them to attain their dreams of buying property and building a proper household. They sense they will symbolically get rooted in the village, the local culture and the people through having property and being seen as a 'decent' household. Asylum is, thus, not only an economic strategy but also a way for faster achievement of social recognition in the village. A few excerpts from interviews with my Roma interlocutors demonstrate that asylum intertwines social, economic and cultural dimensions, which largely motivates repeated attempts, even after being declined.

> I have worked only one month in my life as a registered worker. That is all I have ever worked officially in Serbia. I have been 18 years on an unemployment bureau and they have never found me a job. If I had a job, I would buy a house much sooner, I would apply for a loan and wouldn't bother with asylum. (Relja, July 2014, Gaj)

> Since the beginning of the European Union, Roma have lived better because of asylum. Before there was nothing, only great poverty. Now, people seek asylum, earn some money, return to the village and buy a house, land or car. […] The biggest problem is that there is no job here, no one looks at *Cigani*. For instance, no one thinks to offer a job to us. Everyone in the village scratches father's back [the political father, see Chapter 5]. You can't find a single person whom he didn't employ. Many got rich and built nice households thanks to him. But not a single *Ciganin* [male Gypsy] is employed in his company or in the mine. No one wants to employ us. That's why we

apply for asylum. […] If Roma are about to wait for this country to help them, they would starve. That's why we are wise people and go to foreign countries seeking asylum to earn money. (Soja, July 2017, Gaj)

I would like to live here. I feel best here. All the money I earn in the European Union I spend in my country. Sometimes I can't stand it. Asylum is very stressful, your head hurts, you fear constantly, think what will happen next with you and your family […] Of course, I would prefer staying here. This is my country. My mother is old and sick. Imagine if she dies and I'm in Europe and can't come to bury her or be with her. [Mirko continues after a short sigh.] I have always dreamed of having a big house, a car, a wife and a family.
J. D.: *Where did you want to build your household?*
Mirko: Here, of course. This is my country. You go abroad only to earn money. (Mirko, July 2017, Gaj)

While asylum-seeking may improve their living condition on the one hand, it increases social stratification among Roma in the lower village on the other. Almost all Roma who came back bought or adapted their old houses either in the old neighbourhood or in other parts of the village. Some of them first invested in bringing electricity and water to their households. With better financial prospects and a somewhat changed lifestyle, a few Roma wanted to distance themselves from the old neighbourhood and moved closer to the village centre. In the central village there are abandoned households that used to be in the hands of better-off peasants, now deceased, and whose children do not live in the village anymore and want to sell them off. These households are usually run down but they have kept the charm of traditional Banat dwellings. Unlike peasants from the village who are rarely interested in buying such properties, Roma have emerged as new buyers. When I visited the village in July 2017, I learned that several such properties had been sold to Roma who had been deported to Serbia after a rejected asylum application. Old Banat houses are currently affordable to Roma who want, geographically, to become assimilated with the central village. Steva, for example, recently arrived from asylum and bought a house near the centre. He admitted that he 'bought the house far away from *Cigani*', because his experience of living in Germany and knowledge of German had changed him. Steva felt as if he could not identify with Roma from the lower village anymore. Living among non-Roma, for him means embracing a different quality of family life and values. Although this tendency for

Roma to move from the lower village to be closer to the village centre is gradual, it is interesting to see how it changes the structure of a neighbourhood that was traditionally inhabited by non-Roma ethnicities. In perspective, it paves the way for the emerging new generation of *Domaći Cigani* (Domestic Gypsies) – assimilated Roma, who get accepted by the broader village community only when they split up with their tradition and culture, as was the case with *Domaći Cigani* who settled in Gaj a long time ago.

The cost of social stratification among Roma is sometimes manifested in a predictable way, as envy or hatred. A few Roma who had sought asylum abroad for the second or third time have been the targets of envy in the lower village, and reckon that their success with asylum has turned many Roma but also non-Roma against them. Because they were social beneficiaries in Serbia at that time, their neighbours intentionally reported their absence to the local Centre for Social Work. The Centre consequently had to temporarily cancel social benefits to them until they came back to Serbia. In such a way the envious neighbours prevented them from accumulating income at home while being away in a foreign country. The cut in social benefits income, or dealing with the envy of fellow villagers, are insignificant sacrifices in comparison to the long-term gain of Roma who come back from seeking asylum. They build or buy their own houses, some land, and some of them even start up small businesses. This enables a base for remaking their lives, unlike those Roma who do not try the risky and uncertain path of asylum-seeking.

Religious conversions

Religious conversions in Gaj are a relatively recent phenomenon. They started to occur in the late 1980s and intensified as of the 1990s onwards, predominantly among Roma from the lower village, although there are several Serbian families who converted from Orthodox Christianity to Adventism. The neo-Protestants, thus, present alternative denominations in the village apart from Orthodox and Catholic churches. The neo-Protestants (Adventists, Pentecostals, Baptists, Nazarenes, Christian Brethren and others), although established in the nineteenth and twentieth centuries, are usually understood as a new wave of religiosity in Serbia (Djurić-Milovanović 2012). This is a common phenomenon in Eastern Europe that occurred after the fall of communism when state control over religious life and church organization weakened, enabling the rise of nationalisms and religious proliferation (see Borowik 2006; Wanner 2007).

My Roma interlocutors have encountered neo-Protestant denominations in different ways. Some of them have experienced the new religion thanks to the preachers who come to Gaj to visit and serve their small communities.[3] Others came to know more about these denominations while away seeking asylum, during which they were also baptized. It is not known how many Roma and non-Roma in Gaj belong to a neo-Protestant denomination, because an official survey has never been conducted in the village and most of the data rely upon unreliable informal assessments.

There are approximately ten or eleven Roma who are baptized in one of the neo-Protestant churches, and five or six non-Roma who are baptized in the Adventist church. There are also people from the village who regularly attend services and live according to the church rules and raise their children in its religious spirit, but they are not baptized, and so are officially invisible on this side of the religious spectrum. The process of baptizing represents an individual decision within the neo-Protestant denominations. Unlike in the Catholic and Orthodox churches, where baptizing takes place at a young age without the consent of the new members of the community, in neo-Protestant church denominations, baptizing takes place only when adult, self-aware people express their readiness. Baptizing, however, does not represent the necessary condition for practising religion, or even preaching. My interlocutors agreed that the most essential thing for their brothers and sisters in faith was that they accepted the Bible and the word of the Lord. The new religion allows informal preachers and unconventional religious teachings in the village, and it enables neighbours, friends and relatives to informally gather and exchange their understanding of the Bible and the neo-Protestant ethics. The unconventionality that the alternative religiosity provides, exhorts sceptical attitudes toward formal neo-Protestant preachers. Two Roma neo-Protestants believers from the village express their scepticism but also concerns about the formal aspects of the neo-Protestant church, preaching and its organization.

> I was with Pentecostals but I don't belong to them nor to Adventists or Baptists. I am more for the pure word of the Lord and for the original Bible. My pastor, however, belongs to Pentecostals. I don't like when Pentecostals and Baptists film about the poverty and the poor people and later present this to their financiers. The money they get they keep for themselves instead of sharing it with the

poor people. They don't help me when I need help, whereas they preach the opposite. For example, yesterday I had to sort a full yard of *šapurina* [crowned parts of corn] and no one from the brothers and sisters thought to offer a hand, or at least to give me 500 RSD to find help. The main pastor, who preached in my yard and in my house, gets 700 euros salary and he never offers help. Those under him don't get anything. (Believer, July 2014, Gaj)

The difference between Adventists and Baptists is that Adventists don't help the poor. I was with them. They don't want to help them. They give all money to the pastor and not to the poor. He gets everything paid: pension and social contributions, even an apartment and food. While Evangelists and Baptists have similar views and beliefs, they help the poor and have an understanding for those who are sick and miserable. When Baptists see that you are theirs, that you are baptized, then they help you. Their goal is to work with the poor, to spread love and the word of the Lord to convert them. Yet many don't change their religion. Some *Cigani* [Gypsyies] are with them because of their self-interest. (Believer, July 2014, Gaj)

Although the neo-Protestant church indeed addresses mainly the poorest population in the village, it would be wrong to reduce their work to the instrumental reason of attempting to enlarge its congregation through the poor. Likewise, religious conversions in the village cannot be reduced only to the vulgar idea of pragmatic motivations on behalf of some Roma and non-Roma who use the church to improve their financial situation. As Podolinská (2017, 168–76) shows with the example of converted Roma communities in Slovakia, the conversion has caused numerous problems among converts and new struggles within the community. For the converts, their status became even worse than it was in the past. The new religiosity has caused identity and cultural separation from the old community. Converts felt excluded but also self-marginalized, because they have achieved transformations that others could not comprehend. Moreover, they turned their back on traditional religion, which caused fierce disputes in the village. A similar thing happened with Roma and non-Roma in Gaj, whose conversion and religiosity are contested by both the local religious authorities and the local population.

In February 2013, Adventists from Vojvodina organized a series of lectures to promote the beliefs and activities of the church, and to familiarize the population from Gaj with their religious principles.

During the four-day programme, they also addressed the popular stereotypes that many have about Adventists. The meetings took place in the Centre for Culture in the village. The Centre is near the Orthodox church, and every time the meetings started, at 6 p.m., the bells from the Orthodox church started ringing longer than usual. I would not have paid attention to it since I attended only the final meeting, but one of the participants who was present at all the meetings told me that this happened also on the previous days. Moreover, each day, a few people had briefly sabotaged the meetings by making noise and playing loud music in front of the Centre. Although these two acts of disruption indeed may be unrelated, they were not, nevertheless, spontaneous. In a further interview with the Orthodox priest, he admitted that he had ordered the bells to ring at 6 p.m. because he wanted to 'invite the local population to the evening prayer and discuss with them the activities of the sect next door and their intentions' (Priest, July 2013). The alternative denominations are acknowledged by the Serbian constitution. Yet in public discourse, they are often labelled derogatively, as 'sects'– as the local priest did, to create an atmosphere of fear and mobilize people around an alleged jeopardization of traditional religiosity. Later, the priest visited one of the Roma neo-Protestants who had been hosting services from the pastor in his yard to warn him that he was 'committing unpermitted sectarian activities for which he may end up in jail' (Believer, July 2017, Gaj). New believers have similar disputes with their neighbours and friends concerning their religion and beliefs. The broader community doubts their sincerity and argues that their conversion was inspired by lucrative reasons. Their belief is questioned and mocked, and taken as a joke in street gossip. Their religiosity becomes publicly devalued as dishonest, while they become ashamed and stigmatized.

Conversion for those who took this path is not merely a change of religion – it is much more. It implies crucial changes in lifestyle, attitudes, behaviour, beliefs and ethics. Roma converts acknowledge that they have learned to read and write thanks to the new religion. When they converted, they sought to overcome their illiteracy and so be able to read the Bible. One of the believers from Gaj explains his path to personal transformation in the following way.

> When I started to preach, I first asked my community to provide me with CDs and other video materials because back then I didn't know how to read. I first started to preach among children. Then I spoke with everyone: family, friends, neighbours. Whenever I can,

> I speak about the Lord. My motive is to help people who struggle with their poverty, troubles, revenge. I base my preaching on my life experience. People in Gaj live in great sin, poverty, and hatred. (Lay preacher, July 2017, Gaj)

Converting enabled others to remake their lives and start all over again. This does not mean that some of them became better off, but rather that new beliefs and ethics have been a deeply transformational experience that enabled them to embrace different lifestyles.

> Five years ago, I got hit by a car and barely stayed alive. Doctors released me from the hospital because they thought I was going to die. I lay in the bed and prayed. Slowly, I started to walk again. Then I was baptized in Belgrade in our church. When I started to walk again, my husband believed in the miracle and in the new God. He took off our old saint [an Orthodox saint] from the wall and got baptized in the Baptist church like me. My life has changed radically ever since I converted. I don't steal anymore, I don't lie. I feel much better. It wasn't hard for me to change these things and start living differently. Now, I live only from my own work. No more stealing. (Believer, July 2017, Gaj)

New believers also exercise positive attitudes about their Roma language, culture and their ethnicity. They insist on their Roma origin because they feel it is being embraced and valued by the alternative denominations. They have found an acceptance in the community where they can build a 'redefined Roma identity' (Podolinská 2017, 176), freed from negative and stereotypical images of Roma culture usually associated with vices such as smoking, drinking, stealing or promiscuity. They gained dignity, and their lives gained meaning, predictability and roots. This may not be enough to prosper but it paves the way for structural change, or at least for considering it.

One of the reasons why neo-Protestantism has become accepted by Roma also rests in modest expectations from the community and the church. One of the believers explained what keeps her attached to the new church.

> In the previous religion I had to figure out how to collect money and prepare *slava* [celebration of an Orthodox saint protector of the family] so that people in the village wouldn't laugh at me. I celebrated *Velika Gospijina*. But this God doesn't ask anything

special from me. Only to mention and praise him every day. (Believer, July 2017, Gaj)

As neo-Protestants reject idolatry and cults, practising religion is not costly, unlike Orthodox traditional customs such as village and household *slava* that demand financial investments and special feasts, which many Roma cannot afford. Neo-Protestantism, thus, enables believers to practise good household and individual virtues without expensive investments, and yet not to feel ostracized or ridiculed for not taking part in collective religious performances. What is more, the new religion enables them to keep faith and a sense of dignity.

Gleaning

The practice of gleaning in Gaj, as already discussed in Chapter 3 in 'Relationship toward the poor', provides a diversification of income of the poor, enabled by the consent of the landowner. But when gleaning is used as a cover to collect crops from neighbouring unharvested fields – that is, as a strategy for gaining unlawful profit without investing labour or money into production – it is considered theft. Here I focus only on gleaning in its original meaning, as a strategy for the diversification of income of the poor.

In Gaj gleaning usually refers to the gathering of the leftover crops in the fields, but it may also refer to gathering wood in state forests, or coal in Kovin mine that has been left behind by digger machines. Because of their chronic poverty, Roma are the most commonly known gleaners in the public discourse of the village, although poor non-Roma glean as well.

While gleaned coal or wood in state forests satisfies subsistence needs for heating and ends up directly in family consumption, gleaning of crops is an addition to the family budget. Roma sell the collected corn and rarely keep it for themselves, given that they do not have livestock to feed. This might be understood as a slight deviation from the custom because gleaning is originally meant to support the subsistence needs of the poor. But even though Roma sell the collected corn for a profit, the money from it ends up again in family consumption, so eventually comes back to the spirit of the custom. Apart from gleaning, some Roma from the village work as day labourers which increases their summer income, too. In conversation with Roma, I got the impression that they prefer gleaning to day labour because the wages they get from labouring are not satisfactory. Sometimes they need to travel to another village with organized transport, wake up early and be away from home for the whole day. On the other hand, peasants often complain that it is hard to find a day labourer among the Roma, because they usually do not want to work for low wages. Peasants explain this as a direct consequence of the social benefits Roma receive, which do not motivate them to work. Even though this may be part of the explanation, Roma prefer gleaning over day labour because it enables them to earn more than they potentially could with seasonal wages.

When Roma glean, sometimes there might be plenty of leftover corn and they need to employ all family members, including their children. The schoolteacher confirmed that gleaning is broadly practised among Roma as a summer strategy for income generation. During early summer, Roma parents come to ask the teacher's permission to let their children off school for a couple of days to help them in gleaning. In good years some Roma families would glean from four to five tons of corn and would sell it for 'nice money'. This money they either keep as savings or use for buying firewood. This, nevertheless, does not change the fact that many Roma live miserably most of the year, while only during summer months does their income get slightly higher. One of the Roma explained to me what her household income and expenses look like over the year.

> There are many Roma who steal, but there are also those who don't. We are among the latter. Many hardly live and they don't have any other options but to steal. One cannot live on social benefits, particularly not during winter when we have to pay for electricity and firewood. With 13,000 RSD [approximately 110 euros] that we get for social benefits we have to pay either for firewood or for the pig for the winter. We have to find 20,000 RSD [approximately 165 euros] for this. We don't have that money. The situation is somewhat better in the summer months. (Slavica, March 2013, Gaj)

The shopkeeper from the Roma quarter observed that the income of Roma increases during the summer, because they diversify it through collection of waste metal, day labour and gleaning, whereas in winter they rely only on social benefits and spend less. After some turbulent years when the custom was in crisis because of frequent field thefts, gleaning was difficult, and consequently this affected Roma's income and spending. But since 2016, the custom is slowly stabilizing again, and getting in line with the village normative expectations. The regained trust between the landowners and gleaners has opened a possibility for improvement of their condition, at least temporarily.

For Roma, gleaning is not only about the improved financial balance. It is about dignity too. It is true that this practice may not improve their financial situation in the long run, but the decent income they make during the summer, thanks to their invested and manifested labour, equips them with a feeling of dignity. Then, unlike in other periods of the year, they can invest in the consumption and festivities which take place in the village mostly in summer and which are important for maintaining the self-image of good householders. Such investing in social representation matters in the lower village, in the Roma quarter, just as much as in other parts of Gaj.

Does the state contribute to Roma wellbeing?

The state attempts to minimize Roma's vulnerability both on the local and national level by including them in an encompassing welfare system. Such an attempt is indirectly associated with the readmission agreement between Serbia and the EU. Serbia has been obliged to take institutional care of Roma who get deported from the EU. That means that deported Roma get automatically registered as social beneficiaries in the home country until – if ever – they get employment. Such a measure was necessary to prevent further illegal migrants from Serbia from seeking asylum in the countries of the EU. But the measure, however, has never really stopped the illegal migration, and nor has it improved the wellbeing of Roma in the long run.

The provision of state welfare and the expansion of its programmes have raised concerns among some scholars concerning crowding out informal welfare and ways of spontaneous organization, as can be well observed in the local context of Gaj. The arguments mainly focus on the negative effects of the growing state, where the responsibility for the poor gets delegated from the local community to the upper, state level, while the people become demotivated to participate in local life and local mechanisms of support and care. 'Rather than relying on private social networks, the welfare state's citizens rely on the state's responsibility to guarantee social benefits in times of need' (Gundelach et al. 2010, 631). Increased welfare gradually brings social decline because people lose the initiative to get involved in social interaction, which may also result in a passive civil society (see Di Tella and MacCulloch 2002; Gundelach et al. 2010; Cox and Jimenez 1992).[4]

In Serbia the main financier of social services remains the state or the local government, with over 55 per cent, while NGOs make up 23 per cent of the overall share in the provision of social services. Since 2008, the total number of social services financed by the local government has increased as well. The same is true for social beneficiaries. 'Since 2000, the number of recipients of insurance based benefits has almost doubled, regardless of the legal changes making effectuation of the rights stricter' (Vuković and Perišić 2011, 241). Likewise, as of 2000 there is a trend of an increasing number of NGOs that are financed by the state, which work particularly in domains of social protection of youth, Roma, gender equality and social exclusion (Vuković 2013, 67–72).

State welfare in Serbia, however, does not ensure the necessary integration of welfare beneficiaries with the broader community and the labour market. In the micro-society of Gaj this is quite visible. Apart from their feelings of resentment, people from Gaj usually question the effectiveness of state welfare. They commonly stress that Roma receive social benefits based on their ethnicity and that they do not want to work, even though they are capable of working. Such a perspective is confirmed by a social worker from Kovin municipality who reckons that the current system of social benefits does not create a supportive work environment for Roma.

> Together with unemployment benefits and subsidized prices for communal services and electricity, plus child benefit, maternity benefit, parental benefit, etc., they have enough regular income for living. If they need something in addition to this, then they find a way, they will work for a while. Some do not even need to work. They are absolutely demotivated to work. (Social worker, August 2014, Kovin)

The main fracture that the state welfare system caused, according to the local view, is that it impaired the local labour market. The lack of day labourers makes things seriously dysfunctional and problematic in the long run. I have witnessed when peasants were desperately looking for day labourers among Roma, but they were uninterested in work. The other side of the problem is that during the season Roma who work as registered day labourers may temporarily lose their social benefits, so taking up seasonal work may not be a good solution for most of them. The irony is that while Roma represents a significant work potential, the great number of day labourers actually come from different parts of Serbia and not from Gaj or nearby villages. Such a tendency in the long run may aggravate tensions and blame games between Roma and non-Roma and cause irreversible ruptures in the social connections between them that keep this village functional and mutually dependent.

The local community perceives almost all Roma from the lower village, except for *Domaći Cigani* (Domestic Gypsies), as being the main beneficiaries of state welfare. Apart from disdain, this perception also adds to the feelings of resentment in Gaj. It is commonplace that people accuse Roma of being free riders because they do not work and do not contribute to the state budget. Locals blame Roma for receiving social benefits for unemployment, child allowance, and for single parents, the ill and disabled, school-age children and students. Non-Roma feel that, unlike Roma, they did not get any supplementary social support when they may have needed it, even though they work and contribute to the state budget. Jovanka, a middle-aged administrative worker dealing also in agriculture, talking about her own experience, summarizes the common village resentment and objections towards the state support of Roma.

> I feel hurt because the state has always promoted the birth of children. I gave birth to three children, and I have never received child allowance for any of my kids. My kids are now grown-ups who work and pay taxes to this country. On the other hand, I admit it may be chauvinist, but Roma give birth to many children who they don't send to school, they don't work, they don't pay anything to anybody, and yet they get the most help from the state. In comparison to them, some Serbs now live worse than *Cigani* [in this context, it was meant as a derogatory term for Roma]. (Jovanka, July 2017, Gaj)

The essence of the village resentments rests in the perception of an unfair share of social provisions and unequal treatment of the needs of fellow citizens by the state. Such resentment to an extent affects disinterest among villagers in supporting Roma beyond the traditional arrangements such as gleaning. The common understanding is that the deep poverty of Roma should be the responsibility of the Centre for Social Work, not of the locals. I often heard people saying 'State created the problem with Roma, they should fix it', when referring to state welfare as a demotivating factor for work. In many consecutive interviews people expressed similar opinions that the village should not be responsible for Roma. One such was the president of the association of pensioners from Gaj. Referring to the functioning of the association's safety network, the president explained: 'We do not help Roma, although we have Roma members whom we treat equally. Other Roma [non-members] who ask for money or food from us, we direct to the Red Cross or to the Centre for Social Work' (President of the association for pensioners, July 2013, Gaj).

The case of Gaj shows to us that the more the state was intervening in improving Roma wellbeing, the more Roma were crowded out from local and informal welfare networks. At the same time, state social benefits did a bad favour to Roma in the context of the village, because their image has increasingly been connected to that of 'social parasites'. While state social support was meant to improve the social integration of Roma by bringing their and mainstream values closer together, eventually embedding Roma in the community through social relationships and activities and providing meaning, purpose and companionship, the state did exactly the opposite – it set Roma apart from mainstream society. In Gaj, as we can see, state support obviously did not help much with the social integration of Roma nor with the symbolic or material betterment of their livelihoods. State attempts, in other words, did not result in establishing the expected changes in local practices.

Do Roma contribute to rural development?

So, what can Roma do for themselves and for the village in the vicious circle made of institutional and local pitfalls? In the everyday life of Roma, the discrimination, which is social and cultural, but less institutional, manifests in a slim chance of finding gainful employment. It inevitably directs Roma to rely on state social support, which consequently impairs their social image in the village. As attaining the gainful employment is less possible, while relying on state social benefits is socially unfavourable, Roma in Gaj are left with a few options for improving their livelihoods. They, thus, reach out for the solutions that are in their context perceived as only realistic for improving their livelihoods and attaining property, dignity, and social recognition. Improvement of life of Roma through asylum, gleaning, and religious conversion, is not spectacular but it is visible, and when it is visible it in perspective may pave the way for acknowledging Romas' achievements in the local context.

Personal or material transformations of some Roma can be seen and potentially evaluated by the community through the improved condition in their households, families, behaviour, and lifestyle. Furthermore, each increase in Roma income, either through occasional jobs or starting up small businesses, means improved consumption in the village. Upgrading their living standards, either through buying or renovating their old houses, means Roma maintain the dynamics of the real estate market in the village and also create additional jobs for crafts- and tradespeople. All these improvements taken together, no matter how individual or informal they may be, are, in fact, small contributions to the wellbeing of the community, and the circulation of people and capital.

Although from the consumption balance point of view Roma clearly contribute to rural development, there is another question that should be answered. Are these individual improvements, that are important and transformative for persons and their families, powerful enough to change the negative image of Roma in the village? My evidence suggests that there is no correlation between the improved personal and material wellbeing of Roma and their image in society, which in general remains negative. This means that with the continuing negative image of Roma and general public distrust toward them, improvements of Roma condition are relevant only for their isolated community of the lower village in Gaj, but not much beyond it.

Notes

1 For example, the Strategy for social inclusion of Roma (https://pravno-informacioni-sistem.rs/eli/rep/sgrs/vlada/strategija/2022/23/1) and the Strategy for reduction of poverty (https://www.mei.gov.rs/upload/documents/nacionalna_dokumenta/strategija_siromastvo.pdf), as well as encompassing welfare programmes.
2 Most of my interlocutors knew someone who was turned away from EU borders, or experienced it themselves, because the custom authorities assumed they are trying to enter the EU as asylum-seekers. For this reason, they need to be very cautious when it comes to choosing the right border crossing and time.
3 Adventists and Baptists have their churches in Kovin and Belgrade. Since many Roma believers cannot afford frequent visits to these churches, preachers come to them in their villages, and organize services in informal settings, usually at the homes or yards of some of the believers.
4 Arguments for the 'crowding in' hypothesis stress that the state and informal safety nets complement each other. A more generous welfare state can contribute to better informal distribution of help to those in need (Morduch 1999). The cohesive principle that intertwines the state and informal safety nets facilitates the production of social capital and improves the infrastructure of civil society and the institutions (Rothstein 2001; Torpe 2003). There are many interesting pieces of evidence to support both approaches. But Lucas and Stark (1985) offer an alternative approach, according to which complete crowding out of informal welfare is unlikely, because social pressures, norms, self-interest, and altruism participate in its maintenance, regardless of the size of the welfare state.

8
Conclusion

Planning as a precondition of development

After the Second World War many national governments embraced the idea of development, which initiated new politics, new political discourse and new language that was supposed to bring order and standardize otherwise economically, politically and socially diverse regions. Before the appearance of development discourse, regions and countries were pursuing multiple internal, local and regional paths that were supposed to bring growth to communities and countries. The post-war mindset, however, imposed the idea that development should be under the exclusive care of the governments undermining multiple local ways and practices. Even 80 years after the Second World War, development figures as one of the most important political and local topics that is in the command of state institutions and international organizations. These bodies tend to govern development in a range of spheres and regions, from rural to urban.

Like every small country, Serbia reflects global trends. During the socialist times, but also as of 2000 when liberal democratization was supposed to bring political proliferation and divorce from socialist practices, the state has been imposing its role as the main planner for the betterment of rural life. Policymakers continue to believe that a change of rural livelihoods may be achieved mainly through plans and reforms. Such an institutionalist-driven mindset among not only Serbian but also international policymakers reveals a common thinking, that the replacement of old laws and regulations with new ones will improve their application. The idiosyncratic reasoning of policymakers, copied from their role models in the World Bank and international organizations, equates prosperity with the implementation of new regulations and the introduction of new bureaucrats.

The state planning of agriculture and rural life in Serbia, and pretty much everywhere else, apart from cherishing naïve ideas that the world does not move unless it is directed by a smart cohort of policymakers, conceals a profound truth about planning: it does not ensure success, and neither does the involvement of genuinely interested policymakers dedicated to achieving the set goals. It has been almost a rule, as Haripriya Rangan (2000) persuasively demonstrates in her book *Of Myths and Movements,* that 'development [...] has suffered from both bureaucratic apathy and the "plains" mentality of administrators who ... are ignorant about the region, display superficial understanding of its economy and society, and lack a genuine commitment to solving the problems faced by local communities' (168). With such an attitude, even the best-intentioned plans are destined to fail. Yet, in the rural development discourse, the failure is blamed on ill-conceived plans and inconsistently implemented reforms. And policymakers again attempt to find better institutional solutions, which for the past 80 years have taken many forms, but have not found yet the secret balance between state intervention and local compliance. And this is because the policymakers did not change the highly hierarchical pattern of planning, which although masked remains fundamentally the same: the state plans, the local adopts.

The pattern in fact reflects the modernist approach engraved in development plans that contain the idea that policymakers and state institutions, by assuming the position of power, are rightfully entitled to change the behaviour and organization of lives of people who are deemed inferior, undeveloped and less knowledgeable. The planned change is sometimes imposed by force and political mobilization, and sometimes by the application of tools incorporated in diverse state institutions which aim to confront the local population with their backwardness, as one of the notable critics of development discourse Tania Li (2007) points out in her book *The Will to Improve.*

Yet, there is another problem about the development discourse which even notable criticizers such as Haripriya Rangan and Tania Li rarely take into consideration. While they question the concept of development and its roots, as well as the dimension of its historical and practical implementation, they do not question the concept of planning embedded in the idea of development which, in essence, causes all the later problems we talk about. In this book I tried to emphasize that the problem of development lies in the systematic narrowing down of available alternatives of potential carriers of development, and acknowledging their role in enabling development. We gradually ended up in an absurd situation where both political and theoretical horizons became blurred as they cannot see the alternative to planning. In the *Laissez-Faire Peasant* I have attempted to widen the perspective and inspire conversations about alternatives to planning. I have done so by looking at and explaining development from the perspective of those who are, in the discourse of planned rural development, recognized only as exclusive recipients of development or as its victims. That is, peasants, and their mechanisms to enable spontaneous development on the ground.

Development on the ground

Since the very beginning of my research journey one thought has accompanied me all the way: the idea that peasants are largely portrayed as weak and deprived despite the massive failures of rural development projects in Serbia, but also elsewhere. Although peasants are not unrelated to institutional surroundings, one may implicitly conclude this from the literature review. The existing limitations in a theoretical approach to the peasantry point to the fact that aspects such as individual and local values get overlooked in response to peasants' low compliance to the rural development plans. Rather, attention is given to the explanation of the institutional factors that hamper cooperation between the peasants and policymakers. Recognition of the existing theoretical limits, however, may open new avenues in peasant and rural development studies, particularly if the focus shifts from the importance of planning and institutional bottlenecks to the importance of the symbolic components of peasants' livelihoods. It may even inspire reconsideration of power relations in which peasants are traditionally portrayed as weak. In this book, I argued that peasant's ethics have a strong influence on shaping the development of village life but also in redirecting the state plans for rural development.

The peasants' ethics deserves more theoretical attention than it has currently. Slight progress has been made by the recent introduction of the concept of the 'good farmer' that in essence explains the cultural dimension of farming and social change. In the important book *The Good Farmer – Culture and Identity in Food and Agriculture* Burton et al. (2021), demonstrate that the concept of good farmer influences a variety of contexts from the landscape, environment and gender relations, to political resistance. They examine the implicit notions of what is good, which are engraved in both the farming practices and identities of farmers, especially in the context of a complex relation between the farmers and environmental management.

The Laissez-Faire Peasant attempts to, among other things, advance the concept of the good farmer and explain how the combination of the self-perception of peasants, their land ownership, autonomy and dignity, and village ethics – manifested through the laissez-faire mentality – is intrinsically related to determining the success of rural development politics in Gaj, Beli Breg and Malo Bavanište. When the complex web of values and attitudes of villagers intermingles with the requirements of rural policies, most peasants adjust policies to their own liking and abandon those that are not relevant in managing their own life and business. The evidence from my research field also suggests that the same bundle of values determines spontaneous development in the village context.

The local pursuit of such virtues as autonomy and dignity, changes the course of state agricultural reforms, and at the same time is responsible for the thriving of local communities. Peasants embrace and internalize local values that make their conduct recognized by the community. Local exemplary persons matter too. Peasants follow in their footsteps. In such a context, state incentives and policies are of secondary importance because although they materially and formally stimulate successful individuals they do not trigger them.

This book demonstrates through its variety of examples that local arrangements that have evolved around land ownership and spontaneous social order have brought rural policies such as agricultural subsidies, crop insurance, compulsory agricultural pension insurance or establishing producers' associations, among others, to complete failure. Local practices have changed the flow in subsidies funding, shifted its main purpose and made the agriculturally inactive population important recipients of subsidies. Subsidizing peasants on the one hand, and their evasion of state taxes and social contribution on the other, might generate what is called a free rider problem. Looking from the outside, the peasants are free riders because they use subsidies but they do not contribute to society through taxes and social contributions in return. But this is only true if seen from a narrow perspective. The local spontaneous social order and free riding of peasants made the subsidies inclusive for the non-agricultural population, thanks to which many of them have a more decent living than was the case before.

Likewise, individual perceptions of risks and peasants' attitudes toward the state has caused a massive disregard of crop insurance, which has led to a modest market of agricultural insurance and a low number of insured households. Similarly, land ownership, family and kinship arrangements were decisive for peasants' decisions not to contribute to compulsory agricultural pensions, which made them one of the biggest debtors to the state. Direct and unreported sales that peasants practise continue to dominate, despite state attempts to curtail the unreported money flows. Sophisticated peasants' understanding of cooperation led to a blatant failure of producers' cooperatives and associations, despite generous subsidies provided by the state.

The peasants' responses to state reforms and policies demonstrate what is important in the local context and what makes them so resilient: preserving autonomy through land ownership and dignity. The (land) ownership embodies the whole spectrum of values that define life in the village and attributes that lead to social recognition. These values are extended to the broader village population, including Roma. In the scholarship on rural development, it is rarely discussed in what ways non-agricultural, including vulnerable, rural populations are integrated in rural development, either conceived as formal or informal attempts. In Serbia, state rural development in its current form includes, primarily, peasants who are experienced in farming and have capital to start with. In contrast, Roma and their wellbeing are not tied to state rural development plans, because it is believed that they first need to be socially and economically stabilized through state social policies and social inclusion. In this book, I have attempted to show that Roma contribute to rural development in alternative ways through asylum, gleaning and religious conversions, which enable some of them to obtain property and social recognition in the village, and enhance their betterment, which the too-constrained state social policies cannot create nor sustain.

The examples of peasants' and Roma practices bring closer the argument that individual and local values matter not only for fulfilling self-interest but also for establishing affective connections that maintain community interests. They spontaneously run life in the village and manage needs, disputes and conflicts. In the case of gleaning, for example, the local state proved weak in resolving the problem of field thefts. When the peasants took over the responsibility for preventing field thefts, they managed to restore the custom of gleaning. In other words, the local engagement of people and their self-organization attained rehabilitation of mutual trust and the dignity of the landowners, but also of the dignity of the poor. Likewise, the village ethics maintain order, ensure trust transfer (in case of *veresija* or buying and selling practices) and harmonize relationships among the local population, in spite of institutional regulations or expectations. This is particularly important in situations that involve the rural poor, as explained in Chapter 4.

Life in Gaj, Malo Bavanište and Beli Breg, as we can see by now, is subjected to the web of individual and local values and shared attitudes that represent a regulatory framework, which most of the time efficiently maintains order, enables economic cooperation, forward looking and thriving; rewards hard work, and enables the resilience of the village population. The framework also functions to protect the interests of local people and provide conditions for their fulfilment without or despite state regulations.

Why rural development cannot be planned

Rural development projects and agricultural reforms in various countries have been going on for decades, and peasants, contrary to numerous expectations, have neither vanished nor transformed into farmers. Parallel to this, peasants, in historical, ethnographic, economic or sociological accounts, have been continuously portrayed as weak and disadvantaged groups, as if they lived in a vacuum while agricultural reforms and policies were collapsing around them.

The same happened in Serbian countryside. While policies were collapsing one after another over the past several decades, no one really asked what if these reforms failed because of the peasants, and not because of imperfect plans and strategies, or laws. What if non-tangible components such as individual and local values hampered the embracing of the planned change? We could not know why the policymakers' goals and local values do not synchronize – or when they do, why. We could not know what are the crucial variables that determine the level of cooperation of peasants with state rural policies.

The only way to find answers to these questions was to conduct research among the rural population and comprehend their view, rarely included in such discussions, that it may eventually explain the overwhelming discrepancies between state rural plans and local realities. The evidence from field research in Gaj, Malo Bavanište and Beli Breg, and thorough analyses of rural development plans after 2000, suggests two major conclusions. First, policies are most of the time run with a misleading understanding of change. It is believed that change only occurs when it is imported through plans and reforms, and then seeded in the region through the dynamic interplay of state bureaucrats and local actors. The examples of three Serbian villages confute such interpretations. In Gaj, Beli Breg and Malo Bavanište, people develop through their aspirations for maintaining or enlarging their land ownership and properties. It creates the phenomenon of social imitation. There is an ethic of becoming a better, not necessarily richer, peasant – even though these are not mutually exclusive categories – and through that the land is better cultivated and cared for. Social imitation, in a word, creates a virtuous circle in which peasants through mutual affection, cooperation and admiration, push each other to higher achievements. Becoming a dignified peasant implies extrapolating behaviour which cannot only be good for individuals, but it must also be beneficial for the wider community. People's own understanding of life, land ownership, and business, as well as the hopes for a desirable life bring change. In such a context, the outsider's vision of the betterment is not relevant.

Furthermore, conceptualizations of state rural development remain contested in local settings as they do not share crucial values and attitudes found in the daily practices of peasants. Even though rural development has been one of the priorities of Serbian government since 2000, the local and national elite are not genuinely interested in improving what the rural population itself regards as most needed. Instead of the improvement of the road and transport network, irrigation systems, rule of law or liberalization of markets, government efforts have been focused on visible spending such as subsidies, various stimulations and direct investments, and also on incentivizing the expansion of clientelist networks. The state realization of rural development eventually unfolds its corruptive potential by favouring the circles close to the centre of political power. If the structural improvement of political and economic conditions remain sidelined, rural development will occur, but not as systematically as the government expects. Development will be rather a result of isolated individual or regional achievements that depend on local mechanisms that steer development, as is indeed the case today.

We can only speculate as to whether Serbian peasants will need any rural development stimulus if the structural political and economic changes get accomplished. I believe not. Perhaps it will provide them with more security and predictability. Likewise, with an improved rural infrastructure it could be expected that the development of rural regions will become more encompassing and stable. But even in such a hypothetical scenario, individual and local values will continue to play a major role in stirring the aspirations for prosperity because they define the place in which the peasants live their everyday lives.

The second conclusion from the fieldwork research and analyses of rural development plans since 2000 is that development planning is not possible in such complex fields and diverse settings as agriculture and rural life. In the case of Serbia, the intermingling of the two happens in conditions that are not favourable for creating systematic growth, as I have already pointed out, and which create institutional dysfunctionalities, low public trust and a high degree of informality. Even in the scenario of the most carefully planned agricultural policies it is questionable whether it would create growth. This book shows that change and progress cannot be planned, forced or instructed by bureaucrats and policies. Similarly, Banerjee and Duflo (2019) illuminate the unpredictability of growth and demonstrate that it does not really depend always on mainstream factors such as trade liberalization, investments, low taxes, technological innovation, or a technologically equipped and educated population, as are usually given as an explanation of growth in different economic theories. Banerjee and Duflo argue not only that growth is hard to measure, but also that 'it is even harder to know what drives it, and therefore to make policy to make it happen' (Banerjee and Duflo 2019, 166).

In this book, I propose an alternative to the mainstream understanding of what might trigger development, because in rural studies we still do not have a satisfactory answer to the question of why some rural development projects succeed and others do not, even in regions which sometimes share similar features. Since standard explanations of development economics, as Banerjee and Duflo indicate, are of little help, I was led to explore other factors, that are not taken seriously in rural and development studies. In Gaj, Beli Breg and Malo Bavanište I discovered that development and a sense of improvement are strongly related to peasants' ethics, which are embedded in the ontology of land ownership. The ontology of land ownership generates a spontaneous system of informal institutions and norms that meets not only self-interest but also community wellbeing. The ontology of land ownership enables peasants in their rural universe to spontaneously create their own progress, impose new standards and change themselves accordingly. The ontology of land ownership also implies that farming is a labour of love, which relates similarly to many farming communities across the globe. By chance, on a highway between Pennsylvania and Ohio, I once took a picture of the front of the farm silos, where under the big white cross was a message 'Farmers at heart'. The message captures deeper layers of meaning in which peasants are not only utility maximizers, but are also virtuous, skilful and competent in farming and managing risks. It is love for farming, among other things, that forms the basis of their competence and virtue.

Gaj, Beli Breg and Malo Bavanište boil down to the case that peasants' ethos, understanding of life and their nerve are all suited to bring achievement, whereas state planning often hampers their creativity, aspirations and spontaneous order. The peasants are their own bosses, and they do not need to be directed or taught. As François Legendre said a long time ago on behalf of French merchants, leave them alone: laissez-faire, laissez-passer.

References

Acheson, J. M. 1994. 'Welcome to Nobel country: A review of institutional economics'. In *Anthropology and Institutional Economics*, edited by J. M. Acheson, 3–42. Lanham, MD: University Press of America.
Acheson, J. M. 2002. 'Rational choice, culture change, and fisheries management in the Gulf of Maine'. In *Research in Economic Anthropology* 21: 133–59.
Acheson, J. M. 2006. 'Institutional failure in resource management'. *Annual Review of Anthropology* 35: 117–34. https://doi.org/10.1146/annurev.anthro.35.081705.123238.
Acheson, J. M. 2015. 'Private land and common oceans'. *Current Anthropology* 56 (1): 28–55.
Adie. R. F. and G. E. Poitras. 1974. *Latin America: The politics of immobility*. Englewood Cliffs, NJ: Prentice-Hall.
Altieri, M. A. and V. M. Toledo. 2011. 'The agroecological revolution in Latin America: Rescuing nature, ensuring food sovereignty and empowering peasants'. *Journal of Peasant Studies* 38 (3): 587–612.
Appadurai, A. 1986a. 'Introduction: Commodities and the politics of value'. In *The Social Life of Things: Commodities in cultural perspective*, edited by Arjun Appadurai, 3–63. Cambridge: Cambridge University Press.
Appadurai, A. 1986b. 'Theory in anthropology: Center and periphery'. *Comparative Studies in Society and History* 28 (2): 356–61.
Apthorpe, R. 1997. 'Writing development policy and policy analyses plain or clear: On language, genre and power'. In *Anthropology of Policy: Critical perspectives on governance and power*, edited by C. Shore and S. Wright, 34–45. Abingdon: Routledge.
Arce, A. and N. Long. 1993. 'Bridging two worlds: An ethnography of bureaucrat–peasant relations in Western Mexico'. In *An Anthropological Critique of Development: The growth of ignorance*, edited by M. Hobart, 179–208. Abingdon: Routledge.
Archer, R. and K. Rácz. 2012. 'Šverc and the Šinobus: Small-scale smuggling in Vojvodina'. In *Subverting Borders: Doing research on smuggling and small-scale trade*, edited by B. Bruns and J. Miggelbrinkn, 59–85. Wiesbaden: VS Verlag.
Arsić, S., N. Kljajić and P. Vuković. 2012. 'Cattle stock and the analyses of total meat production in the Republic of Serbia'. *Economics of Agriculture* 59 (1): 99–115.
Bakić-Hayden, Milica (1995). 'Nesting Orientalisms: The case of former Yugoslavia'. *Slavic Review* 54 (5): 917–31.
Banerjee, A. V. and E. Duflo, 2019. *Good Economics for Hard Times: Better answers to our biggest problems*. New York: Penguin Random House.
Banfield, C. E. 1967. *The Moral Basis of a Backward Society*. New York: Free Press.
Banić-Grubišić, A. 2011. 'A different guest worker story: Roma guest workers – a transnational minority in transmigration'. *Issues in Ethnology and Anthropology* 6 (4): 1035–54.
Barany, Z. 2002. *The East European Gypsies: Regime change, marginality, and ethnopolitics*. Cambridge: Cambridge University Press.
Barsukova, S. and A. Ledeneva, 2018. 'Concluding remarks to Volume 2: Are some countries more informal than others? The case of Russia'. In *The Global Encyclopaedia of Informality*, Volume 2, edited by A. Ledeneva, 487–93. London: UCL Press. https://doi.org/10.14324/111.9781787351899.
Barth, F. 1966. *Models of Social Organization*. Glasgow: Royal Anthropological Institute.
Barth, F. 1967. 'Economic spheres in Darfur'. In *Themes in Economic Anthropology*, edited by R. Firth, 149–73. London: Tavistock Publications.
Barth, F. 1975 [1955]. 'The social organisation of a pariah group in Norway'. In *Gypsies, Tinkers and other Travellers*, edited by F. Rehfisch, 285–99. London: Academic Press.
Bennett, J. W. 1966. 'Further remarks on Foster's "Image of Limited Good"'. *American Anthropologist* 68 (1): 206–10.

Bentham, J. [1781] 2000. *An Introduction to the Principles of Morals and Legislation*. Reprint. Kitchener: Batoche Books.

Berg, R. L. 1975. 'Land: An extension of the peasant's ego'. *Anthropological Quarterly* 48 (1): 4–13.

Bernstein, H. 2013. 'Food sovereignty: A skeptical view'. Conference paper for discussion at: *Food Sovereignty: A critical dialogue*. International Conference, Yale University, September 14–15, 2013.

Bernstein, H. and T. J. Byres. 2001. 'From peasant studies to agrarian change'. *Journal of Agrarian Change* 1 (1): 1–56.

Blackburn, J. and J. Holland. 1998. *Who Changes? Institutionalizing participation in development*. London: Intermediate Technology Publications.

Blanton, R. E. and L. F. Fargher. 2016. *How Humans Cooperate: Confronting the challenges of collective action*. Boulder: University Press of Colorado.

Bodewig, C. and A. Sethi. 2005. 'Poverty, social exclusion and ethnicity in Serbia and Montenegro: The case of the Roma'. https://documents.worldbank.org/en/publication/documents-reports/documentdetail/855151468102865205/poverty-social-exclusion-and-ethnicity-in-. Accessed 10 March 2018.

Bogdanov, N. 2007. *Small Rural Households in Serbia and Rural Non-farm Economy*. Belgrade: UNDP.

Bokovoy, M. K. 1997. 'Peasants and partisans: The politics of the Yugoslav countryside, 1945–1953'. In *State–Society Relations in Yugoslavia, 1945–1992*, edited by M. K. Bokovoy, J. A. Irvine and C. S. Lilly, 115–38. New York: St. Martin's Press.

Booth, J. A. and M. A. Seligson. 1979. 'Peasants as activists: A reevaluation of political participation in the countryside'. *Comparative Political Studies* 12: 29–59.

Borowik, I. 2006. *Religions, Churches and Religiosity in Post-Communist Europe*. Krakow: Zaklad Wydawn Nomos.

Brass, T. 1991. 'Moral economists, subalterns, new social movements, and the (re-) emergence of a (post-) modernized (middle) peasant'. *Journal of Peasant Studies* 18 (2): 173–205.

Brass, T. 1997. 'The Agrarian myth, the "new" populism and the "new" tight'. *Journal of Peasant Studies* 24 (4): 201–45.

Bridger, S. and F. Pine. 1998. *Surviving Post-Socialism: Local strategies and regional responses in Eastern Europe and the former Soviet Union*. Abingdon: Routledge.

Burawoy, M. and K. Verdery. 1999. *Uncertain Transition: Ethnographies of change in the postsocialist world*. New York: Rowman and Littlefield.

Burt, R. 1992. *Structural Holes: The social structure of competition*. Cambridge, MA: Harvard University Press.

Burton, R. J. F. 2004. 'Seeing through the "good farmer's" eyes: Towards developing an understanding of the social symbolic value of "productivist" behaviour'. *Sociologia Ruralis* 44 (2): 195–215.

Burton, R. J. F., J. Forney, P. Stock and L. A. Sutherland. 2021. *The Good Farmer: Culture and identity in food and agriculture*. Abingdon: Routledge.

Burton, R. J. F., C. Kuczera and G. Schwarz. 2008. 'Exploring farmers' cultural resistance to voluntary agri-environmental schemes'. *European Society for Rural Sociology* 48 (1): 16–37.

Buttel, F. and H. Newby. 1980. *The Rural Sociology of the Advanced Societies: Critical perspectives*. Totowa, NJ: Allanheld, Osmun & Co.

Byres, T. J. 1979. 'Of neo-populist pipe dreams: Daedalus in the Third World and the myth of urban bias'. *Journal of Peasant Studies* 6 (2): 210–40.

Caldwell, M. L. 2009. *Food and Everyday Life in the Postsocialist World*. Bloomington: Indiana University Press.

Cancian, F. 1961. 'The southern Italian peasant: World view and political behavior'. *Anthropological Quarterly* 34 (1): 1–18.

Cartwright, A. 2001. *The Return of the peasant: Land reform in post-communist Romania*. Abingdon: Routledge.

Castelot, E. 2015. 'Laissez-faire, laissez-passer'. In *Dictionary of Political Economy* Vol. II, edited by R. H. Inglis, 534–5. Cambridge: Palgrave.

Chambers, R. 1983. *Rural Development: Putting the last first*. London: Longman.

Chibnik, M. 1980. 'Working out or working in: The choice between wage labor and cash cropping in rural Belize'. *American Ethnologist* 7 (1): 86–103.

Chibnik, M. 2011. *Anthropology, Economics and Choice*. Austin: University of Texas Press.

Cleaver, F. 2001. 'Institutions, agency and the limitations of participatory approaches to development'. In *Participation: The new tyranny?*, edited by B. Cooke and U. Kothari, 36–55. London: Zed Books.
Cogeca. 2010. *Agricultural Co-operation in Europe. Main issues and trends*. Brussels: Cogeca.
Cohen, A. P. 1979. 'The Whalsay croft: Traditional work and customary identity in modern times'. In *Social Anthropology of Work*, edited by S. Wallman, 249–67. London: Academic Press.
Cohen, P. 1967. 'Economic analyses and economic man: Some comments on a controversy'. In *Themes in Economic Anthropology*, edited by R. Firth, 91–117. London: Tavistock.
Cole, W. John. 1985. 'Problems of socialism in Eastern Europe'. *Dialectical Anthropology* 9 (1): 233–56.
Commons, J. R. 1990. *Institutional Economics: Its place in political economy*. New Brunswick, NJ: Transaction.
Cooke, B. and U. Kothari (eds). 2001. *Participation: The new tyranny?* London: Zed Books.
Cosmin, R. 2009. 'Border tricksters and the predatory state: Contraband at the Romania–Serbia border during the Yugoslavian embargoes'. *Focaal* 54: 49–63.
Cox, D. and E. Jimenez. 1992. 'Social security and private transfers in developing countries: The case of Peru'. *World Bank Economic Review* 6 (1): 155–69.
Cramer, J. K. 2016. *The Politics of Resentment: Rural consciousness in Wisconsin and the rise of Scott Walker*. Chicago: University of Chicago Press.
Ćurković, V. 2013. 'Finansijska Podrška Države Proivodnji Organske Hrane: Velika razvojna šansa Srbije'. PhD thesis. Belgrade: Univerzitet Singidunum.
Čurović, O. 1998. 'Agrar i svojinska transformacija'. In *Agroekonomika* 27, 3–9. Novi Sad: Institut za ekonomiku poljoprivrede i sociologiju sela, Poljoprivredni fakultet.
Dalton, G. 1969. 'Theoretical issues in economic anthropology'. *Current Anthropology* 10 (1): 63–102.
Dargan, L. and M. Shucksmith. 2008. 'LEADER and Innovation'. *Sociologia Ruralis* 48 (3): 274–91.
De Soto, Hernando. 2001. *The Mystery of Capital: Why capitalism triumphs in the west and fails everywhere else*. London: Black Swan Books.
Diković, J. 2014. 'Neither peasant, nor farmer: Transformations of agriculture in Serbia after 2000'. *MARTOR* 19: 149–62.
Diković, Jovana (2015). 'The practices of landownership in Vojvodina: the case of Aradac'. In *Property in East Central Europe: Notions, institutions, and practices of landownership in the twentieth century*, edited by Hannes Siegrist and Dietmar Muller, 268–89. New York: Berghahn Books.
Diković, J. 2016. 'Gleaning: Old name, new practice'. *Journal of Legal Pluralism and Unofficial Law* 48 (2): 302–21.
Diković, J. 2017. 'Tradicijsko privređivanje'. In *Etnologija i antropologija: 70 izabranih pojmova*, edited by Lj. Gavrilović, 332–8. Belgrade: Službeni glasnik.
Diković, J. 2023. 'Prudent resilience of farmers'. *Journal of Rural and Community Development* 18 (3): 153–74.
Dimić, Lj., D. Stojanović and M. Jovanović. 2009. In *Srbija 1804–2004: Tri viđenja ili poziv na dijalog*, 13–115. Belgrade: Serbica.
Di Tella, R. and R. MacCulloch. 2002. 'Informal family insurance and the design of the welfare state'. *Economic Journal* 112 (481): 481–503.
Djurić-Milovanović, A. 2012. '"How long have you been in the truth?" Expressing new forms of religiosity: Romanian neo-Protestants in Serbia'. *Ethnologia Balkanica* 16: 163–77.
Du Boulay, J. and R. Williams. 1987. 'Amoral familism and the image of limited good: A critique from a European perspective'. *Anthropological Quarterly* 60 (1): 12–24.
Dumont, L. 1986. *Essays on Individualism: Modern ideology in anthropological perspective*. Chicago: University of Chicago Press.
Edelman, M. 2013. 'What is a peasant? What are peasantries? A briefing paper on issues of definition'. Prepared for the first session of the Intergovernmental Working Group on a United Nations Declaration on the Rights of Peasants and Other People Working in Rural Areas, Geneva, 15–19 July, 2013.
Ellis, F. 1988. *Peasant Economics: Farm households and agrarian development*. Cambridge: Cambridge University Press.
Ellis, F. 2000. *Rural Livelihoods and Diversity in Developing Countries*. Oxford: Oxford University Press.
Elster J. 1989. *The Cement of Society: A study of social order*. Cambridge: Cambridge University Press.

Elster, J., C. Offe, U. K. Preuss and F. Bönker. 1998. *Institutional Design in Post-Communist Societies: Rebuilding the ship at sea*. Cambridge: Cambridge University Press.

Emery, S. B. 2010. 'In Better Fettle: Improvement, work, and rhetoric in the transition to environmental farming in the North York Moors'. PhD thesis. University of Durham, Department of Anthropology. Available from http://etheses.dur.ac.uk/379/.

Emery, S. B. 2014. 'Hard work, productivity and the management of the farmed environment in anthropological perspective'. In *Contemporary Issues in Management*, edited by L. Hamilton, L. Mitchell, and A. Mangan, 90–104. Cheltenham: Edward Elgar.

Emery, S. B., 2015. 'Independence and individualism: Conflated values in farmer cooperation?' *Agriculture and Human Values* 32 (1): 47–61.

Emery, S. B. and J. R. Franks. 2012. 'The potential for collaborative agri-environment schemes in England: Can a well-designed collaborative approach address farmers' concerns with current schemes?' *Journal of Rural Studies* 28 (3): 218–31.

Ensminger, J. 1998. 'Anthropology and the new institutionalism'. *Journal of Institutional and Theoretical Economics* 154 (4): 774–89.

Ensminger, J. and J. Knight. 1997. 'Changing social norms: Common property, bridewealth, and clan exogamy'. *Current Anthropology* 38 (1): 1–24.

Epstein S. 1967. 'Productive efficiency and customary systems of rewards in rural South India'. In *Themes in Economic Anthropology*, edited by R. Firth, 229–51. London: Tavistock.

Erić, M. 1958. *Agrarna reforma u Jugoslaviji 1918–1941*. Sarajevo: Veselin Masleša.

Fehr, E. and S. Gächter, 2002. 'Altruistic punishment in humans'. *Nature* 415 (6868): 137–40.

Ferguson, J. 1992. 'The cultural topography of wealth: Commodity paths and the structure of property in rural Lesotho'. *American Anthropologist* 94 (1): 55–73.

Ferguson, J. and A. Gupta. 2002. 'Spatializing states: Toward an ethnography of neoliberal governmentality'. *American Ethnologist* 29 (4): 981–1002.

Finke, P. 1995. 'Kazak pastoralists in western Mongolia: Economic and social change in the course of privatization'. *Nomadic Peoples* 36–7: 195–216.

Finke, P. 2003. 'Does privatisation mean commoditisation? Market exchange, barter, and gift giving in post-socialist Mongolia'. In *Anthropological Perspectives on Economic Development and Integration*, edited by N. Dannhaeuser and Cynthia Werner, 199–223. Leeds: Emerald Group.

Forsyth, T. 2005. *Encyclopedia of International Development*. Abingdon: Routledge.

Foster, G. 1965. 'Peasant society and the image of limited good'. *American Anthropologist* 67 (2): 293–315.

Fox, K. 2011. *Peasants into European Farmers? EU integration in the Carpathian Mountains of Romania*. Münster: LIT Verlag.

Gaćeša, N. 1984. *Agrarna reforma i kolonizacija u Jugoslaviji 1945–1948*. Novi Sad: Matica Srpska.

Gaćeša, N. 1995. *Radovi iz agrarne istorije i demografije*. Novi Sad: Matica Srpska.

Ganev, V. I. 2001. 'The separation of party and state as a logistical problem: A glance at the causes of state weakness in postcommunism'. *East European Politics & Societies* 15 (2): 389–420.

Ganev, V. I. 2007. *Preying on the State: The transformation of Bulgaria after 1989*. Ithaca, NY: Cornell University Press.

Ganev, V. I. 2013. 'Post-accession hooliganism: Democratic governance in Bulgaria and Romania after 2007'. *East European Politics and Societies and Cultures* 27 (1): 26–44.

Geertz, C. 1968. *Agricultural Involution: The process of ecological change in Indonesia*. Berkeley: Published for the Association of Asian Studies by University of California Press.

Giordano, C. 2010. 'Multiple modernities in Bulgaria: Social strategies of capitalist entrepreneurs in the agrarian sector'. *Eastern European Countryside* 16 (1): 5–24.

Giordano, C. 2012. 'The anthropology of Mediterranean societies' In *A Companion to the Anthropology of Europe*, 1st edition, edited by U. Kockel, M. N. Craith and J. Frykman, 13–31. Oxford: Blackwell.

Giordano, C. and N. Hayoz (eds). 2013. *Informality in Eastern Europe: Structures, political cultures and social practices*. Lausanne: Peter Lang.

Giordano, C. and D. Kostova. 2002. 'The social production of mistrust'. In *Postsocialism: Ideals, ideologies and practices in Eurasia*, edited by C. Hann, 74–92. Abingdon: Routledge.

Giordano, C. and D. Kostova. 2006. 'Multi-cultural relations in rural Bulgaria'. *Eastern European Countryside* 12: 31–49.

Goldschmidt, W. 1971. 'Independence as an element in pastoral social systems'. *Anthropological Quarterly* 44 (3): 132–42.

Grandits, H. 2012. 'Kinship and the welfare state in Croatia's twentieth-century transitions'. In *Household and the Family in the Balkans: Two decades of historical family research at University of Graz* (Volume 13), edited by K. Kaser, 453–78. Münster: LIT Verlag.

Granovetter, M. 1973. 'The strength of weak ties'. *American Journal of Sociology* 78 (6): 1360–80.

Granovetter, M. 2005. 'The impact of social structure on economic outcomes'. *Journal of Economic Perspectives* 19 (1): 33–50.

Grzymala-Busse, A. and P. J. Luong. 2002. 'Reconceptualizing the state: Lessons from post-communism'. *Politics & Society* 30 (4): 529–54.

Gundelach, B., M. Freitag and I. Stadelmann-Steffen. 2010. 'Making or breaking informal volunteering: Welfare statism and social capital in a sub-national comparative perspective'. *European Societies* 12 (5): 627–52.

Haidt. J. 2013. *The Righteous Mind: Why good people are divided by politics and religion*. New York: Vintage Books.

Hall, R., M. Edelman, S. M. Borras Jr., I. Scoones, B. White and W. Wolford. 2015. 'Resistance, acquiescence or incorporation? An introduction to land grabbing and political reactions "from below"'. *Journal of Peasant Studies* 42 (3–4): 467–88.

Haller, T. 2010. 'Between open access, privatisation and collective action: A comparative analysis of institutional change governing use of common-pool resources in African floodplains'. In *Disputing the Floodplains: Institutional change and the politics of resource management in African floodplains*, edited by T. Haller, 413–43. Leiden: Brill.

Halpern, J. and B. Kerewsky-Halpern. 1972. *A Serbian Village in Historical Perspective*. New York: Holt, Rinehart, & Winston.

Halpern, J. and J. Brode. 1967. 'Peasant society: Economic changes and revolutionary transformation'. *Biennial Review of Anthropology* 5: 46–139.

Hann, C. 2002. *Postsocialism: Ideals, ideologies and practices in Eurasia*. Abingdon: Routledge.

Hann, C. and K. Hart. 2011. *Economic Anthropology: History, ethnography, critique*. Cambridge: Polity Press.

Hann, C. (ed.) with the 'Property Relations' Group. 2003. *The Postsocialist Agrarian Question: Property relations and the rural condition*. Münster: LIT Verlag.

Hardin, G. 1968. 'The tragedy of the commons'. *Science* 162 (3859): 1243–8.

Hart, K. 1973. 'Informal income opportunities and urban employment in Ghana'. *Journal of Modern African Studies* 11 (1): 61–89.

Heiss, J. P. 2015. 'Assessing Ernst Tugendhat's philosophical anthropology as a theoretical template for an empirical anthropology of the individual'. *Zeitschrift für Ethnologie* 140 (1): 35–55.

Helliwell, J., R. Layard and J. Sachs. 2012. *World Happiness Report*. New York: Earth Institute Columbia University.

Henrich, N. and J. Henrich. 2007. *Why Humans Cooperate: A cultural and evolutionary explanation*. New York: Oxford University Press.

Higgott, R. A. 1983. *Political Development Theory: The contemporary debate*. London: Croom Helm.

Hivon, M. 1998. 'The bullied farmer: Social pressure as a survival strategy?'. In *Surviving Post-Socialism: Local strategies and regional responses in Eastern Europe and the former Soviet Union*, edited by S. Bridger and F. Pine, 33–51. Abingdon: Routledge.

Hobart, M. 1993. *An Anthropological Critique of Development: The growth of ignorance*. Abingdon: Routledge.

Hobsbawm, E. 1973. 'Peasants and politics'. *Journal of Peasant Studies* 1 (1): 3–22.

Holland, J. and J. Blackburn. 1998. *Whose Voice? Participatory research and policy change*. London: Intermediate Technology Publications.

Hollander, J. A. and R. L. Einwohner. 2004. 'Conceptualizing resistance'. *Sociological Forum* 19 (4): 533–51.

Holling, C. S. 1973. 'Resilience and stability of ecological systems'. *Annual Review of Ecology and Systematics* 4: 1–23.

Humphrey, C. 1997. 'Exemplars and rules: Aspects of the discourse of moralities in Mongolia'. In *The Ethnography of Moralities*, edited by S. Howell, 25–47. Abingdon: Routledge.

Humphrey, C. 2002. 'Subsistence farming and the peasantry as an idea in contemporary Russia'. In *Post-Socialist Peasant? Rural and urban construction of identity in Eastern Europe, East Asia and the former Soviet Union*, edited by P. Leonard and D. Kaneff, 136–39. Basingstoke: Palgrave.

Isić, M. 1995. *Seljaštvo u Srbiji 1918–1925*. Belgrade: INIS.

James, W. 1899. 'On a certain blindness in human beings'. In W. James, *Talks to Teachers on Psychology – and to students on some of life's ideals*, 229–64. New York: Metropolitan Books/ Henry Holt and Company.

Jancsics, D. 2018. 'Brokerage (general)'. In *The Global Encyclopaedia of Informality: Understanding social and cultural complexity*, Volume 2, edited by A. Ledeneva, 205–8. London: UCL Press. https://doi.org/10.14324/111.9781787351899.

Janjetović, Z. 2005. *Between Hitler and Tito: The disappearance of the Vojvodina Germans* (2nd revised edition). Belgrade: Selbstverl.

Joseph, G. M. 1990. 'On the trail of Latin American bandits: A reexamination of peasant resistance'. *Latin American Research Review* 25 (3): 7–53.

Kay, C. 2009. 'Development strategies and rural development: Exploring synergies, eradicating poverty'. *Journal of Peasant Studies* 36 (1): 103–37.

Keane, W. 2016. *Ethical Life: Its natural and social histories*. Princeton: Princeton University Press.

Kearney, M. 1996. *Reconceptualizing the Peasantry: Anthropology in global perspective*. Boulder, CO: Westview Press.

Kennedy, J. G. 1966. 'Peasant society and the image of limited good: A critique'. *American Anthropologist* 68 (5): 1212–25.

Kerkvliet, B. J. 1990. *Everyday Politics in the Philippines: Class and status relations in a Central Luzon village*. Berkeley: University of California Press.

Kligman G. and K. Verdery. 2011. *Peasants Under Siege: The collectivization of Romanian agriculture, 1949–1962*. Princeton: Princeton University Press.

Kornai, J. 1992. *The Socialist System: The political economy of communism*. Oxford: Clarendon Press.

Korovkin, T. 2000. 'Weak weapons, strong weapons? Hidden resistance and political protest in rural Ecuador'. *Journal of Peasant Studies* 27 (3): 1–29.

Kostić, C. 1969. *Sociologija sela*. Belgrade: Izdavačko informativni centar studenata.

Kovacs, K. 2015. 'Advancing marginalisation of Roma and forms of segregation in East Central Europe'. *Local Economy* 30 (7): 783–99.

Krasznai-Kovacs, E. 2019. 'Seeing subsidies like a farmer: Emerging subsidy cultures in Hungary'. *Journal of Peasant Studies*, 48 (2): 387–410.

Landolt, G. and T. Haller. 2015. 'Alpine common property institutions under change: Conditions for successful and unsuccessful collective action by Alpine farmers in the Canton of Grisons, Switzerland'. *Human Organization* 74 (1): 100–11.

Ledeneva, A. 1998. *Russia's Economy of Favours: Blat, networking and informal exchange*. Cambridge: Cambridge University Press.

Ledeneva, A. 2006. *How Russia Really Works: The informal practices that shaped post-Soviet politics and business*. Ithaca, NY: Cornell University Press.

Ledeneva, A. (ed.). 2018. *The Global Encyclopedia of Informality*, vols 1–2. London: UCL Press.

Leeds, A. 1977. 'Mythos and Pathos: Some unpleasantries on peasantries'. In *Peasant Livelihood: Studies in economic anthropology and cultural ecology*, edited by R. Halperin and J. Dow, 227–56. New York: St Martin's Press.

Lekić, B. 2002. *Agrarna reforma i kolonizacija u Jugoslaviji 1918–1941*. Belgrade: Udruženje ratnih dobrovoljaca 1912–1918.

Lemarchand, R. and K. Legg. 1972. 'Political clientelism and development: A preliminary analysis'. *Comparative Politics* 4 (2): 149–78.

Leonard, P. and D. Kaneff. 2002. *Post-Socialist Peasant? Rural and urban construction of identity in Eastern Europe, East Asia and the former Soviet Union*. Basingstoke: Palgrave.

Leutloff-Grandits, C. 2006. *Claiming Ownership in Postwar Croatia: The dynamics of property relations and ethnic conflict in the Knin region*. Münster: LIT Verlag.

Lewis, O. 1951. *Life in a Mexican Village: Tepoztlan restudied*. Urbana: University of Illinois Press.

Li, T. M. 2007. *The Will to Improve: Governmentality, development, and the practice of politics*. Durham, NC: Duke University Press.

Lipton, M. 1977. *Why Poor People Stay Poor: A study of urban bias in world development*. London: Temple Smith.

Locke, J. and P. Laslett. 1999. *Two Treatises of Government*. Cambridge: Cambridge University Press.

Lowe, P., J. Clark, S. Seymour and N. Ward. 1997. *Moralising the Environment: The social construction of farm pollution*. London: UCL Press.

Lucas, R., and O. Stark. 1985. 'Motivations to remit: Evidence from Botswana'. *Journal of Political Economy* 93 (5): 901–18.
Macfarlane, A. 1978. *The Origins of English Individualism: The family, property and social transformation*. Cambridge: Cambridge University Press.
Majdin, Z. 2012 (11 October). 'Pogled na smrdljivi sir i još bolje'. *Vreme*. https://vreme.com/vreme/pogled-na-smrdljivi-sir-i-jos-bolje/. Accessed 1 March 2017.
Maksimović-Sekulić, N., J. Živadinović and L. Dimitrijević. 2018. 'Concerns about hamonization process of Serbian agricultural policy with EU standards'. *Economics of Agriculture* 65 (4): 1627–39. https://doi.org/10.5937/ekopolj1804627m.
Martinovska-Stojcheska, A., A. Kotevskaa, N. Bogdanov and A. Nikolic. 2016. 'How do farmers respond to rural development policy challenges? Evidence from Macedonia, Serbia and Bosnia and Herzegovina'. *Land Use Policy* 59: 71–83.
Marx, C. 2018. 'The system made me do it. Strategies of survival'. In *The Global Encyclopaedia of Informality*, Volume 2, edited by A. Ledeneva, 487–93. London: UCL Press. https://doi.org/10.14324/111.9781787351899.
McCloskey, D. 1991. 'The prudent peasant: New findings on open fields'. *Journal of Economic History* 51 (2): 343–55.
McCloskey, D. 2006. *The Bourgeois Virtues: Ethics for an age of commerce*. Chicago: University of Chicago Press.
McCloskey, D. 2010. *Bourgeois Dignity: Why economics can't explain the modern world*. Chicago: University of Chicago Press.
McCloskey, D. 2016a. *Bourgeois Equality: How ideas, not capital or institutions, enriched the world*. Chicago: University of Chicago Press.
McCloskey, D. 2016b. 'Max U versus humanomics: A critique of neo-institutionalism'. *Journal of Institutional Economics* 12 (1): 1–27.
Medina, G. and C. Potter. 2017. 'The nature and developments of the common agricultural policy: Lessons for European integration from the UK perspective'. *Journal of European Integration* 39 (4): 373–88.
Medina, G., C. Potter and B. Pokorny. 2015. 'Farm business pathways under agri-environmental policies: Lessons for policy design'. *Estudos Sociedade e Agricultura* 23 (1): 5–30.
Mencher, J. (ed.). 1983. *Social Anthropology of Peasantry*. Bombay: Somaiya Publications.
Menger, C. 1892. 'On the origins of money'. Translated by C. A. Foley. *Economic Journal* 2: 239–55.
Mijatović, B. 2010. *Penzijsko osiguranje poljoprivrednika*. Belgrade: USAID Sega projekat.
Milošević, S. 2008. 'Agrarno pitanje—"sveto pitanje": Ideološki okvir međuratne agrarne reforme u Jugoslaviji'. *Tokovi istorije* 1-2: 149–71.
Milošević, S. 2016. 'Agrarna Politika u Jugoslaviji (1945–1953)'. PhD thesis. Belgrade: Fakultet za filozofiju, Univerzitet u Beogradu.
Milovanović, M. 2016. 'Mogući Efekti Integracije u EU na Poljoprivredu Srbije'. PhD thesis. Novi Sad: Univerzitet u Novom Sadu.
Mintz, W. S. 1973. 'A note on the definition of peasantries'. *Journal of Peasant Studies* 1 (1): 91–106.
Mises, L. 2007. *Human Action: A treatise on economics*. Indianapolis: Liberty Fund.
Morduch, J. 1999. 'Between the state and the market: Can informal insurance patch the safety net'. *World Bank Research Observer* 14 (2): 187–207.
Morris, J. and A. Polese. 2014. *The Informal Post-Socialist Economy: Embedded practices and livelihoods*. Abingdon: Routledge.
Mosse, D. 2001. '"People's knowledge", participation and patronage: Operations and representations in rural development'. In *Participation: The new tyranny?*, edited by B. Cooke and U. Kothari, 16–35. London: Zed Books.
Murtazashvili, I. 2013. *The Political Economy of the American Frontier*. Cambridge: Cambridge University Press.
Narotzky, S. 2016. 'Where have all the peasants gone?'. *Annual Review of Anthropology* 45 (19): 1–18.
Naumović, S. 1995. 'Srpsko selo i seljak: Između nacionalnog i stranačkog simbola'. *Glasnik Etnografskog instituta SANU* 44: 114–28.
Naumović, S. 2009. *Upotreba tradicije u političkom i javnom životu Srbije na kraju dvadesetog i početkom dvadest prvog veka*. Belgrade: Institut za filozofiju i društvenu teoriju.

Nef, J. 2003. 'The culture of distrust in Latin American public administration' [conference paper]. *Public Administration: Challenges of Inequality and Exclusion Miami (USA)*, 14–18 September 2003.
Novaković, A. and M. Radojević. 2014. 'Experiences and perspectives of direct democracy in Serbia'. Working paper presented at the conference *Direct Democracy in East-Central Europe*, Andrássy Gyula German Speaking University & Pázmány Péter Catholic University, Budapest.
Okely, J. 1997. 'Non-territorial culture as the rationale for the assimilation of gypsy children'. *Childhood: A Global Journal of Child Research* 4 (1): 63–80.
Ostrom, E. 1990. *Governing the Commons: The evolution of institutions for collective action*. Cambridge: Cambridge University Press.
Pandian, A. 2009. *Crooked Stalks: Cultivating virtue in South India*. Durham, NC: Duke University Press.
Papić, R. and N. Bogdanov. 2015. 'Rural development policy: A perspective of local actors in Serbia'. *Ekonomika Poljoprivrede* 62 (4): 1079–93.
Pavković, N. 2009. *Banatsko selo: Društvene i kulturne promene Gaj i Dubovac*. Novi Sad: Matica Srpska.
Pavković, N. 2014. *Studije i ogledi iz pravne etnologije*. Belgrade: Etnološka biblioteka.
Pavlović, M. 1997. *Srpsko selo 1945–1952: Otkup*. Belgrade: ISI.
Pejanović, R., D. Glavaš-Trbić and M. Tomaš-Simin. 2017. 'Problems of agricultural and rural development in Serbia and necessity of new agricultural policy'. *Economics of Agriculture* 64 (4): 1619–33.
Pešić, M. and A. Novaković. 2008. *Sloboda i javnost: Određenje, problematizacija i značaj*. Belgrade: IPS.
Podolinská, T. 2017. 'Roma' label: The deconstructed and reconceptualized category within the Pentecostal and charismatic pastoral discourse in contemporary Slovakia'. *Journal of Nationalism, Memory and Language Politics* 11 (2): 146–80.
Popkin, S. L. 1979. *The Rational Peasant: The political economy of rural society in Vietnam*. Berkeley: University of California Press.
Popov, J. 2002. *Drama na Vojvođanskom selu (1945–1952): Obavezni otkup poljoprivrednih proizvoda*. Novi Sad: Platoneum.
Rangan, H. 2000. *Of Myths and Movements. Rewriting Chipko into Himalayan history*. London: Verso.
Redfield, R. 1947. 'Folk Society'. *Journal of Sociology* 52 (4): 293–308.
Redfield, R. 1956. *Peasant Society and Culture*. Chicago: Chicago University Press.
Robbins, J. 2015. 'Ritual, value, and example: On the perfection of cultural representations'. *Journal of the Royal Anthropological Institute* 21 (S1): 18–29.
Robbins, J. and J. Sommerschuh. 2016. 'Values'. In *The Cambridge Encyclopedia of Anthropology*, edited by F. Stein, S. Lazar, M. Candea, H. Diemberger, J. Robbins, A. Sanchez, and R. Stasch. https://doi.org/10.29164/16values.
Rothstein, B. O. 2001. 'Social capital in the social democratic welfare state'. *Politics and Society* 29: 207–41.
Ruegg, F. 2013. 'Social representations of informality: The Roma case'. In *Informality in Eastern Europe: Structures, political cultures and social practices*, edited by C. Giordano and N. Hayoz, 297–319. Lausanne: Peter Lang.
Ruegg, F., R. Poledna and C. Rus. 2006. *Interculturalism and Discrimination in Romania: Policies, practices, identities and representations*. Berlin: LIT Verlag.
Rushdie, S. 1991. *Imaginary Homelands: Essays and criticism 1981–1991*. London: Penguin.
Sachs, J. 2005. *The End of Poverty: Economic possibilities for our time*. New York: Penguin.
Sahlins, M. 1972. *Stone Age Economics*. Chicago: Aldine-Atherton.
Said, E. W. 1978. *Orientalism*. New York: Pantheon.
Schwarcz, Gy. 2012. 'Ethnicizing poverty through social security provision in rural Hungary'. *Journal of Rural Sociology* 28 (2): 99–107.
Scoones, I. 2009. 'Livelihoods perspectives and rural development'. *Journal of Peasant Studies* 36 (1): 171–96.
Scott. J. 1977. *The Moral Economy of the Peasant: Rebellion and subsistence in Southeast Asia*. New Haven: Yale University Press.
Scott, J. 1985. *Weapons of the Weak: Everyday forms of peasant resistance*. New Haven: Yale University Press.

Scott, J. 1986. 'Everyday forms of peasant resistance'. *Journal of Peasant Studies*, 13 (2): 5–35.
Scott, J. 1987. 'Resistance without protest and without organisation: Peasant opposition to the Islamic Zacat and Christian tithe'. *Comparative Studies in Society and History* 29 (3): 417–52.
Scott, J. 2009. *The Art of Not Being Governed: An anarchist history of upland Southeast Asia*. New Haven: Yale University Press.
Scott, J. and B. Kerkvliet (eds). 1986. 'Everyday forms of peasant resistance in South-East Asia'. *Journal of Peasant Studies* 13 (2): 1–3.
Searle, J. 1995. *The Construction of Social Reality*. New York: Free Press.
Searle, J. 2006. 'Social ontology: Some basic principles'. *Anthropological Theory* 6 (1): 12–29.
SEEDEV. 2017. *Konkurentnost poljoprivrede Srbije*. Belgrade. https://www.seedev.org/publika cije/Konkurentnost_poljoprivrede_Srbije/Konkurentnost_Srbije_Analiza.pdf.
Seligson, M. and J. Salazar. 1979. 'Political and interpersonal trust among peasants: A re-evaluation'. *Rural Sociology* 44 (3): 505–24.
Shanin, T. 1973. 'The nature and logic of the peasant economy: A generalisation 1'. *Journal of Peasant Studies* 1 (1): 63–80.
Shanin, T. 1983. 'Defining peasants. Conceptualizations and de-conceptualizations: Old and New in a Marxist Debate'. In *Social Anthropology of Peasantry*, edited by J. P. Mencher, 60–87. Bombay: Somaiya Publications.
Shirky, C. 2008. *Here Comes Everybody: The power of organizing without organizations*. London: Penguin.
Shubin, S. 2006. 'The changing nature of rurality and rural studies in Russia'. *Journal of Rural Studies* 22: 422–40.
Sikor, T. 2006. 'Land as asset, land as liability: Property politics in rural Central and Eastern Europe'. In *Changing Properties of Property*, edited by F. von Benda-Beckmann, K. von Benda-Beckmann, and G. Melanie Wiber, 106–25. New York: Berghahn Books.
Sikor, T. and C. Lund. 2010. *The Politics of Possession: Property, authority, and access to natural resources*. London: Wiley-Blackwell.
Silvasti, T. 2003. 'The cultural model of the "good farmer" and the environmental question in Finland'. *Agriculture and Human Values* 20: 143–50.
Silverman, S. 1979. 'The peasant concept in anthropology'. *Journal of Peasant Studies* 7 (1): 49–69.
Slijepčević, R. M. and I. Babić. 2005. *Real Property Rights in Serbia*. Berlin: Berliner Wissenschafts-Verlag.
Smith, A. [1776] 1976. *The Wealth of Nations*, vol. 4. Chicago: University of Chicago Press.
Solnick, S. 1998. *Stealing the State*. Cambridge, MA: Harvard University Press.
Spoor, M. 2012. 'Agrarian reform and transition: What can we learn from "the east"?' *Journal of Peasant Studies* 39 (1): 175–94.
Statistical Yearbook of the Republic of Serbia. 2016. Belgrade: Statistical Office of the Republic of Serbia.
Statistical Yearbook of Yugoslavia 38, 1991. Belgrade: Savezni zavod za statistiku.
Stavriani K., M. Partalidou, and A. Ragkos. 2014. 'Young farmers' social capital in Greece: Trust levels and collective actions'. *Journal of Rural Studies* 34: 204–11.
Stewart, M. 2002. 'Deprivation, the Roma and "the underclass"'. In *Postsocialism: Ideals, Ideologies and practices in Eurasia*, edited by C. Hann, 133–57. Abingdon: Routledge.
Stewart, M. 2013. 'Roma and gypsy ethnicity as a subject of anthropological inquiry'. *Annual Review of Anthropology* 42: 415–32.
Stock, P. V. and J. Forney. 2014. 'Farmer autonomy and the farming self'. *Journal of Rural Studies* 36: 160–71.
Stock, P. V., J. Forney, S. B. Emery and H. Wittman. 2014. 'Neoliberal natures on the farm: Farmer autonomy and cooperation in comparative perspective'. *Journal of Rural Studies* 36: 411–22.
Stock, P. V. and S. Peoples. 2012. 'Commodity competition: divergent trajectories in New Zealand pastoral farming'. In *Rethinking Agricultural Policy Regimes: Food Security, climate change and the future resilience of global agriculture*, edited by R. Almas and H. Campbell, 263–84. Leeds: Emerald Group.
Strategija poljoprivrede i ruralnog razvoja republike Srbije za period 2014–2024, Ministartsvo poljoprivrede i zaštite životne sredine, Republika Srbija.
Subić, J. 2005. Radna snaga u poljoprivredi Srbije. *Industrija* 3: 79–88.
Šućur, Z. 2003. 'Razvoj socijalne pomoći i socijalne skrbi u Hrvatskoj nakon Drugog svjetskog rata'. *Revija za socijalnu politiku* 10 (1): 1–22.

Sutherland, L. A. 2010. 'Environmental grants and regulations in strategic farm business decision-making: A case study of attitudinal behaviour in Scotland'. *Land Use Policy* 27: 415–23.

Swain, N. 2000. 'The Rural Transition in Post-Socialist Central Europe and the Balkans'. Max Planck Institute for Social Anthropology Working Paper No. 9. Halle/Saale: Max Planck Institute for Social Anthropology.

Swain, N. 2016. 'Eastern European rurality in a neo-liberal, European Union world'. *Sociologia Ruralis* 56 (4): 574–96.

Thelen, T. 2011. 'Shortage, fuzzy property and other dead ends in the anthropological analysis of (post)socialism'. *Critique of Anthropology* 31 (1): 43–61.

Thelen, T., A. Thiemann and D. Roth. 2014. 'State kinning and kinning the state in Serbian elder care programs'. *Social Analysis* 58 (3): 107–23.

Thiemann, A. 2014. '"It was the least painful to go into Greenhouse Production": The moral appreciation of social security in post-socialist Serbia'. *Contemporary Southeastern Europe* 1 (2): 24–41.

Thiemann, A. 2017. 'Shrinking capitalism, "milky ways", and the moral appreciation of Serbia's "living village"', *Glasnik Etnografskog instituta SANU* 65 (2): 387–402.

Thiemann, A. 2023. 'Infrastructuring "Red Gold": Agronomists, cold chains, and the involution of Serbia's raspberry country'. *Ethnos Journal of Anthropology* 89: 289–311.

Thompson, E. P. 1971. 'The moral economy of the English crowd in the eighteenth century'. *Past and Present* 50 (1): 76–136.

Thompson, P. B. 1995. *The Spirit of the Soil: Agriculture and environment ethics*. Abingdon: Routledge.

Thorner, D. 1986. 'Chayanov's concept of peasant economy'. In *A. V. Chayanov on the Theory of Peasant Economy*, edited by D. Thorner, B. Kerblay, and R. E. F. Smith, xi–xxiii. Manchester: Manchester University Press.

Tieffenbach, E. 2010. 'Serle and Menger on money'. *Philosophy of the Social Sciences* 40 (2): 191–212.

Tochitch, D. 1959. 'Collectivization in Yugoslavia'. *Journal of Farm Economics* 41 (1): 26–42.

Tocqueville, A. de. 1838. *Democracy in America*. New York: George Dearborn & Co., Adlard and Saunders.

Todorović, V. 2001. *Denacionalizacija između nacionalizacije i privatizacije*. Belgrade: Službeni list SRJ.

Torpe, L. 2003. 'Social capital in Denmark: A deviant case?' *Scandinavian Political Studies* 26: 27–48.

Tošić, D. 2002. *Kolektivizacija u Jugoslaviji 1949–1953*. Belgrade: Službeni list SRJ.

Turner, B. 2015. 'Exploring avenues of research in legal pluralism: Forward-looking perspectives in the work of Franz von Benda-Beckmann'. *Journal of Legal Pluralism and Unofficial Law* 47 (3): 375–410.

Van der Ploeg, J. D. 2008. *The New Peasantries: Struggles for autonomy and sustainability in an era of empire and globalization*. Abingdon: Earthscan.

Van der Ploeg, J. D. 2010. 'The peasantries of the twenty-first century: The commoditization debate revisited'. *Journal of Peasant Studies* 37 (1): 1–30.

Van der Ploeg, J. D. 2014. 'Peasant-driven agricultural growth and food sovereignty'. *Journal of Peasant Studies* 41 (6): 999–1030.

Van der Ploeg, J. D. and G. Van Dijk (eds). 1995. *Beyond Modernization: The impact of endogenous rural development*. Assen: Van Gorcum.

Vander Zanden, J. W. 1959. 'Resistance and social movements'. *Social Forces* 37: 312–15.

Vasiljević, D., B. Radulović, M. Babović and S. Todorović. 2018. *Komasacija kao neiskorišćeni potencijal. Efekti primene, prepreke i mogući značaj komasacije poljoprivrednog zemljišta u Srbiji*. NALED. https://naled.rs/htdocs/Files/01428/Komasacija-vodic-web.pdf. Accessed 8 August 2024.

Verdery, K. 1996. *What Was Socialism, and What Comes Next?* Princeton: Princeton University Press.

Verdery, K. 2002. 'Seeing like a mayor: Or, how local officials obstructed Romanian land restitution'. *Ethnography* 3 (1): 5–33.

Verdery, K. 2003. *The Vanishing Hectare: Property and value in postsocialist Transylvania*. Ithaca, NY: Cornell University Press.

Vincent, J. 1983. 'Political consciousness and struggle among an African peasantry'. In *Social Anthropology of Peasantry*, edited by J. P. Mencher, 177–91. Bombay: Somaiya Publications.
Vlajinac, M. 1929. *Moba i pozajmica. Narodni običaji udruženog rada: Opis, ocena i njihovo sadašnje stanje*. Belgrade: Srpska kraljevska akademija.
Volk, T. 2010. *Agriculture in the Western Balkan Countries*. Halle: IAMO.
Volk, T., M. Rednak and E. Erjavec, 2010. 'Western Balkan agriculture and agricultural policy: cross-country overview and comparison'. In *Agriculture in the Western Balkan Countries*, edited by T. Volk, 7–37. Halle: IAMO.
Volk, T., M. Rednak and E. Erjavec. 2014. 'Cross-country analysis of agriculture and agricultural Policy of Southeastern European countries in comparison with the European Union'. In *Agricultural Policy and European Integration in Southeastern Europe*, edited by T. Volk, E. Erjavec and K. Mortensen, 9–37. Budapest: FAO.
Von Benda-Beckmann, F. 1993. 'Scapegoat and magic charm: Law in development theory and practice'. In *An Anthropological Critique of Development: The growth of ignorance*, edited by M. Hobart, 116–33. Abingdon: Routledge.
Von Benda-Beckmann, F. 2002. 'Who's afraid of legal pluralism?'. *Journal of Legal Pluralism and Unofficial Law* 34: 37–82.
Von Benda-Beckmann, F. and K. von Benda-Beckmann. 2006. 'The dynamics of change and continuity in plural legal orders'. *Journal of Legal Pluralism and Unofficial Law* 53–4: 1–45.
Von Benda-Beckmann, F., K. von Benda-Beckmann and A. Griffiths (eds). 2009. *The Power of Law in a Transnational World: Anthropological enquiries*. New York: Berghahn Books.
Vukosavljević, S. 1983. *Istorija seljačkog društva III. Sociologija seljačkih radova*, edited by R. Lukić. Belgrade: Srpska akademija nauka i umetnosti.
Vuković, D. 2013. 'Social economy, civil society and the Serbian welfare system'. In *Cooperatives and Social Enterprises in Europe and in Transitional Contexts*, edited by S. Cvejić, 62–79. Belgrade: Sociological Association of Serbia and Montenegro and the Institute for Sociological Research.
Vuković, D. and N. Perišić. 2011. 'Social security in Serbia: twenty years later'. In *Welfare States in Transition: 20 Years after the Yugoslav Welfare Model*, edited by Stambolieva M. and Stefan Dehnert, 228–62. Sofia: Friedrich Ebert Foundation.
Wallace, C. and R. Latcheva. 2006. 'Economic transformation outside the law: Corruption, trust in public institutions and the informal economy in transition countries of Central and Eastern Europe'. *Europe–Asia Studies* 58 (1): 81–102.
Wanner, C. 2007. *Communities of the Converted: Ukrainians and global evangelism*. Ithaca, NY: Cornell University Press.
Ward, C. and Mary C. Rawlinson. 2017. *Routledge Handbook of Food Ethics*. Abingdon: Routledge.
Weber, M. 1930. *The Protestant Ethic and the Spirit of Capitalism*. Abingdon: Routledge.
White, C. P. 1986. 'Everyday resistance, socialist revolution and rural development: The Vietnamese case'. *Journal of Peasant Studies* 13 (2): 49–63.
Wilk, R. 1996. *Economies and Cultures: Foundations of economic anthropology*. Boulder, CO: Westview Press.
Wolf, E. 1955. 'Types of Latin American peasantry: A preliminary discussion'. *American Anthropologist* 57: 452–71.
Wolf, E. 1966. *Peasants: The place of peasantry in society*. Hoboken, NJ: Prentice-Hall.
Wylic, L. 1961. *Village in the Vaucluse: An account of life in a French village*. New York: Harper Colophon Books.
Wynne-Jones, S. 2017. 'Understanding farmer co-operation: Exploring practices of social relatedness and emergent affects'. *Journal of Rural Studies* 53: 259–68.
Yalçin-Heckmann, L. 2010. *The Return of Private Property: Rural life after agrarian reform in the republic of Azerbaijan*. Münster: LIT Verlag.
Yalçin-Heckmann, L. 2014. 'Informal economy writ large and small: from Azerbaijani herb traders to Moscow shop owners'. In *The Informal Post-Socialist Economy: Embedded practices and livelihoods*, edited by J. Morris and A. Polese, 165–86. Abingdon: Routledge.

Index

agency 22, 74
agrarian condition 50
agrarian economy 28
agrarian maximum 37, 42–3, 45
agrarian reform xiv, 3, 22
　see also First agrarian reform; Second agrarian reform
agrarian thought xvii
agriculture xiii, 1–25, 28, 36–51, 54–58, 65, 68, 79, 83, 93–122, 133, 137, 158–184, 188–204, 208, 214
　agricultural associations 20, 79, 81–2, 153
　agricultural development xi, 45–6, 127
　agricultural households xi, 44, 48–9, 98, 100, 106–7, 110, 117–18, 181
　agricultural machinery 21, 41, 159, 163, 174–5, 177
　agricultural pensions 14, 95, 120, 129–30, 154, 211
　agricultural policies 4, 12, 17, 23–4, 94–5, 110–11, 117, 158, 214
　agricultural politics 3
　agricultural producers 21, 25, 41, 43, 47–9, 58, 79, 98, 100–1, 107, 117, 131, 158, 166
ajvar xiii, 104
amoral familism 29
Ana and Damjan's story 171–3, 179, 182
anti-revolutionary theory 31
asylum 191–6, 205, 211
asylum-seeking 24, 191–5
attitudes 3, 11, 23, 51, 60, 64–5, 90, 95–6, 119, 124, 167, 179, 196, 198, 199, 210, 212–13
　peasants' attitudes 6, 90, 210

Austrian School of Economics 10, 12
　Austrian economists 13
Austro-Hungarian empire xvi, 17, 25
autonomy vii, 1, 3, 5–6, 9, 16–7, 22–4, 29–30, 35, 51, 53–9, 78, 83, 109, 124, 129, 152, 158, 173, 177, 179, 210–11
　autonomous actions 4
　peasants' autonomy 6, 16, 55, 57–8, 78
　sense of autonomy 3, 6, 16–7, 22, 29–30, 53–5, 59–60, 82, 130

bačija xiii, 114
Bačka 25
backwardness 25, 29, 90, 208
Banaćani xiii, 164, 170, 177–8, 189
Banat xiii, xvii, 2, 17, 25, 37, 75, 164–5, 167, 170, 175, 177, 183, 189–90, 194
Banerjee, A. 214
Banjaši xiii, 190
barter 10, 110
Barth, F. 145
Beli Breg xvii, 17–9, 22, 25, 43–4, 58, 61, 66, 96, 103, 105, 108–9, 122, 158–9, 175–8, 181–3, 210, 212–15
Bentham, J. 179
Bogdan's story 168–70, 179, 182
brokers 106–7, 140
buša xiii, 54

capitalism 25
　capitalist farm 30
career politicians 135
Češka beseda (Czech association) xiii, 124, 127
Chayanov, A. 30–1, 51

church 39, 65, 138, 140, 143, 164, 196–7, 199, 206
   Adventist church 150, 196
   Catholic church ix, 19, 195–6
   council 138, 174
   Orthodox church 138, 195–6, 198
   neo-Protestant church 196–7
Cigani xiii, 189, 191, 193–4, 197, 204
   Čergari xiii, 190
   Domaći Cigani (domestic Gypsies) xiii, 188–9, 195, 204
   'domesticated' Roma xiii
clientelism 9, 23, 36, 49, 130, 133, 139, 155, 183–5
   clientelist networks xiv, 1, 134, 145, 152, 155, 184, 213
coercion 32, 40–2, 60, 109
collective action 10–12, 14, 16–17, 29
collective good 12–14
collective rights 73
collective wellbeing 14
collectivism 29
   methodological 10, 16
collectivization 34, 39–41, 45
Common Agricultural Policy (CAP), *see* European Union
common good 13, 16, 29, 90, 127–8, 130
communist party 39, 90
   communists 38–9
communitarianism 32
compulsory delivery 39–41
confiscations 40
consent 11, 25, 73, 196, 200
conservation 14, 48, 63, 158
cooperation xiv, 4–5, 7, 11–12, 24, 50, 76–8, 89–91, 110, 118, 125, 165–6, 179, 183, 209, 211–13
cooperatives 40–2, 44–7, 49–50, 58, 76–8, 82–4, 94, 121, 211
   and agricultural cooperatives 78, 177
   peasant work 39–40
   private 49, 57, 105, 167
corporate agriculture 34

corruption 1, 9, 130
čova xiii, 73
credit on trust, *see* veresija
cronyism 9, 130
crowding-out theory 202, 206
customary disrespect 3, 109

Danube (River) 17, 99, 159, 175, 183, 190
day labourers 160–1, 163, 177, 188, 189, 200, 203
decision-makers 139
   decision-making 5, 79, 84, 124, 136
De Gournay, V. 4
democratization process 133, 155, 207
   democratic pluralism 135
   transition 155
   voting system 134
de-peasantization 34
dependency 31, 33–5, 57, 66, 78
deprivation 34–5, 187
development xvii, 1, 10, 12, 22–5, 29, 32–4, 36, 45, 47–50, 53, 86, 90, 93–4, 109, 117, 130, 133–4, 141, 150, 158–9, 166–7, 178–182, 185, 207–9, 213–14
   concept 25, 93, 208
   discourse 207–8
   programs 10
   rhetoric of (development) 140
   scholarly criticism of (development) 130
   scholarship 1
   studies 214
   theories 34
developmentalism 34
dignity 3, 7, 24, 58, 66, 68, 70–1, 84, 87, 120, 158, 164, 173, 177, 188, 199–200, 202, 205, 210–11
   of ownership 63, 65–6, 68
distrust 6, 23, 29, 39, 53, 79, 81–4, 87, 108, 117–19, 183, 206
   distrustful societies 155
   interpersonal 81, 86, 153
   of the state 81–3, 86, 103, 109, 119

diversification 74, 170
  of income 200
domaćin, see household
Dragan's story 167–8, 179, 182
Duflo, E. 214

Eastern Europe 1, 35, 82, 93, 133, 142, 187, 195
economic sanctions 1, 45, 165
elections 36, 88, 102, 134–8, 141, 143, 146, 148–51, 153, 156, 171, 175
  local 127, 144, 146, 153, 156
  municipality 150–1, 153
  republic 149–50
elites 23, 133–4, 137, 142, 150, 184, 213
  local 125, 134–55, 176
  political 36, 133, 135, 137
Ellis, F. 27
emic ideas 5, 157
endogenous development 23–4, 94, 157–8, 182, 185
entrepreneurs 18, 20, 150, 169, 178
  entrepreneurial actions 7, 125–6, 130, 140, 166–7, 169, 173, 178
environmental protection 48
ethos 11, 29, 90–1, 215
European Union (EU) 112, 117, 191, 193–4
  agricultural policies 48, 95
  CAP 48, 86, 95, 110, 124, 126
  integration 48
  IPA 48
  IPARD 48
  pre-accession funds 48
exemplary persons 180, 210
expansion, institutional (bureaucratic) 9, 23, 130, 135, 155
  of elites and clientelist networks 133, 155, 213
expelled Germans 38–9
expropriation of land 39, 43

family farm 7, 27, 30, 54, 56, 69
  economy 30
'farming self' 6

field theft 74, 119–20, 201, 211
Fijakerijada ix, xiii, 61
First agrarian reform 36–8
formalists 31–2
formal rules 3, 12, 109
freedom 5, 32, 59, 187
  of action xiv, 5
free rider 12–14, 127–9, 204, 210

Gaj ix, xiii–xv, xvii, 17–9, 21–2, 25, 40–1, 43–5, 50, 53–68, 70–8, 80–9, 95–106, 108–10, 112–15, 117–29, 134–41, 143–8, 150–5, 158–78, 180–3, 188–206, 210, 212–15
Gajački kotlić ix, xiv, 62–3, 77
gazde, see household
gleaning (*pabirčenje*) xiii–xv, 24, 69, 73–5, 120, 190–1, 200–2, 204–5, 211
'good farmer' xvii, 209–10
Goran's story 165–7, 179, 182
Green Plan 44–5
growth 56, 93, 101–2, 111, 154–5, 166, 179, 182, 207, 214
guest workers 188

household ix, xiv–xvi, 5, 18, 21–2, 28, 36, 41, 43–6, 49, 57, 58, 60, 63–4, 66–9, 71, 77–8, 80, 90, 94–5, 97–8, 101, 104, 106, 108, 110, 112, 115, 117–18, 122–3, 129, 158, 160–5, 166–8, 171, 174–5, 177–8, 180–1, 189, 193–4, 200–2, 205, 211
  agricultural household xi, 44, 48–9, 77, 98, 100, 106–7, 110, 117–18, 179, 181
  domaćin xiii–xiv, 67
  gazde xiii–xiv, 67, 70, 76, 90, 98, 161–2, 166, 168
  householder xiii–xiv, 60, 65–7, 77, 161, 164, 174, 181, 202
  peasant household 21, 42, 45
  peasant-worker household 42

identity 8, 15, 59, 79, 153, 177, 187, 191, 197, 199, 209

import–export 102
individualism 5–6, 22, 29, 32, 53, 75–9, 81–2, 90–1, 130
  methodological 10, 12, 16
informality 12, 109–10, 187, 214
informal norms and rules 12, 214
  arrangements 86
  economy 108–9
  exchange 9, 139
  markets 108–10, 128
  practices 109–10, 133
  and settings 12, 206
  trade 103, 107–9
  unreported economy 103
  welfare 202, 205–6
infrastructure 36, 49–50, 82, 88, 93, 100, 113, 127, 133, 140, 143, 176, 182–4, 206, 213
institutionalism 10
institutions 1, 3, 9–12, 14–15, 17, 25, 29, 32, 98, 109, 130, 133, 142, 155, 157, 180, 183–5, 206–8, 214
  institutional change 1–2
  institution-building 9–12, 14, 17
Instrument for Pre-accession Assistance (IPA), *see* European Union
insurance 36, 59, 80–1, 83, 88, 117–20, 123–4, 129, 203
  agricultural insurance 95, 117–20, 129–30, 211
  crop insurance 23, 79–81, 210
  insurance companies 80–1, 117–19
  pension insurance 23, 98, 120–4, 210
Ivica's story 173–5, 179, 182

Jefferson, T. 58–9
Journal of Peasant Studies 28

laissez-faire vii, xiv, 1–6, 12, 14–17, 22, 24, 97
  formative elements of 23, 79, 90, 118
  laissez-faire, laissez-passer 4, 215
  laissez-nous faire 4

mentality vii, 1–24, 51, 53–90, 118, 130, 210
  practices vii, 23, 93–130
land xi, xiii–xiv, xviii, 1–3, 6–9, 14, 18–9, 21, 27–8, 30–2, 35–45, 48–51, 54–60, 63–5, 67–8, 73, 75–6, 79, 82–4, 86, 89–90, 97–8, 100–1, 113, 115, 117, 119, 123, 127–8, 130, 137, 153, 156, 158, 160–3, 165–9, 171, 173–8, 180–2, 188–9, 193, 195, 210–13
  landless peasants 9, 28, 33, 37, 41, 73
  landowners xiv, 37, 39, 67–8, 73, 79, 100–1, 123, 200, 202, 211
  land ownership 6, 8–9, 17, 37, 39, 51, 55, 58–60, 68, 101, 130, 152, 158, 179, 210–11, 213–14
  love for land xviii, 54, 55
  ontology of land ownership 214
land consolidation 82–3
land fund 37, 39, 42
lease 21, 86, 100, 112–13, 115, 123, 153, 156, 161, 165–6, 168, 173, 177, 182
  land leasing contracts 89, 100
Legendre, F. 4, 215
Li, T. 208
liberal-democratic shift xv
  change 48
liberalization 44–5, 131, 213–14
  economic liberalization 45
liberty 53, 58–9
  personal liberty 54, 59
limited good, image of 29
livelihoods 9, 24, 34, 191, 205, 207, 209
livestock xiii, xv, 21, 47, 49, 66, 74, 84, 98–9, 106–8, 111–17, 123, 129–30, 162–3, 175, 181–3, 200
  breeders xiii, 58, 74, 77, 98–9, 106–8, 111–15, 117, 162–3
  farming 111, 113, 130
  livestock farms 107–8
local arrangements 23, 100–2, 129, 210

local as resource 94, 129
local development 158, 173
local politics vii, 23, 25, 133–56
Locke, J. 59

Malo Bavanište xvii, 17–19, 22, 25, 43–44, 61, 63–5, 83, 89, 96, 103, 105, 109, 122, 158–9, 175, 177–8, 181–2, 210, 212–15
market economy 7, 27, 31–3, 35, 58, 90, 94–6, 100, 109, 182
  marketplaces 104–5
  opportunities 16, 57
Maruška's story 160–2, 182
Marxism 28
  Marxist legacy 28
McCloskey, D. xvii, 7, 180
mentality (*mentalitet*) xiii–xiv, 5–6, 79, 87, 163, 208
  Banat mentality (*banatski mentalitet*) xiii, 5, 76
  peasant mentality (*seljački mentalitet*) xv, 5
  see also laissez-faire
methodological collectivism, *see* collectivism
methodological individualism, *see* individualism
migration 18, 35, 121, 177, 189
  illegal migration 202
Ministry of Agriculture 20, 25, 48, 77, 79, 86, 94–5, 98–9, 101, 110, 117, 122, 153, 158, 184
Mises, L. von 4–5, 8, 179
moba xiv, 63
modernization 94
  paradigm 34, 94
  peasants' modernization 35
monopolies 49, 183
moral economy 51, 74, 90
multiparty system 142, 151
municipality xv, 21, 58, 68, 74, 80, 82–3, 86, 112–13, 118, 120, 124–8, 135–6, 139–44, 146, 148, 150, 163, 166, 172, 180, 203
  commissions 135–6, 140, 144
  council 135, 140, 153

neo-institutionalism xvii, 12–13
  neo-institutionalists xvii, 1
neo-liberal 94
neo-populism 25
neo-Protestants 18, 189, 195–200
  Adventists 151, 195, 196–8, 206
  Baptists 195–7, 206
  baptizing practices 196
  sect 198
nepotism 134
newcomers (*došljaci*) xiii, 63–4, 160, 167–8, 171, 175, 177–8
normative order 11–2,
  framework 11

okućnica xiv, 40, 57
ownership 3, 8–9, 24, 38, 40, 49, 53, 66, 68, 73
  and collective ownership xvi
  feudal 38
  self-ownership 59
  state 49

pastures ix, 14, 20, 49, 74, 112–13, 115–16, 183
patron–client relationship 32, 142, 155
  patronage coalitions 142
pauperization 28, 50
peasants (*seljak, paor*) vii, ix, xv, 20, 1–53, 55–60, 63–4, 66–8, 71–87, 89–114, 117–24, 127–31, 134–8, 150–5, 160, 163, 166–8, 171, 180, 182–4, 188–9, 194, 201–15
  condition 34–5, 154
  dependence 33
  deprived and powerless peasants 2
  ethics 7, 17, 22, 209, 214
  hardworking peasants 75
  new peasants 35, 189
  political action 30
  peasant dilemma 31
  peasant economy 28, 30–3
  peasant studies 15, 22, 28–9, 34, 81, 90

peasants (*seljak, paor*) (*cont.*)
  peasantry 2–3, 22, 27–31, 33–6, 50, 60, 82, 90, 102, 109, 152, 154, 209
  peasant-worker (*polutani*) xv, 42–3, 171
  resilience vii, 1, 3–4, 110, 130
  as victims 1–3, 182, 209
  world views 5
  see also household
periphery 3, 23, 88–9, 109, 167
  life on the periphery 6, 88–9
planners 24, 37, 48, 94
Polanyi, K. 31
policymakers 2, 9, 24–5, 157–8, 207–9, 212
political father 142–56, 193
political parties 14, 36, 134, 142, 146, 154
  Serbian Progressive Party (SPP) 14, 36, 134, 136, 139, 141–2, 146–54, 156, 170, 183
Popkin, S. L. 32–3
postdevelopmentalism 34
post-socialist rural areas 124
post-socialist rural change xvii
post-socialist rural literature 1, 24
post-socialist Serbia 45–9
post-socialist states 90, 108–9, 134
post-socialist transformations 1, 24, 133
post-socialist villages 1
poverty 34–5, 73, 93, 163, 173–4, 187, 193, 196, 199–200, 204, 206
  rural poor 28, 212
Pre-accession Assistance for Rural Development (IPARD), *see* European Union
privatization 1, 3, 14, 35, 47–9
productivism 57
  productivist mindset 109
professionalization
  of elites 134, 146
  of peasants 34
property xv, 8–9, 24, 36–7, 40–1, 43, 45, 47, 50–1, 59, 64, 67, 75, 82, 84, 121, 141, 162, 166, 177–8, 188, 191, 193, 205, 211
  Agrarian Land Fund of Common People's Property 42
  and collective (*društvena svojina*) property xiii, 45, 47, 73
  common property 32
  commons 14
  private property 14, 32, 37–9, 58–9, 68, 73, 77, 79
  property relations 36, 39, 51
  property rights 14, 25
  village 115
  state 47
purposive action 8

Rangan, H. 208
religiosity 174–5, 195–8
religious conversion 191, 195–200, 205, 211
  converts 197–8
rent-seeking practices 9, 23, 49, 130, 133, 185
re-peasantization 34–5, 50
reputation 11, 65–6, 69–71, 75, 87, 90, 148–9, 167–8, 173–4, 177
resentment 88, 127–8, 203–4
  village resentment 204
resettlement (*kolonizacija*) xiv, 18, 37–9
  resettled people (*kolonisti*) xiii–xiv, 37
resilience xviii, 3, 51, 58, 72, 212, *see also* peasants
resistance 14–17, 25, 33, 40, 43, 209
resources xv, xviii, 6, 9, 14, 29, 32, 59, 91, 95, 123–4, 133–4, 138–40, 143–4, 152, 156, 185
  political resources 144
restitution 42, 45, 47, 82, 139
Rista's story 176–9, 182
Roma vii, xiii, 8–9, 18, 22, 24, 71, 74, 99, 150, 160, 162, 174, 187–206, 211

rural development vii, 2, 4, 9–10, 17, 23–4, 48–9, 94, 124, 126, 129, 130, 133–4, 139–41, 152, 154–5, 157, 180–5, 187–8, 205–6, 208–14
  policies vii, 23–4, 48, 90, 93–131
  programmes 9, 188
  projects 94, 157, 183, 209, 212, 214
rural population 1, 20, 23, 27, 48, 60, 94–5, 102, 124, 128, 157, 184–5, 211–13

safety nets 206
  see also informal welfare
scattered fields 83
scepticism 5–6, 22, 53, 79–82, 118–19, 196
Second agrarian reform 18, 38–45, 82–3, 90
Second World War xvi, 18–19, 25, 38, 93, 207
self-governance xvii
self-interested actions 11, 13
self-regulating system 5, 65, 69
self-sufficiency 30
Serbian Progressive Party (SPP), *see* political parties
Shanin, T. 27
shepherd ix, xiii, 74, 114–17, 162–3
Slav population 18
  Slav origin 37
slava xv, 61, 90, 126, 199, 200
  village slava (*seoska zavetina*) xv, 62–3, 76, 78, 190
  Spasovdan xiii, xv, 61, 63
Smith, A. 13
smuggling practices 99
social benefits 154, 195, 201–5
  social beneficiaries 190, 195, 202–3
socialism 35, 39–40, 77, 99, 171
  collapse of socialism 35, 143
socialist agrarian policy 42
socialist economies 109
socialist production 42
social recognition 24, 162, 173, 177, 179, 191, 193, 205, 211

South-eastern Europe 114, 124
sovereignty, economic, and food 7
spontaneous actions 4–5, 11, 15, 23
spontaneous change 158
spontaneous development 24, 209–10
spontaneous mechanism 89
spontaneous social order 12, 97–101, 121, 123, 210, 215
spontaneous system 10, 214
spontaneous wellbeing 4
Srem 25
state xiv, 1, 3, 6–10, 18, 22–5, 31, 34–42, 44–5, 47–8, 50–1, 80–4, 86, 88–90, 94, 96–7, 101–3, 107–114, 117–19, 121–2, 124, 127–30, 133–5, 151, 153–55, 163, 178, 180, 183–5, 187, 202–5, 207–11
  post-socialist 90, 134
  socialist 1, 24, 39
  weak state 1, 86, 155
  welfare 35, 202, 206
stock exchange 103
storage xvi, 57–8, 83
  storehouses (*žitnice*) xvi, 58, 103
subordination 29, 31, 33, 50–1
subsidies 7, 14, 23, 48–50, 83–4, 89, 95–102, 111–13, 117, 121, 123–4, 128–31, 154, 166–7, 179–81, 210–11, 213
subsistence 28, 60, 200
  agriculture 176
  production 28, 35, 200
substantivists 31–2
summer ranch (*salaš*) ix, xiii, xv, 74, 106–7, 112–17, 161–3
supon, see *bačija*

taxation 36, 83, 84
  local taxes 14, 127
  progressive taxation 41
  samodporinosi xv, 127–8
tenants 100, 173, 176
thriftiness 63–5, 163
thriving from scratch 158, 178

top-down narratives, organization, approach 94, 157
tractors 20–1, 44–7, 65, 161, 171, 176–7
trade 5, 23, 42, 48, 57–8, 89, 98, 102–10, 128–30, 178, 180, 183, 214
  direct trade 103, 108, 110, 128
  via Facebook 104–5
  price of land 51, 167
  trade of land 41–2
  vendors 104
  see also informal trade
transactions 101, 106, 110, 139, 142, 155–6, 193
trust xv, 45, 63, 69, 70–2, 75, 78, 80–1, 85–6, 98, 122, 149, 153, 165, 183, 202, 211, 214

underrepresentation 34
urban bias 93
utilitarianism 152, 179
utility maximizers 3, 214

values 2–4, 8–10, 12, 15, 20, 22, 24–5, 60–1, 69, 90, 134, 145, 167, 175, 179–80, 187–8, 190–1, 194, 205, 210–11, 213
  individual 179–82
  local 3, 5, 9, 12, 14, 23, 51, 60, 122, 130, 158, 179–82, 209–13
  village values 170–1
Vasa's story 162–4, 179, 182
veresija (credit on trust) xv, 63, 69, 70–3, 75–6, 78, 109, 211
village xiii–xvii, 1–5, 8–12, 14, 17–22, 24–5, 29–30, 39, 42–3, 47, 50–1, 54–5, 57–8, 60–78, 81, 83, 85–90, 95, 97–100, 102–6, 109, 112–15, 117–18, 120–1, 124–30, 134–6, 138–44, 146–56, 158–71, 173–84, 187–91, 193–206, 209–13
  central village (Gaj) 17–18, 160, 164–5, 171, 176, 194

lower village (Gaj) 159, 189–91, 194–5, 202, 204, 206
upper village (Gaj) 159, 171, 189
village associations 23, 95, 124–7, 129–30, 139
village council (*Mesna zajednica*) xiv, 104, 120, 135–6, 138, 140–2, 148–9, 151, 170
village councillors 136, 140–1, 143
village ethics 3, 6, 12, 22, 53, 60–75, 130, 159, 210–11
virtue ethics xvii
virtues 63, 65, 159, 180, 210
  collective 180
  individual 200
Vojvodina, Autonomous Province of xi, xiii–xv, xvii, 2, 4, 12, 17, 24–5, 37–9, 41–2, 49, 181, 183, 187, 197
voting 25, 135, 145, 150, 152, 154
  system 134
  voters 128, 146, 148, 150, 171, 184

welfare 32, 74, 133, 202–6
  customary welfare 73
  system 202–3
  see also informal welfare; state
wellbeing 14, 22, 74–6, 90, 93–5, 97, 124, 159, 162–3, 170, 175, 202–6, 211, 214
  of community 74, 214
  local 4–25
  see also spontaneous wellbeing
Wolf, E. 28, 31, 51
work, hard 7, 63–5, 68, 74, 158, 161–3, 168, 174–7, 179–80, 212
workers xv, 18–19, 28, 34, 37, 42–3, 137, 145, 160, 171, 175
  see also guest workers
World Bank 180, 207

Yugoslavia xiv, 36–9, 41–6, 51, 82, 120, 127, 189, 191

Yugoslavia (*cont.*)
　Federal People's Republic of Yugoslavia 38
　Interwar Yugoslavia 36, 38
　Kingdom of Serbs, Croats and Slovenes (SCS) 25
　Kingdom of Yugoslavia 24–5
　Second Yugoslavia xiv–xv
　Socialist Federal Republic of Yugoslavia 25, 38, 45
　socialist Yugoslavia xiii, xv, 18, 24, 38, 42

zadruga xv–xvi, 41
zimnica xiii, xvi, 104–5, 123

www.ingramcontent.com/pod-product-compliance
Lightning Source LLC
LaVergne TN
LVHW050008140426
836100LV00010B/58